1986 14.95

Crime in Trinidad

Crime in Trinidad

CONFLICT AND CONTROL IN A PLANTATION SOCIETY 1838–1900

DAVID VINCENT TROTMAN

THE UNIVERSITY OF TENNESSEE PRESS / KNOXVILLE

First Edition.

The paper used in this book meets the minimum requirements
of the American National Standard for Permanence
of Paper for Printed Library Materials, Z39.48-1984.
Binding materials have been chosen for durability.

Library of Congress Cataloging-in-Publication Data

Trotman, David Vincent, 1946–
Crime in Trinidad.

Thesis (Ph.D.)—The Johns Hopkins University, Baltimore.
Bibliography: p.
Includes index.
1. Crime and criminals—Trinidad—History—19th century.
2. Plantation life—Trinidad. I. Title.
HV6875.7.A44 1986 364′.972983 86-7092
ISBN 0-87049-491-0 (alk. paper)

For Mother Edith; Aunty May; Althea, and Mansa and The Casablanca Steel Orchestra

Contents

Tables: Criminal Statistics

Acknowledgments

This study originated as a doctoral dissertation submitted to the Department of History at the Johns Hopkins University, Baltimore, Maryland. I deeply appreciate and acknowledge the comments and criticisms of my joint supervisors, Professors D.W. Cohen and F.W. Knight. I also wish to thank publicly the Programme in Atlantic History and Culture at the Johns Hopkins University for the financial support that made possible the original research for this study. The staffs at the numerous research centers in England and in Trinidad and at the Inter-Library Loan Office of York University, Toronto, were helpful and did their usual efficient jobs. I also acknowledge the comments made by Ato Sekyi-Otu and Althea Prince, my colleagues at York University, Toronto. Secretarial services at York University did a commendable job in having the manuscript ready in readable typescript for the publishers. Last, but certainly not least, I wish to express thanks to my friends in Toronto who at various times were patient enough to listen to unsolicited expositions on some of the themes of this study.

Crime In Trinidad

CHAPTER ONE

Introduction

This is a study of crime and its relationship with the political economy of the multiethnic plantation society that was nineteenth-century Trinidad. It posits that the nature and demands of the plantation system had a profound effect on the rate, pattern, and characteristics of criminal activity in nineteenth-century Trinidad and suggests that by looking at crime, the historian comes closer to understanding the nature of the nineteenth-century plantation system as it operated in Trinidad. The study argues that crime in that nineteenth-century society clearly reflected the conflicts and tensions inherent in the system.[1] The argument is not that without the plantation system there would be no crime. Nor is this study an attempt to justify criminal activity then or now or to make political heroes of all those convicted of crime in the nineteenth-century.

The underlying assumption is that crime is essentially a social phenomenon and that each society produces a crime rate and pattern that is peculiar to itself.[2] My purpose, therefore, is not simply to try to find the historical roots of crime or merely to look for the biological or psychological cause of crime. The study is concerned instead with the organic linkages and relationship between the structural organization of plantation society and the pattern and nature of criminal activity. It argues that the societal structures of inequality and domination inherent in the plantation society facilitated the development of activity that was labeled criminal.

The study also suggests that certain crimes that are of universal incidence may have a particular pattern and rate that draw their singularity or peculiarity from the nature of the political economy and society. For example, violence and theft may be, broadly speaking, universal phenomena—that is, they have occurred in every time and clime—but the particular rate and pattern of violence and theft in any one society is intimately related to the nature of that society. Therefore, an understanding of the rate and pattern of violence and theft in the nineteenth-century plantation society must first begin with an understanding of the plantation system as it operated in nineteenth-century Trinidad. This study does not claim that without the plantation system there would have been no crime—rather, it sees crime as the mirror in which are reflected the problems of the plantation-influenced economy and society in postemancipation Trinidad.

Crime and society in nineteenth-century Trinidad illustrate the divergence between the old planter elite and the newly emergent sectors in the postemancipation reconstruction of Caribbean society. This study examines crime in order to explore the social history of postemancipation Trinidad and the patterns of conflict and control in a plantation society.

This book also attempts to fill a lacuna in the growing body of historical scholarship from the English-speaking Caribbean. Studies of the slave society dominated the published scholarship of the area. This desire to examine the dynamics of slave society is understandable in an area that was dominated by the slave system for at least two hundred years and that still experiences its effects today. The outstanding studies by Elsa Goveia, Orlando Patterson, Edward Braithwaite, Richard Dunn, Carl and Robert Bridenbaugh, Barry Higman, Michael Craton, and others have expanded our knowledge of the origins of modern Caribbean society.[3] They have thereby enriched our understanding of the contemporary society by making contributions to the plural-society debate.[4]

On the one hand, Goveia and, later, Braithwaite have argued for the early establishment of a Creole society that developed a modus vivendi permitting the long tenure of the slave system and tenacious enough to survive well into the modern period. On the other hand, the picture of social failure painted by Patterson for Jamaica, and later supported by Dunn and the Bridenbaughs for the entire seventeenth-century Caribbean, provide historical support for those who argue that the society was held together by force, lacked social will, and cooperated only in the marketplace. The first group emphasizes accommodation, while the other highlights conflict as endemic to the society.

These concerns also dominate the scholarship of the postemancipation period throughout the Caribbean. Both Phillip D. Curtin and Douglas Hall have examined Jamaica in the three decades after emancipation, but they arrive at different conclusions.[5] Curtin argues that while a Creole ideology developed during the slave period, the changed conditions of postemancipation society undermined that ideology, placing the society on a path of confrontation that culminated in the Morant Bay riots and set the pattern for the development of a plural society. Hall, on the other hand, argues that instead of inevitable class and race conflict, the dependence on the sugar industry by both white planters and the black peasantry provided the mechanism for social cohesion. Alan Adamson's study of Guyana stresses the inevitability of race and class conflict in a society where the planter class employed fiscal, technological, and political strategies to frustrate the development of the peasantry, while a later work by Walter Rodney challenges this view.[6]

Trinidad, the focus of the present study, has been unevenly served in the historical scholarship. The slave period, perhaps because of its short duration, has not received the full-scale treatment that the institution in the other territories has been given. Eric Williams' effort lacks scholarly rigor, and the author, without apology, claims that it was not conceived as a work of scholarship but as the manifesto of a subjugated people.[7] James Millette provides valuable information, especially about the free coloreds, but his concern is with the process by which Crown Colony government was established, and he therefore pays minimal attention to slaves and slavery.[8] Donald Wood's short chapter serves as a teasing introduction to the post-emancipation period, but the author pleads that it was difficult to reveal anything more about the slaves, since they were enfolded in anonymity.[9] Bridget Brereton's chapters provide new information summarized from a number of unpublished manuscripts but repeats some of the older questionable generalizations.[10] The study by Vidia Naipaul is not done with the usual paraphernalia associated with historical scholarship, but it is by far the best introduction to the social history of slave society in Trinidad, flawed only by the author's obvious obsession with demonstrating that West Indian history is one of futility and lack of achievement.[11] But a study of slave society in Trinidad would be intellectually rewarding to any enterprising historian. The short tenure of slavery, the rapid development of the economy, the massive importation of both African and Creole slaves, and the numerous ethnic groups provide intriguing variables for the study of the complexities of accommodation and social control in a frontier slave society.

The period following emancipation is better served in the literature. Donald Wood's study of the early postemancipation period is a thorough examination of conflict between the English and French elite for control of the frontier plantation society. The author argues that the religious and political controversies that he discusses meant little to the great majority of urban- or rural-based Creoles.[12] But such an argument assumes that the controversies were only drawing-room conversation items, existed in a social vacuum, and had no immediate or long-term importance. The very fact that a large segment of the population had no input into the political process meant that the decisions of the elite were of extreme importance to the disenfranchised. They may not have participated in the debate, but the effect of these decisions on their lives evoked responses from them that, in turn, had an effect on the further decisions of the elite. The present study contends that the quarrel of the elite had their repercussions on the disenfranchised masses, and their effects are reflected in the record of criminal activity both for 1838–69, the period studied by Donald Wood, and for the remaining years of the century, examined by Bridget Brereton.[13]

Brereton's focus like Wood's in on race relations, and in particular on the emergence of a nonwhite middle class. Earlier, Wood had suggested that "the gradual augmentation from below of the colored and Negro middle classes in the peaceful remaining years of the nineteenth century" was worthy of study and Brereton made this a crucial theme of her work.[14] But the emphasis on augmentation from below influenced her study's focus on accommodation, since the mobility of blacks and coloreds depended in large measure on the extent to which they accommodated to the colonial order. For Brereton, crime becomes merely an "inescapable part of urban lower-class life." She further argues that in many ways the true gulf in the society was between those who were respectable and those who were not, rather than between whites and nonwhites. As she herself admits, respectability was "proved by a certain life-style and especially by command of European culture and manners."[15] But this life-style was considered a natural attribute of whites; nonwhites could only aspire to it and constantly had to prove their respectability. It is precisely because those attributes that were considered nonrespectable were seen as congenitally nonwhite and were invariably labeled criminal that crime was inescapable for those segments of the population who *would not* or who *could not* accommodate. The last decades of the century were not "a time of sunset calm,"[16] and the emergence of the nonwhite middle class was accomplished at the expense of the criminalization of large segments of the black lower class and their East Indian compatriots.

A study of crime offers an opportunity to examine both the pattern of conflict and the process of accommodation in a changing nineteenth-centurv plantation society. Although some scholars have made notable contributions to the study of other aspects of conflict—slave revolts and labor disputes, for example—the study of crime is virgin territory in Caribbean scholarship. After the pioneering work by the anthropologist Chandra Jayawardena, which deals with disputes and their resolution in British Guiana, there have been few attempts to explore the nature of conflict in Caribbean societies from a criminological perspective.[17] A recent anthology of papers, though concerned more with policy issues, is a welcome publication.[18] Historians have neglected this topic, and they have not given the whole complex of law and crime the attention it deserves. Three recent examples have sought to provide the historical background for an understanding of the particular patterns of crime in contemporary Guyana. These articles have located "the well springs" of criminal activity in the nature of plantation society in Guyana, and this constitutes a promising beginning for the historical study of crime in the Caribbean.[19]

The historical scholarship on crime in other areas has not been particularly helpful in an examination of crime in nineteenth-century Trinidad. Although the scholarship outside of the Caribbean has grown voluminous in recent years, it is uneven in quality. Furthermore, there are serious methodological problems that bedevil any attempt at a comparative analysis of deviance. Most of the better studies are based on European societies in the process of industrialization.[20] There are no studies of crime in any society that is comparable to Trinidad. Even though in England, for example, large segments of the population were still disenfranchised, the society was politically autonomous; England was also economically independent and was an industrial rather than an agricultural society; and class divisions notwithstanding, the absence of racial divisions (the Irish diaspora also notwithstanding) made England a far more culturally homogeneous society than could ever be claimed for nineteenth-century Trinidad. But the British studies were valuable in providing warnings about the pitfalls of using statistics and other kinds of data when talking about the incidence of crime.[21] They were also useful for their treatment of the development and role of some of the law enforcement agencies, since in large measure, penal systems, jurisprudence, and the organization of the police were imported to colonial Trinidad from metropolitan England.[22]

The studies available on crime and related subjects in other colonial societies were also of only limited value,[23] because of the unique nature of the colonial experience in the Caribbean.[24] In the colonial societies of Africa and Asia, a foreign order was imposed on an already existing social and political structure, but in the Caribbean, a longer experience with colonialism involved the decimation of the indigenous population and the creation, under forced circumstances, of a new society. In Africa and Asia, a large part of the colonial conflict involved the struggle to prevent the death of the old society; in the Caribbean, the colonial conflict involved the struggle to resist the birth and development of a new society that was neither African nor European. Since all colonial societies experienced the imposition of law enforcement agencies from the metropole, however, those studies that examined the nature and function of these agencies in the colonial situation were of value.[25]

I have been extremely cautious in using contemporary criminological theory to analyze the past. It is conceptually dangerous, if not intellectually dishonest, to impose motives and explanations derived from twentieth-century analyses on the peoples of the past. The insights of the twentieth century are useful as guides, but they must be used with utmost caution and with a conscious effort to protect the autonomy of the past. Furthermore, the bulk of criminological theory has been invariably concerned with devising strategies to control crime and criminals. If anything, my theoretical inclination in this study leans towards those scholars who are concerned with understanding crime as a social institution intimately linked with the political economy.[26]

At any rate, the nature of the evidence used in this study precludes indulgence in rash judgments. The study depends primarily on official documents and partially on the use of local newspapers—the latter a source that was fruitfully mined by Brereton. The behavior of the lower class is well documented in these sources, but the views and explanations advanced are essentially those of the articulate elite. It is a vulnerable base from which to make definite assertions about the beliefs and values of a group of people who left little written record of themselves. A much more secure base would have been an extensive examination of the folklore, calypsos, and oral testimony of the "illiterate." But this data, which has its own peculiar methodological problems, is scarce for the nineteenth century. Therefore, the study makes only reluctant claims to writing history from the inside or from the bottom up and concentrates instead, on the role played by the phenomenon of crime in the entrenchment and expansion of the political economy of the plantation system in nineteenth-century Trinidad.

The plantation system itself changed over time, and the rate, pattern, and characteristics of crime reflected the historical development of the system. This study concentrates on the second generation after the end of the slave system, that is, the period 1870–1900. There are two main reasons for this. In the first place, Trinidad in the period 1870–1900 was a much more mature plantation system than in the period immediately following emancipation. But it was a mature giant with clay feet. Circumstances beyond the control of the plantocracy exacerbated the conflicts and tensions normally present in any plantation society and gave clearer relief to the structural contours of Trinidad society and its relationship with crime. Second, a study of crime must ultimately depend on statistics. Although statistics tend to be a cold and impersonal and prone to numerous errors, they are a far more accurate barometer of criminal activity, if intelligently used, than the impressionistic evidence taken from informants other than the criminals themselves. The statistics for crime in nineteenth-century Trinidad are far more reliable and consistent for the post-1870 period than for the period 1838–69.

By far the most reliable source for the extent of criminal activity would have been police reports for the period, but these are neither consistent nor reliable for nineteenth-century Trinidad. Police returns were furnished monthly for each district and were generally more correct for the pre-1873 period than those taken directly from the magistrates' courts. Statistics from the courts compiled at the end of the year were carelessly kept and usually riddled with statistical errors and minor but irritating computation flaws. Few magistrates kept proper records, particularly those who were not so fortunate as to have efficient court clerks. The errors are numerous, especially for the pre-1873 period, although from 1874, increased and efficient staff as well as standardized methods of reporting decreased the margin of error.

Since some police stations served as magistrates' courts, sometimes the magistrate simply referred to the police returns when compiling his annual report. But because of the size of the police force and the unavailability of police stations in every district, many complainants waited until court day to lodge their complaints directly with the magistrate. Therefore, the total number of cases reported to the police would be considerably less than the total cases before the courts as indicated in the returns from the magistrates. In 1872, for example, the police records listed 10,561 reported cases; the records from the magistrates showed 10,779 cases, and this did not include the cases from the district of St. Joseph.[27] In fact, during the 1890s the discrepancy between police and court records was sometimes as high as four thousand cases.

The police returns, published as *Trinidad Council Papers*

(TCP), generally coincided with the prison returns. After 1873 new regulations required an annual report compiled by the inspector of prisons to replace the sketchy report previously compiled by the superintendent of prisons, the official in charge of the day-to-day administration of the prisons.[28] Since the posts of inspector general of police and inspector of prisons were held by the same individual, there was no discrepancy. The annual report on the prisons served as a general comment on the police and on crime. This combined reporting was so routine that in 1891 the new inspector general of police—who did not hold both posts simultaneously as his predecessor had—complained of difficulty in writing a separate annual report for the police, since there were no previous police reports to serve as a guide.[29]

The statistics on crime in nineteenth-century Trinidad refer mainly to the total number of cases before the courts, the total number convicted and the disposition of these convictions, and the total number committed to prison. These statistics have their limitations, and the further removed they are from the actual commission of the offense, the less reliable they are as indicators of the extent of criminal activity. Nonetheless, they are of some value in the analysis of crime. They are therefore used with reservations and always with the understanding that each statistic is really a convenient shorthand that substitutes for a real human being and his actions. These actions represented the conflict between, on the one hand, a plantocracy bent on defending and extending a system of production and a way of organizing society and, on the other, a disenfranchised and unorganized working class equally determined to create a new life for itself out of the wreckage of slavery, despite the continued domination of the plantation interests.

CHAPTER TWO

The Structure of the Society

The island of Trinidad is 1,864 square miles in area and is situated thirteen miles off the coast of Venezuela.[1] In the nineteenth century, the bulk of the population lived around the major plantations, which were located on the plains of the western seaboard, but increasingly during the century, the residential patterns shifted to the urban centers of Port-of-Spain in the north and San Fernando in the south. There were also settlements in the rural areas and in the foothills of the three mountain ranges that trisected the island. These rural settlements first provided havens for escaped slaves and then for those former bondsmen who preferred, after emancipation, to get as far as possible from the scene of their former servitude. These inland settlements, as well as those that lay nearer to the southern, northern, and eastern seaboards, were very often inaccessible and therefore isolated from the major settlements. Some of these areas were separate worlds with little contact with the rest of Trinidad. In some of them the police, the parish priest, and the schoolmaster formed a triumvirate of influence that encouraged the belief that these officials were demigods. In one instance, the village of Mayaro was divided between supporters of the magistrate and those of the parish priest. The rivalry between these factions was so intense that the groups rioted in 1867.[2] But even in those isolated areas where there were no conflicts, the representatives of the law, the church, and the school were a formidable combination of state authority and models of European civilization.

Poor communications—that is, an atrocious road system that was impassable during the rainy months of the year—contributed to this isolation. The three-and-a-half mile journey from Port-of-Spain to the village of Maraval involved crossing a winding river that became a raging torrent after an ordinary shower. The rural roads were so bad that government officials usually traveled in a group, each member of the party equipped with a cutlass, a light rope, and a strong fishing line. The bridges across rivers were in disrepair, and while on one inspection tour along the north coast, the commissioner of police and his party encountered seventeen bridges that collapsed under them.

The development of a proper road system, the opening up of rail communication, and the establishment of a telegraph service ended much of this isolation and were considered crucial to the efficient administration of justice. The trip from Port-of-Spain to Toco, which took four days in 1874, was reduced to one day with the opening of the railway line to Arima in 1876. The development of proper roads reduced the eight-mile journey between the warden's house in Sangre Grande and the police station at Manzanilla from seven hours to under one hour. Many of the offices of the district wardens, who also served as magistrates, were located along the railway line or within a short distance from it. The railway also reduced the trip between Changuanas and Couva, two major settlements of plantation labor, to about twenty-five minutes. Formerly, the magistrate who served both areas traveled by sea, with an overnight stay in Port-of-Spain, to get from one to the other during the wet season. The railway line to Arima in the east was opened in 1876, the line to San Fernando in the south in 1882, and the Princes Town extension further south in 1884. The railway developments, and the abolition of the tollgate that controlled the eastern entrance into the city in

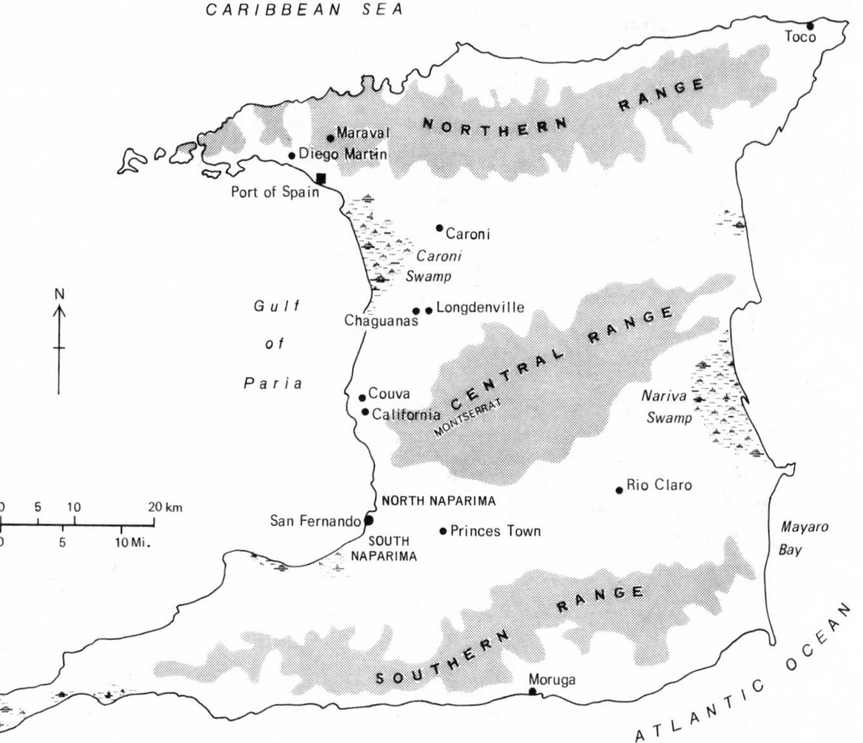

The Island of Trinidad

1878, coincided with and facilitated the rapid shift of the population from the rural to the urban areas in the late nineteenth century. By the end of the century better communication facilities ended the isolation of the plantation belt and undermined the belief that these plantations were worlds unto themselves.[3]

Plantation agriculture dominated the economy of Trinidad. But the system of production, whose Caribbean beginnings can be dated at around 1600, did not come to Trinidad until 1787. The Cedula of Population in 1787 set in motion the process that transformed a backwater of the Spanish Empire into the newest sugar plantation frontier. The sugar revolution that had swept the Caribbean in stages since the seventeenth century was repeated in Trinidad only in the late eighteenth century. Trinidad moved from an island with a single mill in 1787 to one with 159 sugar works that produced 7,800 hogsheads of sugar in 1797. Sugar increased from 9 percent of the total value of commercial crop production in 1786 to 50 percent in 1793.[4] The abolition of the slave trade in 1807, slave emancipation in 1838, and the equalization of sugar duties in 1846 all put momentary checks on Trinidad's rapid development. But by 1870 all the structural outlines of the typical plantation economy, that is, the monopolization of land and capital and the coercion of labor in the production of a staple for export to a distant market, were already fully developed in Trinidad. It is these characteristics—its need to monopolize land, its dependence on a vulnerable external market, and its reliance on a coerced labor force—that make the plantation system criminogenic.

The plantation economy based on the production of a tropical staple for export to a metropolitan market and using a tightly disciplined labor force is extremely vulnerable. It thrives best where political and social dominance gives it complete control over land, the labor force, and capital and where it has unrestricted access to and monopoly of the importing market. The availability of large tracts of land, unalienated by the sugar interests, undermined the attempt at complete control of the labor force in Trinidad after slavery. The era of free trade signaled by the passage of the Equalization of Sugar Duties Act in 1846 exposed the sugar economy to stiff competition from slave-grown sugar exported by Cuba and Brazil and from subsidized beet sugar from Europe. It became increasingly difficult to obtain adequate capitalization for the cane-sugar industry in the late nineteenth century. Therefore, despite increased production in its fairly fertile soils, Trinidad, along with the other British West Indian sugar-producing colonies, experienced the effects of decreasing returns from sugar during the late nineteenth century because of the persistent decline in the price of sugar on the world market.[5]

Despite these changed conditions, the sugar interests sought to make Trinidad a typical plantation society. This combination of external and internal pressures forced the sugar interests to seek ways to expand the output from the labor force, and in the process of striving for the typical or ideal plantation society, the plantocracy criminalized large segments of the population.

In the nineteenth century cocoa emerged as the major challenge to sugar's position as the chief money earner in the economy. Sugar products, which accounted for 87 percent by value of the native products exported in 1854, fell to as low as 40 percent by 1886. The value accrued from sugar exports fell from £718,555 in 1870 to £596,415 in 1895. Total cocoa exports rose from just under £8 million in 1875 to over £24 million in 1888—a threefold increase in twelve years. The value of cocoa exports increased from slightly under £160,000 in 1875 to just over £714,000 in 1888—a fourfold increase in value in twelve years. Cocoa was a minor crop grown chiefly by Spanish peons on the slopes of the Montserrat hills. But after the Spanish and French planters were ousted from their dominance of Trinidad's society and sugar economy, the French shifted to cocoa cultivation, and this formed the basis of their economic and political resurgence in the late nineteenth century.[6]

The plantation system made Trinidad a heterogeneous society. In its drive to recruit both labor and capital, the plantocrats created a multiethnic society and set in train a pattern of cultural conflict that had an impact on crime in Trinidad. In the late eighteenth century Spanish Trinidad was a frontier society. It had a low level of export staple production, vast uncultivated land resources, and a low population density. This attracted French planters, who brought African slaves and initiated the process of social and demographic changes that has been labeled the sugar revolution. From their economic and demographic vantage positions, the French became the new elite. They changed what was originally a backward colony of Spain, with a declining Amerindian population and a few enslaved Africans, into a bustling, French-dominated plantation society.

The conquest of the colony by the British in 1797, shortly after the French influx and the French-dominated transformation, complicated the problem of cultural conflict. The English newcomers gradually ousted the French from their dominant position and gained political and economic control. The institution of Crown Colony government in 1810 guaranteed political control and facilitated British domination of the economic life of the colony.[7] British control of the new sugar frontier attracted British capital, and British planters transferred slaves from some of the older territories to the new colony. But political and economic domination did not immediately or necessarily bring cultural control, and the English elite therefore sought to eradicate the French influence and to impose English cultural domination to match their economic and political control.

The end of the slave trade in 1807, which was the major source of imported labor, and the subsequent emancipation of the labor force in 1838 set the stage for the introduction of further cultural elements. The need in the postemancipation period for a large, unskilled labor force encouraged the promotion of an indiscriminate immigration policy that not only rapidly increased the overall population but also exacerbated the problem of cultural conflict. The immigrants in the postemancipation era came from almost all corners of the globe—Africa, China, Portugal, India, Venezuela—and from the nearby British and French West Indian colonies.[8] They came with different cultural "baggages" and influenced the cultural landscape in various ways. In some cases, the different cultural strains were clearly distinguishable, but more often than not those strains became blurred as the immigrants adjusted to their new environment. In the process, they made their contribution to a developing Creole cultural complex.

Anglicizing this multicultural society to make the colony English in name as well as in fact was a major concern of the English elite and the cause of an intense Anglo-French conflict. But this was largely an intraclass rivalry between the English and French elites for the opportunity to control those institutions that set the cultural tone of the society. Therefore, some of the battles raged around the relationship between church and state and whether education was to be religious or secular. This rivalry with the French occupied the attention of the English elite for the first thirty years after emancipation. The Anglophiles had a combined advantage in their ability to exploit the Crown colony system, which gave them political clout, and their domination of the sugar sector of the economy, which gave them economic leverage. By 1869 a number of compromises in the major areas of conflict had been made, and although the island was still described as English in government but French in language and Roman Catholic in religion, the French influence, though not completely eliminated, was certainly on the wane.[9]

This conflict was largely a struggle between two segments of the same class who, though they differed in language and religion, shared a common belief in the plantation system and the role of non-Europeans in the plantation society. The French furor over education, language, and religion masked their unsuccessful struggle to maintain control over the sugar industry. But they were eventually replaced, and the industry was dominated in the postemancipation period by a combination of local and London-based absentee English interests. The French then shifted into cocoa cultivation, an industry first developed by peasant proprietors but increasingly, in the late nineteenth century, controlled by large plantation owners. As major cocoa growers, they soon revealed how much they were committed to the plantation economy and society by their collusion with the English sugar plantocrats on important issues.

In the late nineteenth century, the cultural conflict shifted from this Anglo-French rivalry to a conflict between the value system represented by the Creole cultural complex and the values of a plantation elite that was often influenced by its version of a Victorian moral code. This late-nineteenth-century conflict was more one between classes, since the expressions of Creole culture that the elite attacked were in fact the values and institutions of the unpropertied and disenfranchised masses of the colony. Sometimes, race and class lines became blurred when segments of the elite opportunistically supported the lower classes. In their struggle to reform some of the more glaring political and social inequalities of the colonial system, segments of the elite exploited the embryonic sense of Creole nationalism. As the tropical representatives of Victorian morality, they pursued a policy of anglicization. The behavior of the disenfranchised may indeed have affronted the moral sensibilities of the elite, but behind the moral outrage articulated lay the fear that the Creole value system and its institutions would provide a rallying point for a real assault on the colonial plantation order.

The system of beliefs, values, behavior, and institutions that has been collectively described as the Creole cultural complex was a heterogeneous composition. It developed as a result of the responses of the constituent immigrant groups to the situations of the new society. But the process of creolization and the manner of contribution to the emerging Creole culture were determined by the dynamics of the plantation system. The socioeconomic possibilities available in the new society determined the extent to which the various groups were able to retain, adapt, or reinterpret their "cultures." Although the non-European immigrants were the numerical majority, they were sociologically subordinate and made their adjustments to the new society—and hence their contribution to the Creole culture—within the parameters determined, in large measure, by the dominant European elite. And even though the elite condemned the behavior of the masses and praised the supremacy of the British way of life, they too made serious modifications in their imported moral code to suit the demands of the plantation society.

The representatives of European culture were a heterogeneous group divided by nationality, religion, and language and with different opportunities for influencing the Creole culture. Even the reputedly English group was divided by nationality in a manner that coincided roughly with class divisions. By 1870, the English held all the influential positions in the state bureaucracy. They owned the bulk of the sugar estates and therefore dominated the nominated element of the Legislative Council. All appointments to the senior civil service were in the hands of the Colonial Office and the local governor, and the English elite therefore controlled all the official seats in the council and were in the senior positions in all major civil service departments.

The movement of British planters and their English-influenced slaves into Trinidad and the injection of British capital also brought a team of middle-level management. These were the overseers and managers on the estates and clerks in the commercial houses and were, in the main, Scottish and Irish. Although many of them tended to be transients rather than settlers, they were the immediate representatives of British culture and the group with which the lower classes made constant contact. The Irish dominated the middle-level ranks of the police force and were in the forefront of the anglicization and anti-Creole campaign. They therefore influenced in crucial ways not only the Creole cultural institutions but also the masses' perception of what was British.

What gave these groups the appearance of a homogeneous unit, however, was their commitment to an ideology of skin color and race. In the plantation society the whites were a numerical minority, and this encouraged the development of an ideology that emphasized race at the expense of class.[10] It was an attitude that had its origins in the slave society, where security demanded unity based on race and therefore deemphasized class differences. In the postemancipation period this attitude decreased slowly, but among the English the prevailing anti-French sentiments served to encourage a blind allegiance to things British. It was reinforced by real British imperial supremacy. England in the nineteenth century was the workshop of the world. Her ships roamed worldwide carrying British manufactures not only to Europe but to those parts of the world that had been subjugated by her armies and those dominated by her financial superiority.[11] The intellectual justification for this supremacy was derived from a crude interpretation of Charles Darwin's theory of evolution. The British believed that their material supremacy was due to some innate quality of the British race and was therefore a vindication of their cultural institutions.[12] British might became British right and served as a unifying bond among the English-speaking elite against the nonwhite majority.

There was also a closing of the ranks among the French in order to resist the British thrust for dominance. The first wave of French settlers had come from the French islands of Martinique, Guadeloupe, St. Lucia, Dominica, and St. Vincent. They were attracted to the potential of the new frontier and had been pushed from their old homes by hurricanes, failing sugar crops because of soil exhaustion, and debts and bankruptcy. Later on, as some of these territories came under British rule, French planters found life under a Spanish Catholic government far more attractive than restricted living under a

British Protestant administration. As the repercussions of the French Revolution spread to the Caribbean, many more political refugees found a haven in Trinidad. In the closing years of the eighteenth century, republicans fled St. Lucia and Martinique and royalists left Guadeloupe and Saint Domingue for Trinidad. The slave revolution in Haiti sent Frenchmen of both ideological persuasions to Trinidad. Later in the century they buried their ideological differences and rallied in defense of the French language and the Catholic religion.

In a short time, by sheer numerical superiority, that segment of the population that was of French influence—whites, free coloreds, free blacks, and slaves—was able to put a Gallic stamp on what was originally a Spanish colony. The demographic impact was evident: the free population increased from 2,550 in 1782 to 6,627 in 1797 and the slave population from 2,462 to 10,009 over the same period. French speakers dominated this population. The population in 1802 was approximately 28,000: 20,464 slaves, 5,275 coloreds, and 2,261 whites; among the whites, the English, Spanish, and French speakers were approximately 29, 22, and 48 percent respectively, and among the coloreds the figures were 11, 33, and 55 percent. In 1802 more than 53 percent of the free population were French in orientation, and 16 percent were English.[13]

Census statistics are not the best guide to cultural influence in a society, and those of the nineteenth century are particularly unreliable in this area. The census of 1821 was the last that made any clear distinctions between British, Spanish, and French inhabitants. In that census the total population was 39,400, and the figures for the free population listed the British inhabitants at 50 percent, the Spanish at 31 percent, and the French at 19 percent: as in 1802, no corresponding figures were given for the slave population.[14] The rapid increase in the British segment is understandable, but the rapid statistical decrease of the French element is inexplicable. There is no doubt that many more English speakers flocked to the island after the capitulation of 1797 was secured by the Treaty of Amiens in

1801. But the drastic demographic reduction of the French is mysterious. Some French settlers may have left, but there is no evidence of any massive emigration from Trinidad—harassment of the French under British rule or the tightening of liberal policies, particularly those towards free coloreds, notwithstanding, Trinidad was still a frontier society with room to maneuvre and, to put it crudely, to make money.

The census of 1822 contains the first use of the term *Creole* to describe a large segment of the population. According to the census of 1822, this group constituted approximately 46 percent of a population of 15,589 free inhabitants.[15] But there is no indication of the major cultural influence among these Creoles; that is, there is no distinction made as to their language or religion that hint at cultural preferences. The succeeding censuses are equally unrevealing about the extent of French influence: the first sophisticated census in 1851, and its decennial successors, still does not give categories that permit the reliable plotting of French influence. The statistics on religious affiliation and school attendance are the only indices that could be used as a guide to continued French influence, but these have their limitations. It is quite likely that English administrators deliberately deemphasized the extent of Gallic influence in the Anglo-Saxon governed colony and recorded vaguely the size of the various national and cultural components of the population.

One other possibility is that the decrease was due largely to a reduction in the size of the free colored and free black population. This group had been predominantly French and, like the free whites, had been attracted by the social and economic possibilities in Trinidad. But during the first few years of British rule, new regulations placed many social and economic restrictions on this group and withdrew many of the liberal policies of Spanish rule. Some may have emigrated, but there is no evidence to support this. More importantly, many may have decided to disassociate themselves from the French in the hope that this evidence of support for the English could be used as a bargaining position to alleviate their situation. This group and their descendants were more Creole, in the strictest sense of the term, than most of the other groups, and they played an important role in the cultural conflict of the nineteenth century. They became an important broker group, and their struggles and attitudes in large measure influenced the role and development of the Creole institutions among the masses.[16]

The various West African ethnic groups contributed the most to the Creole complex because they constituted the largest and oldest of the immigrant groups. This African influence had its roots in the use of slave labor in the development of the plantation system. The slave segment of the population grew rapidly: from 310 in 1782 to 10,000 in 1789, and it reached 20,761 in 1806, on the eve of the abolition of the slave trade. During the slave period the slaves came from two sources. One stream was imported directly from Africa; the others were transferred from older slave societies, first by French planters and later by English settlers, particularly in the period after the abolition of the slave trade.[17] Therefore, although the plantation society in Trinidad had such a late start in comparison to other areas in the Caribbean basin, a large percentage of the subjugated population in Trinidad had already made some kind of primary adjustment to slavery elsewhere in the Caribbean. But there was also a large segment of the slave population that came directly from Africa and therefore was in the process of making both a primary adjustment to slavery and a secondary adjustment to their new locale. Furthermore, a number of Africans, free blacks, were among those who occupied that precarious niche between free whites and enslaved blacks.[18] There were also some free coloreds who had more cultural links with the African sector than with the whites. They too made their contribution to the "African" element of the Creole culture, but theirs was a specific contribution determined by their peculiar situation of being free and nonwhite in a slave society.

The Africans were drawn from various parts of West Africa, but because of Trinidad's late development, the regional origins of this population differed both from population profiles typical of earlier periods and from patterns typical of the British slave trade of the same period. According to a census of 1813 approximately 55 percent of the slave population was listed as born in Africa. They came from the Bight of Biafra, Central Africa, Senegambia, the Gold Coast, the Bight of Benin, the Windward Coast, and Sierra Leone, in that order of proportional representation. But these are merely geographical descriptions that indicated more the points of embarkation than the multiplicity of ethnic groups on the West African coast. Among the Africans from the Bight of Biafra, who constituted about 40 percent of the African-born population, were Igbo, Bantu, and Ibibio; predominant among the Central Africans were those known as Kongo; at least 95 percent of those from the Senegambia were Malinke; and those from the Bight of Benin came from the Allada, Chamba, Popo, and Hausa.[19] It is these groups that contributed to the African presence in the Creole culture, and in 1838 at emancipation the African-born still formed a substantial proportion of the population.

The African component was further augmented and revitalized during the postemancipation period. Between 1837 and 1867 slightly more than 10,000 Africans were brought to Trinidad; some arrived as part of a scheme for the resettlement of Africans liberated from ships trading slaves with Brazil and Cuba, and a number of others, particularly Kroos, immigrated as free labor.[20] Like those of their earlier involuntary counterparts, the ethnic origins of these postemancipation African immigrants reflected the sweep of the West African trading areas, but in particular the nineteenth-century concentrations of the trade. Many of these Africans came from the traditional trading areas of Central Africa and from Angola. There were also increased numbers from the Bight of Benin and in particular from among the Yoruba of southwest Nigeria.

Since these Africans came to Trinidad, not as slaves, but as free men, they were in a much better position than enslaved Africans to attempt to transfer and to recreate some of their cultural institutions. Government regulations failed to prevent the settlement of these Africans in patterns that reflected their ethnic origins. They built new communities and recreated some of their cultural institutions—a few of which suffered transformation in the process, but many of which were as close to the original as the new conditions permitted.[21] It is this group—or more precisely, these groups—of free Africans who were able to recreate kinship, religious, and secular patterns and to influence other institutions in such a way that the Creole culture received an unmistakable African stamp.

The creolization of these Africans took place at two levels: on the one hand, it involved homogenization among the various West African groups, and on the other hand, it involved the adaptation of these groups to the dominant cultures. The details of the first process are not very easy to reconstruct historically, but there are sufficient hints to justify the assertion that it took place. Although those groups spoke a number of separate languages, practiced a multiplicity of religious rituals, and had a number of different secular institutions, this heterogeneity masked a cultural commonality. The similarity was to be found, not in those easily identifiable sociocultural forms, but rather in certain underlying principles and values. It is these underlying "principles" that provided the mechanism for homogenization of the disparate West African groups and the basis for the African contribution to the Creole culture.[22]

The demographic disparities within the African populations would have forced some kind of accommodation among the various groups. During both the slave trade and the postemancipation migration of Africans, none of the groups was large enough or sufficiently balanced sexually to permit total endogamy. The preference during the slave trade was for young males, and this led to a female-deficient population; the postemancipation immigrants were not only predominantly male but also extremely young, many of them children of tender ages. Many Africans had to find mates outside their own ethnic group, either among the other Africans or among the Creoles. Those Africans who came at impressionable ages, unless they were socialized in communities or families that emphasized their cultural traditions, either were subject to Creole customs or practiced, from fading memories, extremely truncated versions of their own traditions. They too would have made marriage choices based on Creole customs rather than on their specific ethnic identities. Intermarriage not only undermined separate ethnic identities but facilitated the emphasis on common cultural principles and therefore encouraged homogenization among the various African groups. And since in the West African "cultural heritage," kinship and marriage patterns were closely related to religion, economic association, and other community organizations, intermarriage provided opportunities for further eclectic borrowing, interpenetration of traditions, and the development of the Creole culture.

The adaptation of Africans to the dominant cultures is by far the easier of the two processes to reconstruct historically, and the scholarship is replete with speculations and examples.[23] These adaptations ranged from the attempts to completely abandon all African traditions to the interpretation of European institutions to suit the irrepressible drives of African impulses. They also included syncretisms that forced African traditions to coexist with European practices, sometimes peacefully and sometimes in conflict. Some of those who refused to adapt or failed to make successful adjustments to the new environment were politely ignored or became the butt of unsympathetic comments; others may have ended up in the mental asylum; and still others found themselves in the hands of the law.

One example will suffice to illustrate the latter possibility. In 1856 Jean Louis and Walter Isdale were indicted for the theft of a gilt statue valued at six pounds and a portrait valued at one pound from the chapel of the Roman Catholic convent in Port-of-Spain. One of the accused was arrested when he offered the picture for sale at one of the numerous rumshops in Port-of-Spain. It is quite possible to dismiss the case as that of two imbibers who saw the opportunity to satisfy their alcoholic thirst with the proceeds of the sale of stolen merchandise. But the evidence of one of the sisters of the convent throws some interesting light on some of the problems of cultural adaptation. The nun testified that she saw a black man about the prisoner's size standing in front of a light before the altar. She saw him remove the crucifix, the top of the tabernacle, and the statue of the Virgin Mary. But interestingly enough, the nun found on the altar, where the statue once stood, a goat's head and a colored shirt.[24] There are no answers, but many questions and speculations: Did the accused believe that the goat's head and the colored shirt were sufficient recompense for the gods or spirits of the chapel for the items they removed? Were the items found part of some religious ritual that required the chapel premises? Did the whole transaction merely represent a complete disregard and disrespect for the Catholic religion? Whatever the answers, the two accused were trapped in an unsympathetic social and political system that did not represent their interests.

The political system facilitated the perpetuation of the plantation system and its control over society. The plantation system not only required the monopolization of land, labor, and capital but also demanded that the entire society be "responsive to the needs of the plantations as institutions, with the society's primary responsibility that of supplying low-paid manual labor to the estates."[25] The success of this domination of society depended on political control that facilitated the manipulation of the lawmaking and law-enforcement agencies of the society. The control of the assembly system in other territories made this a simple matter. The Crown Colony system in Trinidad, despite all its claims to the contrary, prevented this political dominance only in theory. It made this dominance only irritatingly inconvenient at the worst of times but never totally impossible.

The Colonial Office, as advisers to the British Parliament, viewed the Crown Colony system, with its metropolitan-appointed governor and his nominated council, as an impartial administrator and the special protector of the poor. But there were important variances between theory and practice. In the first place, the idea that the "very existence of these colonies, as civilized communities is dependent on the continuation of the sugar cultivation, for which they are peculiarly fitted by nature"[26] was shared by both the local sugar interests and the erstwhile protectors of the population in the Colonial Office. This meant that they were in fundamental agreement on the nature and purpose of the society, although on occasion they differed on the mechanism by which this goal was to be achieved and the details of policy.

Furthermore, the sugar interests had direct access to, and therefore opportunity to influence, the policymakers at the Colonial Office through the operations of their powerful lobby, the London-based West India Committee. In fact, this lobby not only attempted to influence the appointment and tenure of governors (and sometimes succeeded in doing so) but often consulted the appointee prior to his assuming office. During his term they also sought continuous consultations with the governor, the chief executive officer in the colony. The growth of absentee ownership in the sugar sector made this overseas lobby extremely important. In 1887 almost half of the island's sugar production was in the hands of four absentee owners; and in 1896, thirty-six of the fifty-six operating sugar plantations in Trinidad were owned by nonresidents, and eight of these absentee-owned plantations were owned by the influential London-based Colonial Company.[27] This constituted an extremely powerful external lobby based at the seat of power.

This external lobby was complemented by the domination

of the local political structure by plantation interests. Already biased to the view that the colony should be exporters of plantation-produced staples, the political structure of the Crown Colony included a nominated element that was dominated by the very interests from whom the natives were to be protected. The metropolitan-appointed governor received advice from a nominated council that was drawn from representatives of the planting interests, based on the rationale that as holders of property they would give rational advice and be the guarantors of the continuation of European civilization. In 1880, the eight nominated members included four sugar planters, two owners of sugar and cocoa estates, one merchant associated with the sugar interest, and one barrister.[28]

Other principal officers of the administration, at different levels of authority and influence, were also connected with this planting interest. In 1884, the chief justice, Sir Joseph Needham, lived on his 433-acre cocoa estate in Santa Cruz, just nine miles from his office in Port-of-Spain. Needham, the chief legal official in the land, not only was a major plantation owner but was also known to give only two days per week to his official duties in order to supervise the management of his plantation.[29] Other senior government officials were also involved in plantation enterprises: M. M. Phillip, the solicitor general, owned 240 acres of cane in Diego Martin; H. C. Stone, the subprotector of immigrants, owned 177 acres of provision grounds, which he rented out on contract; and H. A. Pitt, the registrar general, owned 1,236 acres of sugarcane land in Couva. Even the district wardens who often served as stipendiary justices were connected with the planting interests in the colony. L. B. Pierre, warden and stipendiary justice of the peace, owned 85 acres of cane land in Toco, the district he administered, and at least three other wardens owned cocoa, sugar, or coconut estates.

Although there was conflict between the sugar and cocoa interests (since these two industries were divided along ethnic lines, with cocoa-estate owners predominantly French and sugar-plantation owners English), there was general agreement on the use of labor and the validity of the plantation system. There was often political cooperation between the owners of large cocoa estates who employed indentured labor and their class allies involved in sugar. In fact, the sugar interests benefited from a division between big planters and peasant producers in the cocoa industry. The big cocoa planters were members of the Legislative Council and, since they used indentured labor, tended on crucial issues to vote with the sugar planters. Between 1881 and 1885 the Legislative Council, dominated by sugar planters, reduced the export duty that was levied on sugar to pay part of the cost of immigration. But at the same time they increased the export duty on cocoa. The cocoa planters in the council voted solidly for the increase, since the bulk of the export cocoa at that time came from the estates of small producers who did not use indentured labor.[30]

Against this combination of forces—general agreement on the validity of the plantation economy by both local and metropolitan policymakers, access to the policy-making body in the colony by the planter class, and the actual involvement of the principal administrative officers in the planting enterprise—the large mass of disenfranchised Trinidadians depended on the London-appointed governor to defend their interests. The herculean task of defying both implicit ideology and explicit social and political power in order to protect the powerless required an individual with exceptional qualities. He needed the implicit trust of his superiors at the Colonial Office as well as sterling personal qualities to survive the vituperative campaigns of the local planter-controlled lobby. He needed to see his task as being the active protection and promotion of the defenseless and not merely as the support of the status quo that gave him an untroubled tenure—the prerequisite to other, more lucrative colonial appointments. But, most importantly, he needed to rise above the insidious racism of the nineteenth century that lent support to the idea that the plantation economy based on a nondemocratic colonial system was the most appropriate vehicle for civilizing the non-European population. There were many governors who never tried to promote the interests of their charges; there were some who tried and failed; and there were a few liberal governors and administrators who rose above the general poor quality of metropolitan appointments to give commendable service. But none was able to completely transcend the racism of his time.

Despite the alleged virtues of the Crown Colony system, the plantocracy was therefore able to continue to exercise political and social control over the colony. For example, the planter class was able to use its political clout to secure a labor force through immigration and, as we shall see, to use the law to enforce "distinctive mechanisms of labor force control."[31] Furthermore, with the connivance of the Colonial Office, the planter class was able to commit the local treasury to support financially the introduction of indentured labor to compete with the Creoles in the postemancipation labor market.[32] This indentured immigration was the mechanism used by the planters to frustrate the attempts of the recently emancipated bondsmen to escape the domination of the plantation.

Crown Colony rule left little opportunity for the disenfranchised masses to participate systematically, to influence political decisions in any organized way, and to make themselves feel and act as if they were part of the body politic. They therefore had no choice but to resort to the kinds of activities—withdrawal from the mainstream, constructing alternative institutions, riots, strikes—that ultimately became labeled as criminal.

It is this control of the nondemocratic political system that permitted the dominant elite of the plantation society to influence the rate and pattern of recorded criminal activity in the colony. The underlying assumption here is that crime can be defined as that activity that is labeled illegal in any society and that carries with it certain penalties and punishments imposed by the state. But the power to define what is illegal, and therefore what is a crime, has historically been the prerogative of the ruling class within any society. In the plantation society, the ruling elite defined as criminal those areas of activity they considered inimical to their interests and to the success of the plantation economy. But this does not mean that the ruling class was only narrowly concerned with the pursuit of wealth, although their behavior tends to give this general impression. No doubt some of the criminal laws benefited the elite in the short run. But those laws were often prompted by altruistic concerns rather than only by material considerations—for the elite were also concerned with a conception of order and a way of organizing behavior in society. Their legislation, therefore, cannot be always explained by crude economic determinism.[33]

CHAPTER THREE

Crisis and Adjustment, 1838–1854

The period 1838–69, the first generation after slavery, must not be ignored, despite the problems of locating hard statistical evidence. It is a crucial period of transition from slave labor to wage labor. During those thirty or so years, decisions were made that form an important background for understanding criminal patterns and activity in the period 1870–1900. In particular, between 1838 and 1859 the elite were able to recover from the aftereffects of emancipation and to reconstruct the society in an image that closely resembled the preemancipation period.

On 1 August 1838 some two hundred years of enforced servitude came to an end in the English Caribbean. In Trinidad—the most southerly of the British island possessions and one of its most recent West Indian acquisitions—the system had had a much shorter life span.[1] Trinidad's experience with plantation society began in 1787, so that, in effect, the British Parliament removed the legal basis of the slave society there after only fifty years. By and large, emancipation meant only the end of the legal justification of the slave system. But the act in itself was important, for at one stroke it freed some 23,000 human beings from the shackles of slave labor and converted them into a class of free citizens with the legal right to bargain for the use of their labor: a right that they would exercise to the hilt—both individually and collectively. It is in the exercise of this right and the right to be masters of their own lives that the recently emancipated came into direct confrontation with those who sought to retain as many vestiges of the old order as were legally permissible and concretely possible. The resultant clash and its repercussions form the background against which criminal activity in the postemancipation era must be viewed.

Most social-change movements appear cataclysmic only when the changes they wrought are viewed in hindsight; those who experience the changes as they occur may sense that the society is in a state of flux, but rarely do they have any strong sense of expectations or prescience. There are some developments, however—especially those that are signaled by some piece of legislation that becomes operative on a set date—that send tremors of anticipation and shock waves of expectation throughout the society. Emancipation was one such development where the intent of the act gave a clear indication of the enormity of its consequences.

Like modern-day legislative acts of political independence, the emancipation act brought with it feelings of anticipation and expectation. Emancipation seemed not to mean a mere tinkering with the system, (as amelioration in 1817 had), but appeared rather to strike directly at the very core of the society. For even though the £1 million compensation may have been offered to soften the blow and the four-year period of apprenticeship (1834–38) to have been suggested in order to ease both owner and slave through the trauma of transition, neither device could mask the enormity nor the seemingly irrevocability of the proposed changes. At one stroke it was proposed to create free men from a class of slaves and in so doing to dismantle the social structure that reflected a whole way of life, a way of doing and seeing things. Not only a labor system, not only a social structure that rested on this system of labor, was challenged but also all the justifications that were used to rationalize the system. And even if in hindsight these rationalizations and justifications are revealed to be bankrupt and illogical, on the eve of emancipation they were real—so real that men acted out their lives with these justifications as premise and in so doing reinforced and perpetuated the hegemony of the slave society.

But of course emancipation meant different things to the different classes in the society. The masses of people for whom emancipation meant freedom expected that the legislative act would significantly change the conditions of their lives in immediately recognizable ways. Even though there were slaves with fears and doubts about their future, the vast majority received the news with an understandable joy coupled with hope and expectation. They had a future to make that could hardly be worse than their slave past. Emancipation meant an opportunity to shape their lives and future in ways not previously possible. And with this in mind, they moved to make a reality of the abstract legislative abolition of slavery. At the risk of attempting to sound profound about a rather simple fact—the emancipated could only experience freedom as a fact if they could by their actions demonstrate that the emancipation act irrevocably removed the conditions that had governed their former existence.

For the slave owners emancipation could only foreshadow doom and gloom. A whole civilization was about to collapse, and the society was going to revert to barbarism. On the eve of emancipation one family leaving Trinidad declared with understandable gloom:

> We had now determined upon returning to Europe, there seemed no longer any rational prospect of doing good, in any sense of the word; the toil became insupportable, where the best intended efforts all failed, either for the improvement of the people, or the benefit of the estate. We felt that the really important influence of the proprietor was gone; that even personal security was in danger; and in fine, that there was no longer any incentive to remain. There were

> some good and faithful negroes, . . . but in the event of any rising, their numbers could have been of no avail . . . the certainty that we were no longer safe, and were no longer able to effect any good, determined us to leave.[2]

Biased, uninformed interpretations of postrevolutionary Haiti were used as justifications for this pessimistic outlook—a fine, prosperous society was now in ruins because the slaves seized the direction of their lives from the control of European slave owners. In the opinion of slave owners England was now contemplating to compound the ignorance they saw exemplified by Haiti by actually *giving* slaves their freedom. Emancipation was viewed as an immoral act perpetrated by an uncaring and ungrateful Imperial Parliament that was destined to bring untold ruin and destruction to slave society in the Caribbean.

But long before 1838 the slaves throughout the Caribbean had shown their contempt for the system that governed their lives. Sometimes by attempting open rebellion or more often by recalcitrant behavior that employed subtle and not so subtle action, they demonstrated that they were willing, if they thought the time opportune and the means accessible, to make bids for their freedom, whether individually or collectively.

By their actions they made it quite clear that they understood the meaning and nature of the controversy and debate that raged over their heads. They knew it concerned the conditions of their life—it was about slavery and freedom, and that was the central concern of their lives. As one governor Smith remarked in 1831: "The slaves have an unaccountable facility in obtaining partial and generally distorted information whenever a public document is about to be received which can in any way affect their condition or station."[3]

They construed every major blow to the system—especially insofar as it visibly angered and affected the plantocracy—within the context of their bids for freedom. It was quite easy for them to picture a planter class unwilling to grant them a freedom that they were sure was granted by a distant monarch. As a result, every step on the way to emancipation—abolition of the slave trade, amelioration, apprenticeship—they interpreted as news of their freedom and, when freedom did not materialize, they perceived this to be the result of deliberate obstruction by the planters.

Added to the planters' fears about emancipation were their frustrations created by the brief duration of the slave-plantation system in Trinidad. Utilizing an abundance of fertile land, the system had only begun in Trinidad in 1787; when it came to a swift end in 1838, the potential of the virgin territory seemed to have been unfulfilled. The colonial authorities had removed the supports of the slave society in quick succession—the source of the labor supply in 1807 and absolute control over labor in 1824. The weakened system had only to await the coup de grace—which came in 1838 with emancipation.

External structures and social arrangements may change quite easily as governments abolish the laws that legitimize their existence. It is far more difficult; however, to remove the ideology that supported and rationalized the structure in the first place. Ideas tend to take on a life of their own—very often long after the situation that gave rise to their articulation no longer exists.

On the eve of emancipation, the planter class in Trinidad was heir to an ideology that was at least two hundred years old in the Caribbean. From its origin and development by their lineal and class ancestors on the first sugar plantation in the West Indies, the ideology had taken root and exercised an undisputed dominance over the life and thought of Caribbean society. The dazzling monetary success of the early planters, the "golden age of sugar" in the eighteenth century, nurtured the ideas and ensured their logevity. A way of seeing, a way of doing things, gripped the minds of men so that they could only see the postemancipation period through these old perspectives, and they therefore sought, if not to totally recreate the past, then at least to influence the present in such a way that it corresponded to the essence of the old ideology.

The division of the society based on race and color remained as a by-product of the old system, since no law could abolish that. Then as now, legislation influenced only man's public actions and barely touched the private domain. Throughout the nineteenth century, division according to race and color continued to exercise its baleful influence on the society. But even that was in large measure tempered over time, as race and color distinctions tended to become blurred and class became the more important determinant of social stratification. This is not to say that Trinidad was ever a racial paradise; at any time more often than not, color, race, and class boundaries were coterminous. But given time and opportunity, one could breach the race and color walls that surrounded the source and control of wealth (which was the basis of the class distinctions)—either directly by inheritance or purchase or indirectly by marriage, education, or access to political power.

The inhumanity of slavery might be abolished, the unnatural use of race and color as social determinants might itself be removed publicly in the short run and privately in the long run, but what remained untouched and undisturbed was the organization of the political economy, the essential legacy of the past. Plantation economy and society were based on the idea that a large mass of imported labor should produce a staple crop for export in order to create wealth for a privileged few who dominated society politically, economically, and socially. It was an idea that had seized the imagination of the seventeenth century, had demonstrated its potential for success in the eighteenth century, and was faithfully adhered to in the nineteenth century, despite the changed conditions and the revealed fallacies.

In succinct words of one colonial official, it was a "hypothesis, expressed or understood, that the system of husbandry pursued during slavery was alone suitable to tropical cultivation."[4] As late as 1884 one of its ardent defenders again articulated that idea: "That the very existence of these colonies, as civilized communities is dependent on the continuation of the sugar cultivation, for which they are peculiarly fitted by nature . . . that with the ruin of the sugar industry the European element will promptly disappear, and the great progress made of late years by the emancipated classes will not only be stopped, but without the civilizing influence of European thought and European intelligence they will promptly retrograde."[5]

Whether in 1664, 1774, or 1884, civilization for the Caribbean as the plantocracy understood it meant one and the same thing—it was to be based on the production of sugar by a large labor force tied to large plantations and to be run by either resident European owners or the representatives of absentees. Despite all the new moral clamorings, this concept inherited from the days of slavery was still dominant in the nineteenth century—a monoculture directed by a privileged few and accompanied by the degradation of labor. Emancipation threatened this civilization.

The more pessimistic members of the society saw in the end of slavery not merely a decline in profits and the end of sugar cultivation but also a reversion to barbarism and widespread anarchy. This in fact was their definition of crime. The spectre of Toussaint's Haiti haunted them, and they saw the end of their idea of civilized life. Their comments in the newspapers articulated these fears. The slight skirmish caused by the refusal of labor to return to work on the announcement of the apprenticeship scheme in 1834 was enough to justify all their fears of an impending state of lawlessness and the collapse of the good old days of law and order.[6]

They conveniently forgot, of course, that they had never really experienced total and complete calm in the days of slavery. The slave system was inherently prone to conflict and depended on a large measure of coercion and vigilance to ensure any modicum of success. During slavery the means of providing this coercion was there—now the legal right was taken away, and its moral justifications (although still secretly and sometimes openly supported by some) were publicly ridiculed. Some of them awaited with undisguised eagerness the vindication of their worst fears of holocaust. In fact, emancipation day itself passed quietly, with only the showers of a tropical rainfall to add color to the proceedings.

If the evidence of this reversion to barbarism was to be found in the increase in criminal activity, then the harbingers of holocaust were sadly mistaken. One source that gives us at least a partial picture of the situation is the record of prison committals for 1838–54. Yet these figures do not tell the full story, since the statistics available for 1838–47 give only the number in confinement on a particular date in the year, that is, Michaelmas, 29 September. (See table A.1.) They therefore omit those who were not caught, those who were caught but received short sentences and were therefore released before the count was taken, and finally, those who paid fines rather than serve a term of imprisonment. This latter category is extremely important, since the stipendiary magistrate of St. Joseph reported in 1841 that only one offender in ten was ever committed to jail in default of means of payment.[7] Nonetheless, the figures are useful for giving some indication, however qualified, of the increasing number of people unfortunate enough to find themselves incarcerated on 29 September each year.

Between 1839 and 1843, the crude average was seventy prisoners in confinement on Michaelmas; the average increased by 50 percent to 105 in the period 1844–48 and increased by a further 57 percent to 166 in the period 1849–54 (with 1851 excluded because no figure was available).[8]

But now that the social control agencies, the powers to punish and imprison, were in the hands of the civil authorities, the increase seems rather modest. Furthermore, in the light of the population increases engendered by immigration and the spin-off urban-directed migration, the increase seems even more modest. The estimated population of Trinidad in 1839 was 36,655, and the population of Port-of-Spain was estimated at 11,701. By 1844 the general population had increased to 59,815 and the Port-of-Spain population to 15,609, and the census of 1851 gives the total population as 68,600 and the Port-of-Spain population as 17,205.[9] The population in the chief urban center had increased by 47 percent in the thirteen years from 1839 to 1851.

But what were the magistrates saying about crime in those early days after emancipation? In Port-of-Spain, John Cadiz, the police magistrate and stipendiary justice of the peace reported in 1841 that "During the first year of absolute freedom . . . there were numerous complaints of petty thefts, assaults and batteries, and drunkeness, but I am now happy to say, that complaints of this kind have been reduced to perhaps less than 50 percent. They have become more steady and fixed to particular pursuits, and they are comparatively seldom brought before me for drunkenness." The reports are the same for two other areas with large populations. In St. Joseph the stipendiary justice, J. A. Giuseppe, reported a decline in the petty offenses of assaults, fights, and drunkenness after an initial outburst in the months immediately after emancipation, but at the same time reported a total absence of major crimes. Finally, in Carapichaima, another populous rural area, Andrew David in 1841 agreed with his colleagues' assessments:

> The offences most common with them are assault and batteries and cases of cutting and wounding; petty thefts, and stealing in the dwelling house occasionally occur, burglaries rarely. Two cases of arson have been brought before me, several fires have taken place, some of which were suspected to have been put maliciously but no positive proof could be obtained. During the years 1838 and 1839, the cases of assault and battery, and of cutting and wounding were very frequent; they are less so now, but the change for the better on this point is not so great as should be expected.[10]

Apart from these petty offenses, all the magistrates' reports for the period agreed that crime was not a major problem. A holocaust of social disorder, a reversion to barbarism, a general bloodletting, did not materialize in those first few years after emancipation. When the bloodshed that the planters feared did occur, it was not directed against them. Instead, we begin to see the pattern of implosive violence that is a major characteristic of racially oppressed colonial societies.[11] There was no general epidemic of serious crimes against property, though there were some complaints of minor offenses. In Port-of-Spain, there were reports of nightly robberies between April and October 1839. At first the police suspected a gang of robbers led by one Fayal, but eventually they arrested another individual and the robberies ceased. In rural Mayaro, there were a few cases of cattle poisoning in the latter part of 1839, although it would appear that the sense of panic made a mountain of a molehill.[12]

The newspapers, of course, differed with the magistrates. The media, especially the *Port-of-Spain Gazette,* championed the planter's cause and appear to have exaggerated the extent of criminal activity. They complained that the police cases increased in the town and cited the increasing lengths of the case lists they published in 1839. No doubt the police cases did increase in Port-of-Spain. The magistrate, J. J. Cadiz, tried 41 cases in February 1839 and 121 in May of the same year.[13] But after all, the population in Port-of-Spain had increased, not only by migration from the rural areas but also by the increasing number of West Indian immigrants, who tended to settle in the city first on their arrival, until they moved to the rural areas in the crop season.

Instead of the anticipated chaos, the emancipated made definite responses to the demands and opportunities of the era of freedom. In predictable fashion they sought to escape the domination of the plantation on which they had labored for so long and for so little. They occupied vacant lands, of which there was an abundance in the new frontier society of Trinidad. A number of new settlements sprang up, some of them in almost totally inaccessible areas like Toco; but the vast majority of new villages were in areas within easy access of the two urban areas—Port-of-Spain and San Fernando—and in areas adjacent to major thoroughfares like the main road to Arima from Port-of-Spain.[14] As more estates fell into disuse and were abandoned, the occupation of derelict or fallow estates by squatters increased. Some apprentices bought private lands offered for sale. But the high price placed on Crown lands before 1869 prevented many of them from buying such property, and therefore they had no option but the illegal act of squatting.[15]

Mobile huckstering and permanent retail trades shops also developed as alternative activities to plantation labor. Even during slavery a number of slaves had demonstrated their penchant for retail trades and had established thriving mercantile establishments on the estates.[16] After emancipation, this group increased, and an important internal trade between estates and between villages developed in wares that included both provisions grown on home plots and imported foodstuffs and haberdasheries.[17]

The profusion of mobile hucksters and permanent shops caused no end of concern among some of the planter class, who called for high taxes and licenses to curtail the proliferation of these establishments. The chief complaint was that they were poorly organized and most of them were stocked with inventories worth no more than ten shillings. No doubt some of these shops were poorly stocked and did not display the sophistication in organization and marketing skills of their longer-established and European-owned counterparts. But it was grossly unfair to attribute their shortcomings, as some observers did, to the fact that their rejection of plantation occupations was an indication of their inability to pursue mercantile avocations. One commentator declared: "These shopkeepers, tradesmen and vendors, may be said to have absconded from the agricultural occupations, and as a consequence, are in general, wanting in those qualifications which are necessary to success in their new avocations."[18] Such a view indeed, was part of the intellectual and ideological legacy of the slave past. It was believed that the debilitating and stifling limitations of slavery necessarily constituted the proper training ground for the successful merchant.

Even those who had acquired skills during slavery fled the plantation and formed part of a general movement toward the urban areas by some specific employment groups. Artisans as a group flocked to the urban centers, where opportunities for employment were much better and not as seasonal. Likewise, the number of women seeking employment as domestics in the urban areas also increased.

Still, there was not a complete withdrawal from the estates. Some remained on the estates, attracted by free rent and access to provision grounds; others remained tied to the estates for reasons that may in future challenge the attentions of the social psychologist. In fact, what is even more curious is the behavior of some laborers during the 1840s, when the crisis in sugar prices forced many estates into bankruptcy. Despite the fact that the planter was in ruins and unable to pay wages, some laborers remained on some of these estates and worked for months of their own free will without asking for or receiving wages.[19] Whether these were estates where "humane" treatment in the preemancipation period was being repaid with loyalty in the time of adversity or where the laborers had developed a sense of communal ownership is not quite clear—but it is these strange human responses that sometimes defy simple explanations and baffle the historian.

Even those who did, in fact, remove themselves physically from the estates did not go too far away from the scene of their former servitude. As one writer has suggested, "they had been caught up in that revolution of rising material expectations from life,"[20] and living in a money economy, they needed a monetary income. But they sought to limit the degree of their participation in the money economy insofar as it meant labor on the plantations. Those who occupied lands located near estates preferred to work part-time on the neighboring estates at their own convenience. They preferred task work: that is, specific jobs, rather than regular employment. This gave them sufficient time to work on their own plots and to organize the marketing of their produce. In this way, work on the estates only supplemented either their subsistence gardens or income from other activities. But the overall concern of the laborers was that they have control over their own time and labor.

It is in their attitude toward labor that this concern with independence comes out quite clearly. That attitude bothered the planters more than anything else, for the laborers did not refuse to work, but they worked when and how they felt and no more than they thought was absolutely necessary for the realization of their own aims. The slightest incident that bothered them—the slightest hint at the authority of the planter or the mere suggestion of a return to the conditions of slavery—was cause enough to put down tools and quit the job. This attitude was particularly prevalent among the artisans, the skilled in the factories and the carters in the field. They knew that sugar production depended on their active participation and involvement. They were the crucial links in the making of sugar—those who took the canes from the field to the factory and those in the factory who were involved in the manufacturing process.

The planters declared that the motives advanced by labor to justify their refusal to work were capricious, as indeed a superficial examination reveals them to be. One carter, directed to take canes from one section of the field to another, bluntly refused, although he knew the canes were liable to become sour if left unattended. He simply walked off the job, and the cart and canes remained in the field. His reasons may have been valid. He may have had legitimate objections to the task. Whatever they were, however, they were not recorded. Some carters simply refused to work if they were not allowed to use their favorite animal in the cart.[21] Their colleagues in the fields were also rebellious—they decided when they were going to weed and when they were going to cut canes, and furthermore, they worked only on condition that the decision to work any particular part of the plantation be left up to them.

To exasperated planters, these actions appeared as the capricious behavior of rebellious adolescents. The planters have the final word in the historical record only because they gave themselves the opportunity to articulate their frustrations. We are left only to conjecture about the motives underlying the actions of the recently emancipated, since the voice of labor is conspicuously absent from the contemporary record.

Twenty-one witnesses gave evidence before the famous Burnley Committee on the condition of Trinidad in 1842.[22] There were seven witnesses directly connected with the planting interest as proprietor or planter, three representatives of religious bodies, two magistrates and a barrister; the other nine were all in some way connected with the establishment also—among them, the assistant colonial secretary and agent general for immigrants. Not one laborer was called before the committee.

But then, of course, the record would not be complete without mentioning Frederick Maxwell. This gentleman was the manager of the Philippine estate in South Naparima, which was owned by St. Luce Philip, a medical doctor. The Philip family had brought Frederick Maxwell as a slave from Grenada when he was five. He worked on Concord, another estate belonging to the Philip family, until he was manumitted, and thereafter he became the manager of the Philippine estate. Mr. Maxwell was quick to agree that the laboring population was much better pleased with its present condition, but he was even more vehement in his castigation of labor than any other witness. This was Frederick Maxwell's response to one of the questions:

> Q. If wages were to fall one-half, do you think that the laborers would suffer materially in consequence?

A. No, it would only oblige them to work better; and they would be much happier and better off than they are now, wasting their time in idleness and dissipation.

Maxwell complained about the drunkenness and dissipation of the laborers, but he paid fifty cents (2*s.* 2*d.*) for weeding "a square of sixty feet when the canes are foul, but seventy or eighty feet when in better order, with half a pound of fish and one glass of rum."[23] He was also annoyed that few laborers performed two tasks per day, with many of them only doing three or four in the week and others not more than one. He attributed their reluctance to work to idleness and laziness, and to a preference for living upon their more industrious friends and the plunder of canes from the estates.

Of course Maxwell does not qualify as a witness for labor, even though it may be that the organizers of the enquiry appreciated the publicity value of the testimony of an ex-slave turned manager. Because no actual laborers were summoned to explain or defend their actions to the committee, we can only surmise in hindsight that their actions were not really capricious behavior but serious attempts to test the reality and extent of a recently acquired freedom. Without doubt they knew the strength of their position in a labor-scarce economy, and this prompted not only individual but also collective action. In many instances, attempted exemplary reprisal on one resulted in stoppage of work by the entire gang. They recognized not only the vulnerability of the planter and his utter dependence on them but also the willingness of the ex–slave owner to resurrect, if not the form, then at least the spirit of slavery. They therefore defended their newly won freedom with the only weapon at their disposal—labor power. And perhaps in addition we can only tentatively suggest that in their attempts to decide where, when, and how to work, they aimed at more control over the decision-making process of production.

This attempt to define new relationships in the condition of labor caused a number of laborers to be brought before the magistrates, where they received the full rigor of the law for a breach of verbal contracts as in the two examples below:

> Caleb Quildore and John Charles entered into a contract (verbal) with Lionel Lee, part proprietor of the Orange Grove Estate, in wheeling magass from the mill to the magass house, at the rate of 6*s* currency per diem; that on the 15th day of March, 1841, the chain of the magass carrier got deranged; that defendants were ordered to clear away the magass, in order that the chain might be repaired; they (defendants) wholly refused, and neglected to do as ordered. In consequence of such neglect on the parts of defendants, the mill was stopped for the space of three hours, and a great loss incurred on the part of the proprietor.
>
> Sterrit entered into a verbal contract with William Power, manager of Paradise Estate, to superintend the carts of the Paradise Estate, at the rate of 13 dollars and 40 cents per month. That on the 7th day of the month of January last past, the said William Power received a letter from the proprietor of the said Paradise Estate to send to town a certain number of carts to *receive the baggage of the said O. W. Span;* that on the morning of the 8th January, the manager (W. Power) sent six carts under the superintendence of Sterrit, with directions from him (W. Power) to make inquiry at the countinghouse of Messrs. Gray, Losh and Co., where the baggage of the proprietor was to be found. Sterrit wholly neglected and refused to take out to the Paradise Estate the baggage of the said O. W. Span; the whole of the carts quitted town soon after seven o'clock a.m. without executing the manager's order.[24]

Without going into the validity of these verbal contracts—or for that matter, raising the question of the wide possibility of misunderstanding and misinterpretation—it is quite clear that both Caleb and John, as well as Sterrit and his carters, were aiming at job definition and specialization. The defined for themselves the limits of their participation in the verbal contract. Caleb and John contracted to wheel magass from the mill to the magass house, not to fix deranged chains or to clear magass. The jammed wheels prevented them from fulfilling their part of the verbal contract, but that was not their concern. They were not mechanics, they were carters, and therefore it was up to the proprietor to ensure that the conditions were conducive to the completion of their part of the bargain. In the case of Sterrit he was employed to superintend the carts of the estates insofar as their use pertained to the production of sugar. His duties did not include the transportation of personal baggage, even if that baggage belonged to the owner of the estate. If those were the arguments of the defendants in these two cases they failed to convince the magistrate: for their conduct, William Gray, the stipendiary justice, ordered Caleb and John to pay the sum of nine dollars each, the equivalent of fifteen days labor, to their employers, and Sterrit forfeited one month's wages to his employer.

Caleb, John, and Sterrit were only individual examples of unfortunate skilled workers who were punished by the law for a breach of verbal contract. Many others refused to work but were never brought before the law, because they refused to enter into any but the minimal contractual arrangements. The field laborer in particular would work by the task or at best by the day. In the labor-scarce situation, they held the upper hand and exploited the situation to the fullest. The planters had to tolerate stoppage of work, incomplete tasks, destruction of property in the course of duty, and even plundering of canes. They were afraid to appeal to the magistrates since "so much uncertainty prevails as to the result, so much loss of time by attendance of managers and witnesses, with a great risk of much unpopularity attaching to the former, interfering with his future exertions to procure labor, that it is in general found advisable to pass over even more henious offenses."[25]

The conditions of the market forced planters to pay high wages and also prevented them at times from forming successful antilabor combines. Both in 1841 and in 1842 there were unsuccessful attempts to mount a united front of planters to force a reduction in wages. The two attempts failed because some planters could not see beyond their immediate individual gain and need for labor. They paid the going wage and secured labor at the expense of their colleagues' efforts. It was not until 1844 that the even more drastic decline in sugar prices provided a sufficient stimulus to encourage cooperative action to reduce wages. There were strikes in some places for as long as six weeks, but eventually the laborers accepted the reduction.[26]

Some planters even modified their attitude to law and order to suit the demands of the labor market. They had at first viewed the growth of squatter settlements on Crown lands and abandoned or unused private property as distinct threats to their labor supply and conducive to the instability of society and the growth of disrespect for law and order. They originally tried to pass ordinance 9 in August 1838 "for more effectually preventing persons from settling on or occupying waste and uncultivated lands without authority." But when this did not receive the consent of the Colonial Office, they welcomed the order-in-council of 6 October 1838—which authorized the eviction of squatters, imprisonment of up to six months, and the seizure of their crops—even though it was less draconian than they would have preferred. Yet many planters soon preferred to view squatter settlements adjacent to their estates as potential labor pools rather than nests of criminals. Police action by the zealous law and order advocates, they argued, only drove the squatters into other areas, where some planters were less concerned with the law and more interested in attracting estate labor.[27]

There is no doubt, however, that despite this lax attitude to the law, the plantocracy and its representatives in the Legislative Council sought to use the law to create the legal climate in which they could still control life in postemancipation Trinidad as they had done during the period of slavery. Obviously, their prime concern would be to ensure that legally they would be entitled to demand the labor of the former slaves. Two factors prevented them from using their access to political power to its fullest advantage. In the first place, unlike the older territories with an entrenched planter-dominated legislative assembly, Trinidad was a Crown Colony, which meant the legislative body played, at best, an advisory role to the local governor—and in the final analysis the ultimate authority lay with the distant Colonial Office, which could bypass the ordinances of the local body and rule by order-in-council. Second, during the crucial period of transition, 1838–48, the under secretary of state for the colonies was James Stephen, a man heavily influenced by the current humanitarian movement and well aware of the planters' desire to continue the social relations of the slave society in the era of freedom. Stephen, who saw himself as a watchdog of the interests of the ex-slaves, played an important role in refusing to consent to any bill that included draconian provisions restricting the freedom of the laborers.[28] In 1838, of twenty-one ordinances passed by the Legislative Council in Trinidad, the Colonial Office disallowed eight for this reason, and in at least seven cases orders-in-council were passed as models for legislative action.

One major area of immediate concern was the creation of a police force.[29] One already existed for the urban area, Port-of-Spain, but there was an interest in creating a police force that would put in the hands of the central authorities the formal and informal policing roles that slave owners had exercised in the preemancipation period in the rural areas. Stephen's major objection was clearly to the obvious attempt of the planters "to create private constabularies for the large estates". He also complained about planters who sought to combine "police duties and power with the judicial functions of a magistrate."[30] An ordinance of 1838 that established a system of rural police was given consent but short tenure, and had to be renewed at least seven times between August 1838 and June 1841. An attempt to pass a consolidated and permanent ordinance in 1840 was disallowed. Eventually a consolidated ordinance was passed in 1841 but was repealed by Ordinance 6 of 1849, and the latter remained in force until the end of the nineteenth century. The ordinances of 1841 and 1849 were, in fact, based on a model police code sent by Stephen to the colonies that drew its inspiration from the newly organized metropolitan police system in England.

In 1838 Stephen refused to give consent to Ordinance 4, which sought "to ascertain and regulate the powers of Justices of the Peace in determining complaints between Employers and Laborers and between Masters and Servants, Artifices, Handicraftsmen and Others"; Ordinance 6—"to provide a summary power of punishment for petty thefts"; Ordinance 7—"to provide a summary power of punishment for malicious injuries to property"; Ordinance 8—"for the more effectually preventing persons from settling on or occupying waste and uncultivated lands without authority"; Ordinance 9—"for the more effectual prevention of wilful trespass on lands"; Ordinance 12—"to consolidate and amend the laws relative to Vagrants, Rogues, Vagabonds and incorrigible rogues"; and finally, gave only limited and temporary consent to Ordinance 13—"for the regulation of Hucksters, Pedlars and Hawkers in the several rural Police districts."[31]

In all of these disallowed ordinances the overriding concerns of the planters were quite clear—the protection of property and the imposition of legal restrictions that would limit the options available to the laboring class and thus result in the creation and maintenance of a dependent class of wage earners. The vagrancy ordinance, for example, was vague and had such a broad, sweeping definition of vagrants, vagabonds, and rogues that virtually any individual who was not at work on an estate could be deemed a rogue or a vagabond. Stephen objected to these ordinances because they gave large and almost unlimited powers to a magistracy that was susceptible to the overwhelming influence of the planters.

All of the legislation, including the model codes sent by Stephen, reflected the biases of Victorian England, in particular the concern with the protection of property, the attitude to work, and the latent fear of the masses. But what was important was that in those early years after emancipation, the humanitarian intervention of James Stephen prevented the passage of legislation that contained all the glaring, repressive features formulated by a plantocracy with its back to the wall. This first attempt by the planters to legislate the recently emancipated back to the plantations, and so solve their perceived labor problem, had failed. Other strategies would have to be devised.

If the problem in those early years after emancipation was shortage of, or an uncertainty about, the supply of labor, then the obvious solution was immigration. After all, if immigration and the importation of labor had solved the labor problems of seventeenth- and eighteenth-century West Indian society, then why not those of nineteenth-century Trinidad? It was also in keeping with the age: for if the eighteenth century saw in the slave trade the largest recorded forced migration of people, in the nineteenth century voluntary migration would reach enormous proportions, as the promise of a "new world" in North America attracted the poor, hungry, and dispossessed of Europe. The Trinidad planter recently deprived of his labor sought to attract to Trinidad as many of the would-be migrants as would respond to his promises.

The nearest source were the ex-slaves in the nearby West Indian Islands. They needed no encouragement. In islands like Barbados and Antigua where the land-labor ratio was different from Trinidad, there were few or no alternatives to the low wages the planters offered to the workers. In Trinidad, workers received thirty cents a task at emancipation of 1838, and shortage of labor had forced wages up to fifty cents a task by 1840. This wage scale was an irresistible attraction to Barbadians, who very often, without the option of doing task work, received twenty cents *per day.* So that despite attempts by the plantocracy in the other islands to prevent the emigration of labor, West Indians flocked to Trinidad. Many of them worked only for the crop season and then returned home. Some of them paid their own way; others benefited from a passage scheme paid from the Colonial Treasury. In the two and a half years between January 1, 1839, and June 30, 1841, 2,745 West Indians traveled to Trinidad with their passages paid from the Colonial Treasury. An additional 7,773 immigrants from the British West Indies landed in Trinidad between 1843 and 1856.[32]

But of course it was to Africa that the planters *first* turned to solve their problems; after all, Africa had provided the source of labor that created the wealth and reputation of the West Indies. The idea was well planted in men's minds that African manual labor on West Indian sugar plantations was the tried and unbeatable formula for financial success. Now in this time of need, unimaginative minds turned once more to summon Africa to the rescue. But times had changed, and now the migration had to be of free men.

A number of Africans came as genuine free immigrants from the colony of Sierra Leone, where since 1787 British humanitarians had established a colony to resettle freed slaves. In 1841 the first shipload of 181 passengers arrived in Port-of-Spain. This source very quickly proved unreliable, since for a number of reasons few Africans chose to emigrate from Sierra Leone.

The vast majority of Africans who eventually came to Trinidad between 1834 and 1870 were drawn from another source. Agents working on behalf of the government recruited them from the large number of Africans whom the Royal Navy had rescued from slave ships bound for Cuba, Brazil, and the United States and then sent to Sierra Leone and Saint Helena. Originally these liberated Africans had been given the option of service in the Royal Navy, enlistment in the West India Regiment, or after a period of "apprenticeship," financial assistance in resettling in Sierra Leone. The authorities gradually limited these options and pressured the Africans into emigrating as plantation labor to the British West Indies. Between 1837 and 1867, more than thirty-six thousand Africans, many of them still weak and shocked from the trauma of capture and sale, were taken to the West Indies. Approximately nine thousand reached Trinidad; over seven thousand of them arrived before 1856, the bulk of them (nearly six thousand) arriving between 1840 and 1849.[33]

Even Europe provided immigrants to solve the labor shortage perceived by the planters. Originally the argument was that a large class of yeomen of European stock would introduce into the essentially two-tiered socioeconomic structure inherited from slavery a group of yeomen peasants whose moral and industrial example would be of benefit to the development of the society. But too many things prevented the realization of this ideal. The idea that tropical countries could be worked only by nonwhite labor was well entrenched. The temperate countries provided too many prospects that were more attractive for white emigrants than those in the Caribbean, where industry was nonexistent. And more importantly, in Trinidad, a cautious land policy originally designed to prevent the emergence of a black peasantry was no attraction to poor, land-hungry European emigrants. The days of poor white emigrants making a fortune through swashbuckling or through legitimate pursuits were over—they ended in the middle of the seventeenth century, when, with the enthronement of "King Sugar," it became common currency that nonwhites were destined to labor on large plantations for a few privileged whites, and conversely that whites, because of climatic, racial, and other reasons were to provide only capital and managerial skill.

The majority of those Europeans—Scottish, German, Irish—who did come sought opportunities in areas other than plantation labor. Only immigrants from the Iberian peninsula, where the Portuguese—some of them fleeing religious persecution, all of them trying to escape the droughts, famine, and crop failures that hit the Madeiran wine industry—saw in Trinidad an opportunity for a new start in an agricultural society. It was these Portuguese—used to agricultural labor under a tropical sun—who emigrated to Trinidad. The flow was slow, however. The first group of 200 arrived in May 1846, and the following year another 346 came on bounty; all together, only 1,298 Portuguese came as immigrants to Trinidad. Numerically they couldn't satisfy the planters' expressed need for labor, nor did they make any contribution to the creation of a peasantry.[34]

Meanwhile, the planters' vision had turned and was now focused on the East, and it is the East Indian immigrants who came to the rescue. India, torn by civil strife, wracked by repeated famines and crop failures, provided another attractive source of recruitment for planters, who publicized high wages and painted Trinidad as a paradise for the discontented and dispossessed of the Asian subcontinent. The free movement of labor from one part of the empire to another became another manifestation of the idea of free trade that dominated the nineteenth century. The first boatload of 225 passengers landed in May 1845, and but for a brief two-year break in 1848–49, they arrived in a steady stream until 1917, bringing some 141,615 immigrants in all. Add to this some 2,500 Chinese who came between 1853 and 1866, and the Asian contribution to the attempt to rescue sugar production in Trinidad is complete.[35]

In aggregate, a minimum of forty-four thousand immigrants came to Trinidad in the few years between 1839 and 1861; thousands more were to come in the remaining years of the century. Their arrival had serious implications for the fluid socioeconomic structure of nineteenth-century Trinidad, and quite apart from the obvious demographic impact, the new immigrants brought changes to the pattern of crime in the postemancipation society.

In the first few years after emancipation the level of criminal activity could not really be described as a crime wave, and it certainly did not justify the worst fears of the defenders of slavery, who had predicted a backslide into barbarism. There were few scenes of mass riots, carnage, and the wanton destruction of life and property. The major offenses were petty larceny and drunkenness, with the occasional brawl and fight. But gradually, particularly in the second half of the 1840s, the picture changed—though it still did not by any means approach the mental image that haunted the planters. By 1846, the general complaint was that pilfering had increased "so much . . . as to cause great discouragement to the cultivation of provision grounds, and in consequence the supply of fruits and vegetables is scarce and insufficient. There has been of late also, rather an increase in the grosser crimes."[36]

The concrete evidence to support the contention that there was an increase in crime, especially the grosser crimes, is not conclusive, however. In the fifteen months between January 1845 and March 1846, the stipendiary magistrates, local justices, and courts of petty sessions adjudicated over 3,676 cases; but there is no comparable information for the period prior to 1845 to make this statistic relevant.[37] On the other hand, the average number in confinement at Michaelmas increased from the 1840–46 figure of 83 to 151 in the period 1847–54. Again, however, given the rapid increase in the population, it seems reasonable to expect a corresponding increase in committals.

Furthermore, the years 1846–54 were trying economic times, and insofar as there is a negative relationship between criminal activity and economic conditions, an increase in committals is to be expected. The plantocracy, already suffering from loss of labor and decreasing returns from sugar production, received its rudest shock with the passage of the Equalization of Sugar Duties Act in 1846. From then until 1854, prices continued to decline, but they then leveled off, with a slight increase, between 1855 and 1860. In the midst of this, and deepening the state of chaos, the West India Bank suspended cash payments in December 1847 and closed its doors. Many estates went out of operation, and there were numerous petitions of insolvency. Both planters and laborers were hard hit—the former were unable to pay wages, and many of the latter found themselves unemployed and with useless bank notes on their hands.[38]

During the period 1848–54, the annual committals for offenses against the person fluctuated between 121 and 175 for the first six years before making a dramatic decline to 94 in the seventh year. (See tables A.2 and A.3.) It was the number of committals for assaults that was responsible for this sudden decrease; although the other three types of offenses against the person had all increased above their 1848 figure by 1853, committals for assaults decreased by 50 percent between 1848 and 1854—and in fact between 1853 and 1854.

In the absence of concrete evidence to link increased police activity with decreased committals for assaults, alternative explanations have to be suggested.[39] Since we are dealing with prison committals and not cases either prosecuted or reported to the police, a number of other variables have to be taken into consideration. One of them would have to be the attitude of the authorities toward imprisonment as a punishment for crimes in this category and the possible option of fine in lieu of imprisonment. Some of these assault cases involved a minimum of physical contact between antagonists—as a result, many of them were considered petty and therefore punishable by fine rather than imprisonment. Hence, rather than overcrowding the jails with committals for petty offenses—although this was permissible by law—magistrates may have imposed fines rather than jail terms, and only the more indigent of those convicted ended up in the list of committals.

On the other hand, the other offenses in this category—cutting and wounding, murder and manslaughter, rape—were serious offenses. The latter two were without the option of a fine, and magistrates may have considered cutting and wounding also a grave offense deserving of incarceration rather than a fine. So the figures for committals for these offenses may well show a picture closer to the actual level of commission than the figures for assaults.

Overall, there were 114 committals for the three major offenses against the person. In the first year of the seven-year period, the number committed to prison was 5. It reached a high of 29 in 1853, then dropped slightly to 22 the following year. The rate of committals had increased fivefold in six years. It is fairly safe to say, then, that interpersonal violence increased during this period.

Committals for crimes against the social order decreased between 1848 and 1854. In 1848, 26 percent of all committals were for offenses in this category, and in 1854, the seventh year of the period under review, only 8 percent of all committals were in this category. The average for the period was 223 committals; but there were two major deviations from this average—in 1849, when the total committed was 351, or 138 *above* the average, and in 1854, when the 89 offenders imprisoned were 130 *below* the average figure for the period.

Only one offense within this category showed any signs of definite increase despite the overall tendency of the category towards decrease. Committals for resistance to police climbed from 10 in 1848 to a peak of 50 in 1852 before declining to 34 in 1854. This 1854 figure was still three times the figure for 1848, however. The size of the police force and its composition encouraged this pattern of resistance to the officers of the law and the lack of respect for authority. In 1850 the force numbered only 112 to police a population of 69,600, and in the main, its members were non-Trinidadians.[40] It took a long time for this law enforcement agency, largely alien staffed, to command respect in the society. Magistrates were at pains to impress upon the Creoles the legitimacy of this policing authority and increasingly resorted to imprisonment to underline their point. But until the fledgling agency grew in strength and its composition changed, there was continuous conflict as the indigenous Creole community challenged its authority.

On the other hand, committals for drunkenness declined from 128 in 1848 (a sizable increase in 1849 notwithstanding) to just 20 in 1854. This by no means should lead one to believe that the society experienced a period of sobriety, since these figures are for committals and not convictions. Therefore it does not necessarily mean that people either were drinking less or acquired a greater capacity for alcohol intake before intoxication brought them into contact with the law.

Any number of reasons could account for this decline. By then, the planters had finally been forced to cease giving alcohol as part of the wage packet, and this may have had some effect.[41] Decreased concern about public intoxication may have encouraged a consequent decrease in police activity and hence a decrease in the number sent to jail. Public outcry about moral issues is seldom sustained for any length of time.

But again, given the fact that we are dealing with figures for those individuals who received prison sentences in lieu or in default of payment of fines, it may well be that more people paid fines or that magistrates preferred to impose fines for what they considered a minor offense. In a period of economic distress, however, this should not have been the case. For although more people may have been driven into seeking refuge in alcohol from the economic problems of the times, fewer people would have had the wherewithal to pay the courts or to buy drinks. An alternative explanation may well be that the magistracy was sensitive to the problem and reprimanded and discharged rather than imprisoned or fined indigent drinkers.

The committals for offenses against the social order do not accurately reflect the state of disorder that existed in this period of transition. Committals for riotous behavior is a case in point. The recorded pattern of committals belies the volcanic nature of the society and the ease with which it could erupt as the underlying tensions sought resolution. Nowhere is this better revealed than in the riot of 1849.

There were thirty-five committals for riotous behavior in 1850. The majority of those committed were convicted on charges arising from a riot that had occurred in October of the previous year. An attempt to introduce new prison regulations that called for the shaving of the heads of prisoners, including petty debtors, and that forced the latter to wear prison dress and to work at hard labor had met with stiff public resistance. A crowd broke into the marketplace and selected a deputation to present a set of resolutions on the matter to the governor. An estimated five thousand persons gathered outside the council chambers during the deliberations, and soon a general riot ensued. In the melee, public buildings were stoned, and the crowd refused to disperse despite the reading of the Riot Act. The crowd even stoned the governor's phaeton, although he was not in it at the time, and that night "there were clusters of men in the streets armed with sticks and cutlasses who attacked every police constable and white man."[42]

The riot soon spread islandwide as estates to the eastward of the town were set on fire, causing some £6,000 damage. Other issues were soon raised, and armed proprietors in St. Joseph, annoyed over a proposed territorial ordinance that aimed at new rates of taxation to raise finances in the depressed economy, marched on the warden's office. Eventually, what began as an objection to prison regulations became a two-day islandwide riot as various groups sought redress for their particular grievances during this period of economic distress.

The record for committals for crimes against property do not conclusively demonstrate the usual negative relationship between economic distress and criminal activity. The committals remained roughly the same during the seven years under review. They average 25 percent of the total committals for that period. Only in 1850 do they increase to above 27 percent of the year's total, and only in 1849 do they fall below 22 percent. The bulk of the committals are for petty theft, the category that was common in the early years after emancipation. In fact, of the three principal offenses against property, 97 percent of the total committals were for theft. One observer claimed that incendiarism was on the increase, but there were only 12 committals for arson in the seven years, with 6 of them in two years, 1851 and 1852.[43] On the other hand, committals for burglary (as distinct from petty theft), definitely increased. If the sugar crisis caused widespread distress, it is not reflected in increased committals for property offenses.

Again bearing in mind that we are dealing only with prison

committals and not with convictions or total cases before the court, it can be reasonably argued that the available statistics are not reliable as an index of the extent of criminal activity in this type of offense. Not all cases of burglary and theft are necessarily reported, especially where the victim believes that the chances of apprehending the culprit and bringing him to justice are slim. Given the inadequate organization and the low level of efficiency in the police force at the time, this variable is even more crucial. In fact, in cases where the culprit is known, the victim may not make a report, but instead may deal with the case without recourse to the official authorities.

Nevertheless, crimes against property are useful indicators not only of the effect of economic conditions but also of the extent of social discontent and disorder. Discontented citizens may vent their feelings against property as the only tangible symbol of the source of their discontent. Arson, or the willful destruction of property by fire, is a case in point, but the proof of arson may have been problematic, given the primitive state of forensic science at the time. There were, of course, numerous reports of buildings on fire—but there is no indication of how many of those fires were deliberately set or, given the highly inflammable material used for construction, how many were accidental. The fact is that unless actually caught in the act, arsonists were difficult to apprehend. It is quite obvious, however, that arson may have been more commonly resorted to than is suggested by the rate of committals. As De Verteuil observed: "An African laborer, who may have received an offensive epithet from his employer, or some other trifling injury, will satiate his vengeful passions by firing a magass or curing house, or perhaps the dwelling of the offender."[44]

Houses in which cane refuse was stored as fuel were generally selected, since they were easy to fire, and thus it was less likely that the arsonist would be discovered in the act. This was the reason why smoking on a plantation road was made an offense: By so doing, estate owners reduced the risk of fire on the estates and ruled out accident as a legal defense for those apprehended on charges of arson.

It is in the committal statistics for crimes against the social economy and labor that we notice dramatic increases during the period. In 1849 there were 312 committals for such offenses, or 33 percent of total committals for the year, and by 1854 the number of committals had increased to 650, or 59 percent of the annual total. Imprisonment for debt is most certainly a reflection of the economic conditions. Small planters, merchants, and particularly hucksters, were the ones who were committed. The figures for committals are fairly reliable, since there was no great stigma attached to imprisonment for debt, and debtors generally arranged for their own incarceration and release. Most of the cases of imprisonment for debt were for sums of less than £11, and of 1,140 cases between 1850 and 1854, only 122, or 10 percent, were for sums above that amount.[45]

The other offenses in the social-economy category—breach of contract and offenses against the immigration ordinance—reflect the changing nature of labor relations in the postemancipation society. During the seven-year period under review, they account for 38 percent of the committals for offenses against social-economy ordinances. By 1854, the combined committals for breach of contract (still governed by Ordinance 6 of 1846—Masters and Servants Ordinance) and offenses against the Immigration Ordinance 5 of 1850 was greater than committals for all other offenses combined. This development indicates not only the increasing number of immigrants but the continued efforts of the planter class to control labor in the plantation economy.[46]

In conclusion, it can be said that criminal activity did increase slowly but steadily during the generation after emancipation. Nonetheless, the evidence suggests that preemancipation fears of backsliding into barbarity and society of uncontrolled criminality were not realized between 1838 and

1846. This does not deny that the activities of the Creoles as they responded to the fact of freedom were not deemed criminal, but obviously those activities never reached proportions that seriously threatened the safety of life and property. Between 1847 and 1854 the major increases in prison committals were for offenses against the social-economy and labor ordinances. Committals to prison for crimes against the person and against property remained fairly stable. This pattern probably continued until 1869.

By 1869, however, the society had in large measure adjusted to the trauma of transition. For the plantocracy the problems of labor, if not of capital, had been temporarily solved, and the planters slowly but surely recaptured their commanding position in the society. In 1849, in the midst of the postemancipation crisis, Governor Harris had remarked that emancipation was a "rude shock which disturbs them [and] not only reduces them to a lower place in society but puts them to the necessity of becoming indebted to the lower classes and almost dependent upon their will for assistance."[47] Twenty years later, this period of demoralization and dependence was behind the plantocracy.

The brief space of independence that the Creoles had won for themselves by seizing the time and exploiting the perceived weaknesses of the plantocracy was now being slowly eroded by indentured immigration. Imported labor had rescued the sugar economy from ruins and the plantocracy from destruction. The planter class could now calmly reassert or attempt to reassert its hegemony over the society, a hegemony that emancipation and the loss of control over labor temporarily threatened.

Between 1838 and 1847 the ruling elite had been handicapped in their attempts to deal with the society by the overzealous activity of a secretary of state who had blocked most of their attempts to legislate the re-creation of slave society. In a sense, then, they were restricted in their ability to totally define the boundaries of criminality in the society and to devise methods of controlling crime.

During the first three decades after emancipation, the plantocracy was faced not only with the scarcity of capital and the lack of labor but also with ethnic conflict within its ranks for the right to set the social and cultural tone of the society. This seriously affected their ability to deal with the "lower orders." By 1870 the French Creoles tacitly conceded the loss of dominance in the society and the steam engine of anglicization moved relatively unimpeded to consolidate its total control of the society. With increased access to capital, control of the labor supply, and its chief rivals on the retreat, the English plantocracy could now pay full attention to the control of the lower orders. But the basis of their dominance, the solution to their economic troubles—immigration—was a Pandora's box. The problems created would have serious implications for the character and intensity of criminal activity in the remaining decades of the nineteenth century.

CHAPTER FOUR

Law Enforcement Agencies and the Rate and Pattern of Crime, 1870–1899

In the newspapers, the articulate of the ruling elite continually complained about crime and, like their predecessors in the slave period and immediately after emancipation, they persistently visualized a spectre of steadily increasing criminality perpetrated by "the great horde of uncivilized" with whom they were surrounded and on whom they depended for their wealth. Many of their comments and fears stemmed from a thinly veiled but virulent racism that postulated the inherent and incurable criminality of Trinidadians of African descent and their compatriots, the East Indians. In fact, in the minds of the English and French elite alike, the propensity for criminality correlated with one's racial and ethnic origin.

The elite chose to be dependent on immigration to fill their labor needs, but in their view immigration was a mixed blessing. Many of them argued that Trinidad could not help but spawn increasing crime, since it was a society that was peopled by the scum of every corner of the earth, and this made Trinidad a den of iniquity. As early as 1856 Governor Elliot pontificated that: "The vices of different races of men, suddenly congregated in the same community, and standing to each other in various degrees of ignorance, cunning and moral insensibility, circulated with more rapidity and with more deepseated mischief than any physical contagion to which human nature is liable."[1]

The East Indian immigrants inherited the catalogue of vices that the plantocracy had first ascribed to the African bondsmen and their descendants—uncategorically they were incurable liars, thieves, and drunkards and were untrustworthy. The immigration of West Indians was also viewed with mixed blessings. The report with the Blue Book for 1879 solemnly intoned: "The immigration from the neighbouring colonies although no doubt it may be viewed as an indication of present prosperity in this colony naturally brings with it some evils. It undoubtedly helps to swell the numbers admitted into the Gaols and Hospitals of Trinidad—for a large proportion of those who come to the Island consists of persons who have led a life of idleness and vagrancy elsewhere, and who find a continuance of such habits more congenial to their tastes than following steady occupations."[2]

Others, slightly more enlightened though not necessarily less racist, saw a connection between unstable economic conditions and increasing criminal activity. They claimed, as others have before and since, that there was a direct consequential relationship between a rise in the level of criminal activity and situations of economic crises and unemployment.[3] The presumption was that in times of acute economic crises the normal constraints of society are rejected or ignored, and the necessity for survival forces usually law-abiding citizens to choose illegal means to satisfy their needs and wants. With a population already prone to criminality, the situation was compounded. Newspaper editorials and letters to the editor persistently talked about an increase in crime, and during the 1880s, when a fall in sugar prices created an economic crisis, it was argued that: "Placed between the increased cost of living on the one hand and the difficulty of obtaining work on the other, the labouring man will look about for other means to maintain himself and his family."[4]

But in the nineteenth-century plantation society, the coercive demands of the plantation system *always* produced a high level of criminal activity. Increases in the level of total cases, convictions or prison committals were not necessarily or always directly related only to these changes in economic conditions. The presumed relationship of crime and economic conditions reinforced by racial stereotypes influenced public opinion—insofar as public opinion was represented by letters to the newspapers, exhortations by religious authorities, or cries of calamity from public officials. Law enforcement officials who were also quite aware of the changed or changing economic climate were also well aware of the potential of these new circumstances as preconditions for increased criminal activity. When the public clamored about poor economic conditions, the law enforcement agencies increased their activity and generated increases in the criminal statistics that did not always represent real increased criminal activity.

The evidence from newspapers and some of the articulate members of the elite must be viewed merely as impressionistic and the articulation of their real and imagined fears generated by their knowledge of the conflict-prone socioeconomic system that they chose to be governed by and to govern. In nineteenth-century Trinidad, the problem of separating fact from fiction and self-serving assertions from reality is compounded by the fact that one individual, Lionel M. Fraser, during a long tenure in the civil service served as chief of police, inspector of prisons, and police magistrate and for a brief stint as editor of the influential *Port-of-Spain Gazette*. From 1869 until 1890 this individual held several posts in the criminal justice machinery, very often simultaneously, and from this uniquely advantageous position, he influenced attitudes about criminal activity and the crime rate. Yet it is the statistics compiled by this individual and his successors that constitute the raw material for understanding crime during the nineteenth century.

Statistics were compiled annually by the police, the courts, and the prison officials (see Table A4). Since our evidence and interpretation of the rate and pattern of crime depends on statistics not only compiled by these agencies but, more importantly, generated by them, an understanding of the nature and character of these agencies, how they perceived nineteenth-century Trinidad society, and their role and function in it aids our understanding of crime.

PRISON COMMITTALS

One indicator of the level of criminal activity in the society is, of course, the number of individuals committed to prison. The annual statistics on committals in Trinidad are fairly reliable and consistent for the nineteenth century, particularly from 1855 on. Apart from consistency, the major strength of the record of committals is that it is a clear indication that those imprisoned are those whom the society considered a threat to its well-being. So in a real sense committal rates may tell us much more about attitudes than about the actuality of criminal activity.

But there are some limitations. In the first place the total committed represented only those who were unlucky enough to be caught; therefore, it says as much about the efficiency of the law enforcement agencies as about real crime rates. Those who were caught were in fact only the tip of the iceberg and represented perhaps only one-tenth of the total "criminal" population. Second, some of those who were imprisoned may have been incarcerated because of an inability to pay the fine that would otherwise have served as punishment and prevented their imprisonment. But the decision to imprison may have been affected not only by the magistrate's reading of public opinion from the press but also by the annual reports of the superintendent of prisons and his complaints of overcrowded prisons, which were common in the nineteenth century.

For the thirty-five years from 1870 to 1905, not more than twenty-eight citizens per every thousand of the population were incarcerated in 1877 and not less than sixteen in 1899.

There was a steady increase until 1882, and then a gradual decline for the remainder of the century. The overall picture for the last half of the nineteenth century is a declining rate of annual committals, despite short periods of increases. The peak periods after 1870 are 1874, 1882, and 1894–98, the latter period coinciding with the time of the sugar crisis. The only conclusion that can be derived if one uses only annual prison committals as a measure of criminal activity is that the declining rates suggest a decrease rather than an increase of crime.

The indiscriminate use of confinement in nineteenth-century Trinidad presents another danger in depending on prison committals as an accurate indicator of the rate of criminal activity. Generally, those listed on the prison rolls would also include individuals who were awaiting trial and either had been denied bail or had been unable to provide bail or surety. It also included those against whom no specific charges had been laid, but who were suspected of criminal activity and were imprisoned while the police investigated the charges. Finally, the prison population also included witnesses who were being held in safe custody during criminal trials and those whom the authorities labeled "menaces." In the confusion of the nineteenth century, restriction of freedom by incarceration without due process of the law was not an uncommon occurrence. Before 1875, these non-penal incarcerations formed approximately 10 percent of the prison population, and for the remainder of the century those categories sometimes contributed as much as 25 percent in some periods.

It is quite clear that from 1883 the rate of committals to prison decreased steadily and continued to do so for at least the remaining years of the century. Certainly, this decrease in committals to prison did not reflect a decrease in criminal activity, but rather the gradual abandonment of the prison as the major agency of social control. From very early in his tenure, the ubiquitous L. M. Fraser expressed doubts about the efficacy of the prison system as a means of either deterrence or reform. In one of his early and many attacks against the penal system he bemoaned the lack of severity.

> In the gaol he [the prisoner] is well lodged, and fed at the public expense, with food identical with that which he consumes when at liberty, and clothed (also at the public expense) in a way which to a labourer in the old country would be a mark of disgrace, but which to him conveys no such feeling. He has medical attendance when ill, and what to the Creole and Asiatic is an immense enjoyment, he can sleep from 6 P.M. to 5:20 next morning. The labour to which he is put is not more severe than that to which he has been accustomed on the Estates or roads of the Island, and certainly can in no case be considered penal or even in the light of a punishment. What then does such a prisoner really suffer by imprisonment? The loss of his tobacco, of his rum, and of the means of indulging in the grosser sensual pleasures? I cannot think that this alone acts as a deterrent from crime.[5]

In Fraser's opinion the criminal class neither feared a prison term nor felt disgraced by it, for in many cases imprisonment to the lower classes was not a diminution of personal liberty but in fact an exchange of uncertainty for the security of shelter, clothing, and the certainty of food. He claimed that there was increasing disrespect for the prison and pointed to increasing recidivism as evidence of the inefficacy of the prison system. Echoing the debate then raging in England, Fraser argued that only a severe prison system could combat the ever-increasing crime rate and reformation of the criminal could only be achieved through punishment. During their prison terms those incarcerated should be subjected "to a discipline so severe as to make them feel every hour of their sentence to be one which for their own personal comforts they will not desire to repeat." Quoting Sir Joshua Jebb, a Victorian criminologist, Fraser argued that the elements of punishment were "hard labor, hard fare and a hard bed."[6] Yet despite Fraser's appeals over a twenty-year period, the prison system did not, either by punishment or reformation, make any significant mark on the level of criminal activity.

Nor could it. Although in many areas Fraser's misguided and biased advice was heeded, it was to little avail. The treadmill, the crank, and the shot drill were introduced; despite the controversy surrounding the practice, prisoners were whipped; prisoners were also sentenced to solitary confinement or placed in irons and were employed either at breaking stones, felling trees, or picking oakum. Distinctive prison garb and the shaving of the hair of female prisoners were other methods introduced in an attempt to stigmatize the prison term in such a way that it could act as a deterrent. The already meagre prison diet was reduced, and the withholding of meals was commonly used as a method of prison discipline. Despite these increases in the scale and range of punishment, the number of third time recidivists increased. (See table A.5). On the other hand, the number of *first* committals, like the total committals, declined throughout the nineteenth century, and that is during both the period of relative prosperity, 1870–83, and the period of crisis, 1884–1900.

Fraser and others continued to complain about the prison system and to campaign for prison reform. Among the reforms they advocated was the separation of prisoners. In their view, reformation of the criminal could be achieved and recidivism reduced if the prisoner did not have the opportunity to mix unrestricted with other criminals. The number of people that were incarcerated each year, however, made a mockery of any attempt at segregation. Prison cells were overcrowded, and it became virtually impossible to keep confirmed recidivists from first-timers or to prevent the slow, fragile, but nonetheless persistent development of a sense of caste/class consciousness among those who had been earmarked by the society and its agencies as beyond the pale of redemption.

Reformation or punishment became meaningless goals in a criminal justice system operating in a political economy that demanded the seasonal availability of a large unskilled labor force. Sentences were short; at least 80 percent of all the prison terms were for periods of three months or less, and the bulk of these were for less than a month. (See table A.6)

The sentences were too short either to serve as punishment or to effect reformation. Ideally, a prison term in a plantation society should be severe perhaps, but certainly not too long, for long prison terms removed the labor force and inconvenienced the production of the seasonal crop. In the case of the indentured East Indians, short prison terms during the off-season reduced the size of the planter's wage bill—since under the immigration contract the planter was obliged to provide year-round work for the indentured East Indian; short prison terms during the off-season also shifted the cost and responsibility for shelter and provision from the plantocracy to the state.

The decline in prison committals after 1883, which coincided with the period of crisis, does not by itself represent decreased criminal activity. In addition, it indicates the partial failure of the penology system, a shift in penological thought, and the abandonment of imprisonment as the sole means of social discipline. Instead, we find a shift to the increased use of the monetary fine.[7] It may have been accidental that this shift coincided with the sugar crisis, but it was certainly fortuitous. During the crisis, a beleaguered plantocracy required the services of the labor force in an effort to expand production. They therefore preferred to have labor available rather than in prison. The increased insistence on the fine rather than imprisonment forced the individual to accept the low wages offered during the crisis in order to avoid a term in a prison that was simultaneously increasing in severity. For even though Fraser and others claimed that prison was not sufficiently severe to act as a deterrent, in the long run more people preferred to maintain their liberty rather than exchange it for Fraser's delights.

CONVICTIONS

The convicted fell into four categories: those who were imprisoned peremptorily, that is, where the magistrate ordered imprisonment either because the law allowed no alternative or because the magistrate used imprisonment as exemplary punishment; those who were imprisoned because they could not (or would not) pay a fine that was imposed as an alternative to imprisonment; those who were fined and paid the fine; and last, those who were bound over (and/or whipped) and/or were reprimanded and discharged, but for whom the decision was entered as a conviction without imprisonment or fine. (See table A.7.)

Those who paid fines increased slowly from 44 percent in the 1871–76 period to 51 percent of those convicted in 1895–1900, while those who were imprisoned in default of fines remained close to 13 percent throughout the period. Peremptory imprisonment decreased from 32 percent of the convicted in 1871–76 to 12 percent by the end of the century and reflected the decreased use of the prison as a mechanism of social control. On the other hand, the number of those convicted but neither imprisoned nor fined increased from 10 percent in 1871–76 to 23 percent by the end of the century and indicated an increase in the use of the threatening coercive force of the courts as a mechanism of social control. Overall, no less than forty-five, and at times as many as fifty-eight persons per thousand of the population were found guilty before the courts. (See table A.4.)

Whereas prison committals show an overall tendency to decline in the second half of the nineteenth century, criminal convictions increased between 1870 and 1900. These increases in convictions reflect more the increased competency of the magistracy than increased criminal activity. In the nineteenth century the court system was not only class- and race-biased, unjust and corrupt, but unashamedly incompetent.

Table A.8 gives the disposition of cases before the magistracy.[8] Column 2 gives the rate of cases discharged: that is, those cases that were discharged for want of prosecution either by the police or private citizens or for lack of evidence on which to build a case. There was a steady decrease in this category from approximately 34 percent of all cases in 1870–74 to 23 percent of all cases by the end of the century. It is clear that although increasing numbers of cases were being brought before the courts, many had no evidential basis on which to be tried and were settled outside of the courts prior to trial. Column 3 lists cases tried and dismissed on their merits. This category too shows a steady decrease, moving from approximately 22 percent of all cases at the beginning of the period to 14 percent by the end of the century. This decrease reflects increasing competency on the part of the prosecuting officers of the courts; one notes a steadily increasing rate of convictions returned—from approximately 43 percent in 1870–74 to 62 percent by 1895–99.

There is a reversal of this trend in the disposition of cases before the superior courts. (See table A.9.) Instead of increasing, the rate of convictions decreased slightly, from 62 percent to 59 percent. Acquittals also decreased from 36 percent in 1871–75 to 20 percent during 1886–90, although they increased again to 25 percent at the end of the century. The number of cases that fell through (nolle prosequi)—either because the state or a private citizen refused to proceed with the case from lack of evidence or on the advice of the presiding judge or because the matter was settled privately—increased dramatically from less than 2 percent of all cases in 1871–75 to a peak of 25 percent in 1886–90, but then dropped to 15 percent by the end of the century.

Various reasons and excuses were offered for the high rate of discharges, dismissals, and acquittals in both courts. It was claimed that many of the discharged, dismissed, or acquitted cases were the result of the actions of the lower classes, who were "very much inclined to take out summonses against one another in the state of excitement" but eventually did not proceed with the prosecution. It was also suggested that some magistrates listed as "discharged" cases in which the accused was simply reprimanded and dismissed, although the individual discharged may in fact have been guilty. It was further claimed that in many cases witnesses could not be found or had been bribed and therefore the Crown could not proceed with the case. It was also argued that cases were dismissed because untrained police without professional assistance did not adequately present cases before the courts.[9] Finally, it was claimed that the number of acquittals "was increased by the number of cases of riot and similar offences in which identification is "difficult" and that the court returns listed the acquittal of *each* person tried as though he had been separately indicted, when in fact several persons were often included within the same indictment.[10]

The jury system was blamed the most for acquittals. In superior court cases, "the verdict of the jury must be unanimous, or the jurors [were] confined for twenty-four hours without nourishment until they [came] to a final understanding, or are [were] dismissed on some good ground."[11] The attorney general explained that "the accused can generally manage to secure upon the jury the names of two or three friends whom he can entirely depend upon, and as the jury is discharged if at the expiration of six hours they do not agree, it is not difficult for persons born in the climate to hold out long enough in disagreement to secure the discharge of the jury without giving a verdict."[12] The Colonial Office "doubted whether trial by jury [was] an institution well adapted to countries mainly inhabited by uncivilized races,"[13] although Judge Fitzgerald found no dissatisfaction to express with the criminal juries and scarcely recollected any instance of what he called factiousness.[14] But the attorney general, a Creole with thirty years' experience in the courts, was a better judge of the jury system, and he doubted the efficacy of the system in a society like Trinidad, "composed of elements so various and discordant."[15]

There is no doubt that color and class considerations played an important role not only in the selection of juries but also in their deliberations, and ultimately affected the rate of convictions and acquittals. But juries were used only for indictable offenses in the superior courts; the bulk of cases each year were tried before a magistrate and without a jury. The bulk of the defendants at that level were members of the lower class—black and East Indian—and they did not have the opportunity to use color and class connections in order to manipulate the criminal-justice system to their advantage.

The jury system—riddled by class and color conflicts, and increasingly influenced by a growing Creole nationalism that reacted against some of the glaring inequalities of the colonial system—affected the rate of acquittals in the superior courts. The increasing rate of convictions is a reflection of the increasing competency and size of the bar serving the courts. The bar of Trinidad was a combination of barristers trained in England at the various Inns of Court and a number of attorneys and solicitors trained in Trinidad. Ordinance no. 7 of 1871 permitted the local enrollment of those who, rather than incur the expenses of an education in London, preferred to article in Trinidad after passing an examination in elementary general knowledge regulated by the Supreme Court and a subsequent examination set by the Incorporated Law Society of London.[16] By 1894, as a result of a petition signed by barristers, solicitors, and merchants, Ordinance 17 of 1894 was enacted to amend the 1871 law and restrict the enrollment of locally trained practitioners, or "village lawyers" as they were called. The new ordinance required that in future all solicitors must be duly qualified persons admitted to practice in some part of the United Kingdom.

The petition complained about an overcrowded legal profession and advocated that the time had come for checking the influx of local men. In 1871 there had been ten solicitors in actual practice. After the 1871 ordinance had been in effect for twenty-two years, there were thirty-eight solicitors, twenty-seven barristers, and eighteen enrolled as articled clerks. The attorney general supported the petitioners' accusation of an overcrowded profession, of which the second branch (the solicitors) was "composed in a great measure of men of a comparatively low and uneducated standard, who are absolutely unfit to exercise the responsible functions" of the legal profession. The petitioners, concerned about protecting their monopoly, pompously argued that because it was so easy to enter the profession, "men unfitted for it both by training and education have slipped in—such men will naturally bring in persons of their stamp, who will further tend to lower the tone of the profession."[17]

No doubt the composition and tone of the bar had been changed as a result of the 1871 ordinance. What bothered the petitioners, however, was, not the level of training of the locally trained barristers and solicitors, but that their exclusive club of whites and coloreds was slowly being infiltrated by a few blacks. The monopoly of the nonblacks was being breached, while the myths that surrounded the law that served to make it a nonblack preserve was being debunked by the increasing presence of blacks. This is not to say that the newcomers were flaming radicals; many of them were archconservatives and reactionaries only too happy to be included or considered for inclusion in social circles hitherto denied them because of the color of their skin and their ethnic origin. But the mere existence of a black face—his local training notwithstanding—with the ability and the right to stand before a magistrate or a judge of a high court and eloquently argue the law as if British jurisprudence was his natural birthright was enough to torpedo the bastions of class and color prejudices and to fuel the growing Creole nationalism that was threatening to undermine the nineteenth-century colonial system. In fact, it took a long time for the presence of a phalanx of black or colored practitioners to have anything but a psychological impact on the large number of blacks with cases before the courts. After all, it took money to hire the services of a qualified lawyer, and one still had to face the often arbitrary decisions of a magistrate who was often not only ignorant of the law but often contemptuous of the notion of the impartiality of the law. Furthermore, many of these lawyers supplemented their private practice by working as a state prosecutor on occasion.

The appointment of a solicitor general to assist the police in the preparation of cases before the courts also had its effect on the rate of discharged, dismissed, and convicted cases.[18] This office was well served in the person of M. M. Philip, "a gentleman of color, a Roman Catholic, a man of such astuteness of character, and possessing considerable influence among the class of whom he may fairly be said to be a natural leader," from 1871 to 1888.[19] Philip was a graduate of one of the British Inns of Court and had a large private practice between 1855 and 1871, before he was appointed solicitor general. He brought the same talents that distinguished him as a private practitioner to his job as public prosecutor. He and his closest intellectual rival, Charles Warner, were among the leading legal luminaries of the late nineteenth century. Warner was the attorney general from 1844 to 1870 and had almost single-handedly drafted all the criminal and civil legislation that governed Trinidad in the nineteenth century.[20] Indeed, after his removal from office under charges of misappropriation of funds, he was retained against the government in many cases. Until his death in 1881 he and Philip towered above their associates.

The growing number of colored and black lawyers created legends with their legal skills before incompetent magistrates. Although there were hints of racial and class consciousness, these lawyers were not necessarily radicals prepared to storm the barricades or to destroy the colonial prison walls that were cemented by color and class prejudices. Many of them were active in the movement for constitutional reform, but more so because they felt personally cheated by the system than from any sense of outrage at the injustices daily perpetrated on the majority of the population. Still, some of them used their legal skills to defend members of the lower class and saved a few from ending up in the statistics of convicted or incarcerated.[21]

By the end of the nineteenth century the quality gap between the holders of magisterial office and practitioners at the bar was so wide that H. A. Alcazar, in a debate in the Legislative Council, moved that all future magisterial vacancies be filled only by gentlemen possessing a legal training. Alcazar argued that the increasing complexity of legislation on which magistrates had to adjudicate left the them at the mercy of lawyers. Significantly enough, his examples of complex legislation were the Agricultural Contracts Ordinance, which governed relations between cocoa-estate owners and their quasi-peasant employers, and the Indentured Immigration Ordinance, which governed relations between plantation owners and their indentured employees.[22] But legal training was no guarantee against attempts at control by the plantocracy: a magistrate in San Fernando, who had legal training, had recently run afoul of the plantocracy, who, dissatisfied with his rulings on immigration cases, had him removed and transferred to Barbados.[23] The competent members of the magistracy were resented by the plantocracy, and the incompetent ones were attacked by the lawyers in the courts.

Much of the incompetence in the magistracy stemmed from the backgrounds of those recruited to the bench as stipendiary magistrates.[24] Many of the magistrates had no legal training, and they were often recruited for qualities that were only peripherally connected with their knowledge of the law. There was a preference for English barristers to be appointed as magistrates. A number of Creoles were also appointed, however, but many of them had only a passing acquaintance with the law. John Cadiz wangled an appointment as magistrate in 1865 because of connections he had made while serving as copying clerk at government house. An editorial in the *Trinidad Chronicle* agreed that he knew no law but, in his defense, stressed his family connections and argued that: "It perhaps may be the height of wisdom to make appointments at haphazard and to watch with sagacious patience the doings of a new man who has to administer laws of which he is ignorant, and to perform functions which he has yet to learn. There is no saying what hidden springs of knowledge, energy and judgment may not, under the pressure of necessity, he forced out of such virgin soil."[25]

But whether they were local or expatriate, with no legal training or trained barristers, these magistrates were biased, and their magisterial decisions had a direct influence on the crime rate: that is, on the number acquitted and convicted. Many of their decisions were often arbitrary and based on subjective opinions. This was unavoidable when the magistracy boasted in its ranks individuals like H. P. Hobson, a stipendiary magistrate in San Fernando whose qualification for appointment was, not his legal training (of which he had none), but his supposed acquaintance "with the customs and characteristics of those who frequent[ed] the court."[26] It was not difficult for class and color biases and prejudices to influence magisterial decisions. G. H. Chapman often made his private racist sentiments public knowledge by his comments in the San Fernando court.[27] The residents of Arima petitioned for the removal of L. P. Pierre, whom they claimed crusaded on the bench for the expulsion from the district of all West Indian immigrants.[28] R. D. Mayne was notorious for the arbitrary way in which he dispensed his brand of justice in Port-of-Spain and once, flying in the face of incontrovertible evidence, told a defendant: "You are indeed very lucky, my good woman, that the constable has failed to prove his case against you, otherwise you would have been sent to hard labour, as the ordinance provides, without the option of a fine. But as the case stands, you must pay a fine of two pounds."[29]

Decisions relied less on law and more on blatant prejudice, and racist notions of the character of Africans and East Indians alike prevailed over the facts of the case. The Creole magistrates depended on their notions of class and color characteristics, and the English imports imported racial stereotypes rampant in Victorian England. By their blatant abuse of the law and their position, these magistrates swelled the lists of those convicted.

Corrupt and venal, they turned the magistracy into their private kingdoms. Mr. Jobity in Couva dismissed or postponed cases at will, although this was claimed to be "a dilatoriness which is a frequent fault among creoles." Chapman in San Fernando once had a lady friend sit on the judicial bench with him and take "a loud, boisterous and abusive part in the proceedings."[30] A petition from the residents at Princes Town complained that the magistrate there was a known usurer who not only loaned money at high rates but allowed his friends access to court records.[31] Others misappropriated court funds; in fact, Lionel M. Fraser—the terror of criminals, former commandant of police, and inspector of prisons—was found illegally using money assigned to the court's fund for indigents when he acted as stipendiary justice in St. George East.[32] Many magistrates were addicted to drink and discharged their duties while under the influence of alcohol. When Chapman was finally relieved of his office in San Fernando, he was admitted to the lunatic asylum suffering from mania characterized by the existence of numerous delusions and hallucinations. Medical authorities claimed that the members of the secret societies whom he stated visited him at night were the result of fits of delirium tremens, a condition for which he had been treated five times in one year; the working class may have attributed his visitors to poetic justice and the workings of their gods because of his unjust machinations on the bench.[33]

The superior courts were better served with legal talent, but were as equally biased as the lower courts. It was quite clear that the puisne bench, like their magistrate colleagues, shared the class interests of the plantocracy. In 1845 Governor MacLeod found it necessary to defend the puisine judges against charges of prejudice and bias—he claimed that although they had held property during slavery, they did not mix with the planters, and were men of great talent and unbiased. Their talent was not in dispute; but their freedom from bias and influence, given their background and the nature of the society, was certainly in question. In fact, MacLeod grudgingly admitted that in Trinidad, "where the nearest relatives of the judges practise at the bar, the community cannot divest themselves of the feeling that some bias may occasionally be entertained by the Bench."[34] The problem was not merely collusion between bench and bar, however, but the feeling that the planter class had undue influence on the legal machinery. Three years later MacLeod's successor, Lord Harris, reported that the lower class was still complaining about the unfair application of the law if transgressed by a colored or black man, and their lack of confidence in the system and in the impartiality of the law had shaken their energy.[35]

This feeling of mistrust continued throughout the nineteenth century, and with continued good reason. Many of the planters themselves were justices of the peace.[36] The planters and the judiciary—in fact, the entire legal profession—were connected by blood relationships, by marriage ties, by the old school tie, by membership in the same social clubs, and of course by their common allegiance to the race and color stratification that was an integral part of the ideology that dominated the plantation society. Few of them made any effort to hide these connections. Even the Colonial Office was forced to demand that the magistrate for Caroni—the heart of the sugar belt and the major user of indentured labor—"should be a barrister and one not in any way connected with the island."[37] The physical arrangements of the court often reinforced this feeling of partiality, since special seats were set aside for planters, their attorneys, and "other gentlemen of class," or they sat and mixed with the magistrates even when matters with which they were connected were on trial.[38] Even the court's timetable at times played second fiddle to plantation needs: Magistrate Hobson once postponed the sitting of the Port-of-Spain court to attend the sale of the plantation Lothians, where he was joined by the inspector of police and the other learned counsels of the court.[39]

Both public and private praise and/or condemnation of

court officials bear testimony to the continuation of this collusion. In the recommendation for one official who had applied for promotion, it became necessary to point out that "he administered the law without fear or favor deciding against most wealthy and influential persons and against [his] most intimate friends." The same official was praised for the firmness and the vigor with which he dealt with cases of "obeah" and "squatting," which were essentially lower-class transgressions.[40] Under normal circumstances this should have been redundant. One wonders whether his dealings with his friends and the influential were few and far between, equally vigorously prosecuted, or merely taps on the hands as the ruling class policed itself for fear that blatant discrimination would result in a total disrespect for the rule of law. One puisne judge, Fitzgerald, was accused of an excessive regard for wealth and position, a charge that did not strengthen the public confidence in the strict impartiality of the judicial bench.[41]

Between 1832 and 1900, only five men held the office of chief justice, the highest legal office in Trinidad. Between 1832 and 1869 the office was held by only two men, George Scotland and William Knox—Scotland for seventeen years (1832–49) and Knox for twenty years (1849–69). The three men who then occupied the office for the remainder of the century were, Sir Joseph Needham (1870–85), Sir John Gorrie (1886–92), and Sir John Goldney (1892–99). By their rulings and decisions on simple as well as on controversial cases, these men influenced the criminal justice system both in theory and in practice. By their actions, they demonstrated to all whether the law and the system of justice defended particular class interests or gave reality to the ideal of equality before the law. Of the five nineteenth-century Chief Justices, only Sir John Gorrie demonstrated that though blind, justice ought to protect the weak from the oppression of the strong.

Throughout his tenure in office, Gorrie was in constant conflict with the police, the magistracy, the bar, his colleagues on the bench, and the plantocrats—who saw him as the incarnation of all that was evil. But by his ceaseless efforts on their behalf, he won the respect, admiration, and love of the lower classes in Trinidad, who recognized in him a protector of their interests. Captain Baker, the commandant of police, reported that "vagrants and idlers, the very scum of the population—in the highways and byways openly and loudly proclaim His Honour as their special guardian and protector."[42]

The plantocrats and their locally based allies agitated for Gorrie's resignation and eventually pressured the government to appoint a commission of inquiry into his administration. When he was forced to leave Trinidad, Gorrie was given a tremendous send-off by a huge crowd. The inspector-general of police reported that "the Chief Justice on his departure was surrounded at the time of his embarkation by a clamouring crowd of thieves and prostitutes whose acclamation of himself was mixed with threats against law and order"—but that "the respectable portion of the community" did not participate.[43] The unrestrained reaction of the lower classes to Gorrie's departure was sure testimony of their affection for a man whom many felt and knew was a direct challenge to the corruption and bias that characterized the justice system. But Gorrie was only one man with but a short tenure. He left, and the system continued almost as if he had never been in Trinidad.

One's chances before the courts depended in large measure on one's class, color, and racial origin. The bulk of defendants were, of course, from the working class and were predominantly black and East Indian. In this British colony, one of the central maxims of British jurisprudence was inverted: if he was from a particular class or race, the defendant was assumed guilty until he could prove his innocence. The East Indians felt the brunt of this unjust system. Before the courts, they depended on court-appointed interpreters, who were often found to be giving wrong translations of their statements and pleas.[44] Already predisposed to believe that East Indian was the incarnation of all imaginable criminal vices, magistrates rarely believed either an East Indian plantiff or defendant. The attorney general reported in 1873 that "rightly or wrongly (but I think myself with but too much reason) the testimony of Asiatics is looked upon here as utterly unworthy of credence."[45] In his role as defense attorney in the Abbé Jouin murder trial, M. M. Philip (in 1870, two years before he became solicitor general) asked a jury to place little value on all "coolie evidence," since with "unscrupulous hardihood they violate the most sacred of the sanctions which they represent as binding them to the truth." His colleague in the same trial, Mr. Fitzjames, pontificated that "coolies" were "a class in which truth is rarely found, while on the other hand, falsehood becomes them with a ready means either for the purposes of revenge, or the acquisition of pelf."[46] Given this attitude, there is little need to wonder at the high rate of convictions.

TOTAL CASES BEFORE THE COURTS

In a criminal-justice system where corruption, incompetence, and prejudice were the order of the day and where honest, competent, and unbiased men were not only rarities but sometimes hounded from their jobs, the statistics on convictions and committals cannot be trusted as the sole indicators of the real extent of criminal activity. Instead, we should also take into account the total number of cases before the courts. This figure is a reflection of all those accused of committing a crime, not only by the law enforcement agencies but also by private citizens who believed that an illegal act had been committed that affected their life, property, or rights as a citizen. In the absence of consistent and reliable police reports, it is a figure much closer to the actual crime rate than figures taken from prison committals or of those who were found guilty and convicted.[47]

When viewed in relation to the phenomenal population increases of the nineteenth century, total cases before all the courts show a definite tendency to decrease after 1884. Using 1871 as the baseline, there was an increase from 102 cases per

1,000 of the population in 1871 to 130 per 1,000 in 1876 and then a sudden decrease to 100 in 1878. The figure increased during the period 1893–96 but was still below the 1871 figure. There was again a sudden drop in 1897 and a continued decrease to 78 cases per 1,000 of the population by 1900. Insofar as total cases before the courts reflected criminal activity, therefore, the period 1870–1900 exhibited a definite overall decrease in cases before the courts, and the period of rapid decreases significantly coincided with the period of depression in the sugar industry.

Some of these fluctuations reflected changes in the law. There had been a shift from Spanish law, and although this process of legal assimilation was largely completed by 1850, the impact of the changes was still felt in the late 1860s and the 1870s.[48] Furthermore, there were numerous occasions in the late nineteenth century when Trinidad ordinances were brought in line with English legislation and legal statutes.[49] These changes in the criminal law facilitated increased arrests and therefore increases in the number of cases before the courts. Behavior that had previously been considered within the realm of the law or at least acceptable practice suddenly became illegal, and these administrative changes and streamlining of the criminal code affected the court statistics, and consequently the interpretation of the extent of criminal activity. In fact, the number of offenses for which prisoners were committed throws some light on the expanding legal net that caused slight increases in the number of court cases in some years: for example, the number of offenses listed in the prison records increased from 83 in 1874 to over 146 in 1904.

One attorney general argued that the increased number of cases before the courts in the early 1870s stemmed largely from privately initiated litigation. In his opinion, this reflected growing respect not merely for the law or for the rule of law but for the increased existence of the essentials of litigation, namely, wealth and leisure.[50] If this was the case, then the period after 1884 was one of decreased wealth and leisure. In fact, while there was a great deal of privately sponsored litigation, the bulk of cases before the courts especially after 1874 came, not from private citizens, but from the activities of the Trinidad Police Force, and it is the nature, composition, and behavior of that agency that is important in understanding these fluctuations in the court statistics.

The bulk of the cases came from a police agency that was as biased, corrupt, and incompetent as the courts. This is all the more remarkable since the force was largely undermanned, and despite rapid increases, it did not manage throughout the nineteenth century to keep up with the rapid population increases. (See table A.10.)

The bulk of this police force was located in the two major urban areas, Port-of-Spain and San Fernando. In 1871, in an establishment 245 men strong, roughly 53 percent were stationed in Port-of-Spain, which contained approximately 21 percent of the total island population (See table A.11.) But although the town was laid out in fairly regular blocks that made it relatively easier to police, it was still a difficult task. There were twenty-six miles of streets that were divided into eighteen beats, and each beat was patrolled by three men on individual eight-hour shifts.[51] In many areas, however, policemen did not dare go singly: La Basse, for example, was described as "inhabited by a population so lawless and reckless that no single constable would venture amongst the broken down houses, deep ditches and open wells."[52] Belmont, Laventille, and east of the Dry River were other areas that were virtually impossible to police with single constables by day or night.

San Fernando was no better served, and its police complement was badly distributed and utilized. Hills and unpaved tracks that served as roads made police supervision in the town extremely difficult. In 1865, twenty-eight police and a subinspector stationed at the headquarters in San Fernando serviced both the town, with its population of about 5,000, and the outlying rural districts, with its population continually augmented by immigrant workers. A normal duty roster had sixteen police on sentry duty over the cells—six by day and ten by night; two constables on patrol—one by day and one at night; three constables involved in purely clerical duties; and three constables who served court summons in the county districts, leaving San Fernando at 7:00 A.M. and returning at 6:00 P.M.[53]

Much of this deficiency was partially corrected by the appointment of private rural constables. According to one report, there was a private constable on every estate.[54] Theoretically, they came under the jurisdiction of the inspector general of police, but in fact they were virtually private constabularies.[55] They took orders from and reported only to the estate owner or his attorney. It was therefore unnecessary in many of the rural areas where there were large sugar estates to have a large police complement. In 1883, the district of Chaguanas, located eighteen miles from Port-of-Spain, had a population of 6,114, of which approximately 3,158 were East Indians, the majority under indenture. Yet there were only five policemen stationed at Chaguanas. (See table A.12.) Instead, the district was heavily policed by private estate constables.

But what the police lacked in numbers, they made up in aggressiveness. In fact, they were badly trained and incompetent and masked these failings with an aggressiveness and zeal that resulted in swollen statistics of court cases. One police magistrate, in giving his requirements, expected the policeman to be "a fair scholar and a competent criminal lawyer." But this was asking too much in the nineteenth century—in fact it is a rarity even in the twentieth. The emphasis on the paramilitary character of the organization made it precisely a "force," rather than a service that would attract, encourage, or cultivate men with "the patience of Job or the wisdom and tact of Solomon," such as Magistrate Lovesy envisioned.[56] Instead, coupled with the pattern of recruitment, it encouraged the development of a spirit of antagonism that made the police an alien force in a community that felt itself embattled and under siege.

The military background of all the chief officers during the nineteenth century encouraged the development of this paramilitary and aggressive stance. The four men who headed the organization from 1867 to 1900 all came to the Trinidad police with previous service in the military rather than with experience from the developing professional police forces in Britain. Lionel M. Fraser, who served as chief of police from 1867 to 1877, was an ensign in the Twenty-Fifth Regiment and a lieutenant in the Forty-First Regiment, served in the Crimean War, and finally ended his military career in 1859 as adjutant of the Forty-First Regiment at the military fort in Trinidad. His military background influenced not only the way he organized the police but the attitude toward the public he encouraged among his officers and men.

His successor, Captain A. W. Baker, (1877–88) continued this paramilitary tradition of the police and in fact heightened the tension between public and police that stemmed from the overly aggressive attitude of the police under his command. He, too, had had a military career and had served under Lord Wolsely in the Ashanti wars on what was then Gold Coast. He joined the Trinidad police as Captain Baker in 1877, although on his transfer at the end of his term in 1889, it was revealed that he had retired from the army as a lieutenant but had fraudulently claimed the rank of captain.[57] Under his command the police declared war against the public on all fronts, under the banner of law and order and under the pretext of stemming the tide of rising criminality. The two major riots in late-nineteenth-century Trinidad, the Carnival Riot of 1881 and the Hosein riots of 1884, occurred during Baker's tenure and largely as a result of his aggressive attitudes.

The withdrawal of the regular military troops in 1888 encouraged the further development of the paramilitary character of the police.[58] The year of that withdrawal, Captain

Fortescue took over the acting command of the police from Baker. The latter had been transferred after some public pressure was mounted over the conduct of the police during his administration. Fortescue took over in the midst of the sugar crisis with public opinion of the police at a low ebb, morale and efficiency in the force equally low, and the war with the designated criminals only slightly abated. He too came to the police with the military service background. He had joined the Rifle Brigade in 1855 as an ensign and served in India during the Indian Mutiny (1859). He had seen action at the seige and capture of Lucknow, the affair of Koorsee and the taking of Fort Doomerea and had served on the North West Frontier during the battle of Shubkhudder. After a ten-year stint in the prison services of British Guiana, he was appointed inspector general of Trinidad police in 1889. Even if he had wanted to discontinue the paramilitary orientation of the police, the withdrawal of the regular troops had increased the need for the police to serve as the first line of defense for the elite, who always thought of themselves as living under siege.

Major General F. C. Scott became inspector general in 1898. Scott, like Fraser, had begun his military career in 1854 with the Forty-Second Highlanders during the Crimean War. Like his immediate predecessor, he had seen service at Lucknow during the Indian Mutiny, but his military reputation had really been made in West Africa. He saw service during the first Ashanti war of 1874, and after a ten-year period in England with Her Majesty's bodyguard and as Commander of the Fourth Battalion of the Middlesex Regiment, he returned to Africa in 1891 as inspector general of the Gold Coast Constabulary. During his service in the constabulary, he commanded the Jebu Expeditionary Force that captured the capital of Jebu Ode and took the Awujale and his court prisoner; commanded the Attabubu Expeditionary Force of 1893–94 that repelled the Ashanti invasion of Nkoranza; and commanded the Ashanti expedition of 1895–96, which occupied Kumasi and took the *Asantehene* and his court prisoner. From his service in West Africa, he came to Trinidad to command the police force in a country inhabited by peoples of African descent.

Fraser, Baker, Fortescue, and Scott came to their positions not merely with a military background but in fact with military experience gained from British imperial aggression in Africa and Asia. They came to a country where the economy depended on a labor force composed of the descendants of enslaved Africans and indentured East Indian immigrants. They came to jobs where in the normal course of duty, the majority of the individuals with whom they would come into contact had been psychologically crippled and brutalized by the society in which they lived and either had been forced into or had deliberately chosen a life of crime. Military service in Africa or India was certainly no training ground for developing even minimally liberal attitudes; rather, it encouraged the cultivation of all the racism that characterized the nineteenth century. They allowed all the fears generated by their other colonial experiences to influence their behavior in Trinidad—the Indian Mutiny, the Ashanti wars, the Boxer Rebellion gave rise to stereotypes of treacherous and bloodthirsty Trinidadians.

They themselves believed and encouraged their officers to believe, that they were, if not domestic missionaries, at least charged with being the only defense against Trinidad's slipping into barbarity. After all, they saw Haiti as living proof of the result of letting Africans govern themselves. They treated the lower ranks in the police as the native troops were treated in the colonial armies. They assumed that strict military discipline would provide at least a veneer of civilization, so that the lower ranks could be used as the storm troopers in the war against creeping criminality. Between 1867 and 1884, the number of cases before the courts was at a continually high level and reflected the intensity of the campaigns of the paramilitary police against the public.

Some of the men who made up the second division, the

inspectorate, whom had previous military or police experience; other men had none, like A. Douglas Owen, who was inspector of police in 1874. Owen, the son of an English barrister, came to Trinidad in 1870 as an overseer in the employment of the Colonial Company. After serving two years in that capacity, he resigned and found employment as a clerk in the Colonial Secretary's office. From that position it was not difficult for him to wangle an appointment as inspector of police in 1874.[59] Men of this background who had connections with the planting interest and who joined the police could not help but bring attitudes and prejudices that encouraged the antipublic aggressiveness of the police. Furthermore, although inspectors received 250 pounds sterling per annum plus 50 pounds rent allowance, they were also allowed a portion of seizure and of certain penalties recovered through their information. This practice encouraged corruption, bribery, and the use of one's position and authority for personal aggrandizement by unscrupulous and corrupt inspectors.

It was the senior noncommissioned officers who drilled the Trinidad Police Force (TPF) into shape as a paramilitary force and who brought it continually into conflict with the public. The TPF was from 1867 modeled after the Royal Irish Constabulary (RIC). From its inception, the latter organization was: "Armed and trained to operate as an agent of the central government in a country where the population was predominantly rural, communications were poor, social conditions were largely primitive, and the recourse to violence by members of the public who were 'agin the government' was not infrequent."[60]

The model of a paramilitary organization operating as a police force in a colony, which was the conception of the RIC in Ireland, was transferred to Trinidad. The RIC was a semimilitarized force whose modus operandi was based on the presumption that it operated in a society in which large segments of the population were opposed to the system of law that the RIC was commissioned to defend.

Noncommissioned officers were recruited from the RIC to come to Trinidad at fairly attractive wages and conditions. They brought certain attitudes and prejudices and sought to make the TPF a faithful replica of the RIC. One Irish constable, who was to make a name for himself harassing the lower classes, declared in his self-serving memoirs: "At the time of my appointment I had served sixteen years in the Royal Irish Constabulary, and a special training which I had for three or four years undergone in that force—besides having passed through two huge riots in Belfast—in a great degree specially fitted me for what I had soon to undergo in Trinidad. . . . The crimes in Trinidad in those days surpassed anything I had ever dreamt of."[61]

From 1868 these Irishmen dominated the third-level rank of the TPF and many of them were eventually promoted to the second division, the inspectorate. Under L. M. Fraser they established their right to run the TPF. In fact sometime in 1875, Fraser fell from his horse and struck his head. This accident caused him to lose his nerve and to be unable to exercise full and personal command over the police. He distrusted his second division officers, the inspectors, whom he suspected of wanting to displace him as chief of police. Instead, he began to rely heavily on his Irish sergeants and thus undermined the authority of the Inspectors.[62] As a result, the Irishmen were given the opportunity to completely run the police force and to develop it to their own liking; until he resigned in 1877, Fraser allowed these Irishmen to fashion the TPF. Fraser's successor, Captain Baker, although he exercised greater control than Fraser, also allowed them excessive freedom. For a long time they were a stumbling block to the promotion aspirations of the black and colored enlisted men, since when some of them were promoted to the inspectorate, the vacancies were filled by other Irishmen. Although colonials themselves, the Irish were no less racist than the English and were not slow to develop all the prejudices common to whites in black colonial societies. They quickly acquired bad reputations among the enlisted men, who invariably took their frustrations out on the public.

English senior officers and Irish noncommissioned officers were but part of the foreign element that made Trinidadians view the police as an alien army of occupation. From the very inception of that agency in the postemancipation period, Trinidadians refused to join the police. The working class had had the experience of a police force staffed largely by coloreds during slavery. In the postemancipation period, they therefore rightly distrusted an enlarged organization in which coloreds and whites still played an active and controlling role. Ten years after emancipation, Governor Harris complained that: "No native of Trinidad has ever entered the force; in fact, threats have been held out, that anyone so doing would be denounced; it is therefore necessary to trust any strangers who may present themselves, and hence to offer high wages, much above the rate of those given to labourers and artisans."[63]

The Trinidad Police Force became the refuge for eastern Caribbean West Indians, who fled from low wages and few alternatives to employment on sugar plantations. Barbadians in particular dominated the police force (see table A.13)—some of them were whites and coloreds, but the bulk of them were black.[64] Many of the West Indians were itinerant professional policemen who moved from island to island attracted by higher wage scales or who had barely escaped the law in their own islands.[65] Some were demobilized soldiers of the West India Regiment. Many of these demobilized soldiers saw little difference between soldiering and police work, and indeed, many found that employment in the police afforded them greater opportunity for expressing the authoritarian and sadistic tendencies cultivated by their military training, for which there was no other outlet for expression during peacetime. At any rate, if from emancipation Afro-Trinidadians had refused to join the police force and therefore began the trend of foreign recruitment, by the late nineteenth century the efficacy of a foreign-recruited police agency as a social-control mechanism was obvious.

The East Indian element was the most alienated from this law enforcement agency. According to the census of 1891, there were 70,218 East Indians in Trinidad, of whom at least 35 percent (24,641) had been born in that colony. In the prisons in 1891 there were 1,153 East Indians, or 45 percent of the total number committed for that year. Yet at no time in the nineteenth century were there any East Indians in the police force. In 1865 a letter in the *Trinidad Chronicle* suggested that Afghans or Sikhs should be recruited to the police force, but to do undercover work. The writer emphasized, however, that only high-caste Indians should be recruited, since "experience has shown that confidence reposed in the high caste Indian has rarely if ever been misplaced."[66] More than twenty years later, the chief of police echoed the same sentiment and preference for Sikhs, although no East Indians had yet been recruited.[67] Governor Robinson argued in 1889 that "coolies plot and commit crimes according to methods peculiar to themselves" and recommended that "men from the Indian Constabulary who have had experience in the criminal habits of coolies" be attached to the police force.[68] But the Indian Constabulary, like the Trinidad Police Force, was modeled after the Royal Irish Constabulary. Robinson's intention was not to hire East Indians but rather Irish policemen who had worked in India. The East Indian in Trinidad was left without even the possibility of using racial solidarity with the police to protect him from a brutalizing agency.

Not that there was any racial solidarity between Afro-Trinidadians and the Afro–West Indian members of the police force. For just as the police did not allow color to deter them in their campaign of brutality and oppression, so too, the working class defended themselves and were not blinded by the color of their oppressors. There was open war between the police and the public, and each incident increased the tension and encouraged retaliation from the other side. The level of resentment against the police force was high and was reflected in the number of charges for attacks against the police, resisting arrest, and refusal to comply with official police orders.[69] These were convenient charges that policemen used at will, often tacked on to other charges, to coerce and badger those who dared to question their authority. Nothing was more revealing of the hatred of the police force than the way in which the public took delight in cutting the water hose in order to frustrate attempts at extinguishing a fire at police headquarters in 1881.[70] The police were neither liked nor respected, but were viewed as a force to be resisted whenever possible.

Despite all this show, the force was terribly inefficient, and the police made up for their inefficiency with their brutality. They depended less on the development of detective skills to solve cases than on a network of spies and informers and on information picked up by constables who openly associated with known criminals and prostitutes. They were totally corrupt—accepting bribes, perjuring themselves in court, and even taking part themselves in other illegal activities.

Part of their inefficiency stemmed from the rapid turnover—few lasted more than ten years.[71] In 1895, 32 percent of the police establishment had less than three years' service, and less than 38 percent had over ten years' service. The pay was low, the conditions of work brutal. So much so, the authorities confessed, that one way of combatting the reluctance of nationals to apply was "by showing them that a police constable is cared for, respected and made comfortable by their officers and that his position is an enviable one, and that admission to the force is a thing difficult to obtain and worth seeking for."[72] But that was asking too much of a paramilitary force that attempted enforced celibacy by restriction of the ranks to barracks for long periods. Brutal conditions of work bred brutal men, and the possibilities of the office attracted many who used their power to victimize and oppress the defenseless.

They were a terribly corrupt body of men, and as the *Palladium* remarked, the police was "not remarkable for purity of character in the subordinate members of the Force."[73] Nor, for that matter, in its senior officers: following Captain A. W. Baker's transfer, it was found that that terror of evildoers had embezzled funds from the police canteen. The *Palladium* was quite correct when it complained about "their immoral lives, their want of sobriety and temperance." The Irish NCO's in particular, as Governor Harris had warned earlier, were particularly susceptible to drinking problems.[74] Sergeant-Superintendent Fraser came to Trinidad from Ireland in January 1892 and died of alcohol-related illnesses in September of the same year, still owing the rumshop fifty dollars for drinks; between June and his death in September, he bought or credited seventy-seven bottles of rum and four bottles of whisky. Fraser was probably a lone drinker, since much of the alcohol was bought in half bottles.[75] Many other members of the force were alcoholics like Fraser and frequent habitués of the rumshops.

A small group, the police felt themselves beleaguered, and they initially acted on the defensive in their dealings with a public that resented them. Gradually, under the goadings of their English and Irish superiors, they began to develop a sufficient esprit de corps to be willing to perjure themselves to defend a comrade.[76] Estranged from the policed masses not only by country of origin but also because they did not speak or understand the French patois that was the common language of the masses, they became more and more antagonistic in their dealings with the public.[77] From 1868 to 1884, under the commands of both Fraser and Baker, they ran roughshod over the public and were responsible for the large number of cases before the courts, many of which were discharged and dismissed.

Eventually, in their arrogance, they even dared to touch the colonial sacred cows, and they harassed citizens whose class and color should have protected them from police brutality. Governor Freeling "heard with regret from people of both high and middle class standing in the community of the overbearing and injudicious conduct of certain of the NCO of Police." One Irish policeman, whom Baker called "a talkative and impertinent cockney," even had the audacity "to arrest without warrant a white woman." Others complained about the outrages that respectable townsmen suffered at the hands of "the scum of Barbados from which our Police are notoriously derived."[78] The brutality that for so long had been perpetrated on the lower classes eventually spilled over and touched the upper classes.

After their handling of the carnival riots in 1881, even the *Port-of-Spain Gazette,* hitherto staunch supporters of the police, turned against them and complained that: "Nothing but the removal of Captain Baker, Sgt. Brierly and Sgt.-Major Concannon will restore to our Police Force the confidence of the population. The moral power of the Police, on account of the conduct of their superior officers, is entirely gone; and it is not by brute force that a couple of hundred men are going to keep order among a population of 33,000 one tenth of which at least are habitual violators of the law."[79]

The protests against the police continued to mount, and their handling of the East Indians in the Hosein riots of 1884 did not help their public image. From 1885 until 1892, public pressure forced them to ease up on their self-declared war with the public. This in large measure was responsible for the decrease in cases before the courts from 112 per 1,000 of the population in 1884 to 81 per 1,000 in 1892. Concern expressed over the relationship between the sugar crisis and criminality then encouraged increased police activity, which resulted in a rise in the total number of cases in the years 1893 through 1896. But by the end of the century the rate was down to 77 per 1,000.

The noted criminologist, Sir Leon Radzinowicz, is reported to have said that criminal statistics are rather like bikinis—what they reveal is suggestive and what they cover is vital. The description is rather apt for the criminal statistics of nineteenth-century Trinidad. The statistics on total cases before the courts (convictions, and committals to prison), reveal suggestions about the law enforcement agencies and their relationship with the public; but what they hide is the vital understanding of the nature of crime in the society. Decreasing committals to prison was not an indication of decreasing criminal activity, but rather a reflection of the failure of the penal system and a shift in the favored method of punishment; increasing convictions by the courts were generated, not by any increase in criminal activity, but by the increased competency and streamlining of the courts; and finally, the fluctuations in the number of cases before the courts were in large measure the results of an aggressive and overzealous police force.

An analysis of the nature of the crimes before the courts brings us closer to an understanding of the nature of crime and its relationship to the political economy. (See tables A.14–A.16.) But even more than the fluctuations within the categories, it is the nature of the specific offenses of which these categories are composed that is crucial to understanding the nature of crime in nineteenth-century Trinidad.

CHAPTER FIVE

Crimes against Property

When contemporaries spoke about increasing criminality, as they persistently did in the nineteenth century, they referred in particular to crimes against property and person and not to the bewildering array of criminal variety that faces twentieth-century man. Although the nineteenth-century man was not completely devoid of concern for the sanctity of life, only slowly did he reverse his priorities from an emphasis on the protection of property. In slave societies the concern for human life coincided with the concern for property, since the slave was considered chattel and therefore had to be protected as an investment. In the postemancipation period, since the labor force (real and potential) no longer represented an investment, the concern with real property and its protection became of prime importance.

But this concern with property was intensified because of the nature of the society. In a society where the majority was propertyless and where the continued wealth of the elite depended on their continuing in that state, there was obvious cause for concern. Furthermore, the plantation economy is characterized by its propensity for and its vulnerability to cyclical crises. The natural calamities of hurricanes, tropical storms, and crop failures due to pests and diseases were only one area of concern. More importantly, dependence on a single crop that was produced by a largely coerced labor force for sale to a distant market made the plantation economy extremely vulnerable and prone to repeated boom-and-bust cycles.

It was the knowledge of these structural deficiencies of the plantation economy that influenced the ideas and actions of the elite in Trinidad. They expected, and repeatedly articulated the fear, that in periods of economic crisis men forced by dire circumstances would increasingly turn to illegal means to relieve their distress. They also knew that, in periods of boom in a society where wealth depended on the systematic exclusion of labor from the means to be independent and where the possibilities existed for large sections of the potential labor force to resist inclusion in the labor market, some men would also resort to illegal means to provide themselves with the means of survival. The incidence of crimes against property clearly reflected the level of distress and inequalities in the society and the actions that individuals took as they sought to relieve this distress or to redress the perceived inequalities. It also revealed the actions the elite initiated in defense of their interests and property.

Property cases were nine percent of the total cases before the courts in 1875–79; the proportion increased over the next five year period and reached 14 percent in 1880–84. It increased again in 1885–89 to 17 percent before declining to 15 percent in 1890–94 and a continued decline to 13 percent for 1895–99. What is interesting about this fluctuation is that during the period of crisis, 1887–96, there was a tendency for crimes against property before the courts *to decrease*. (See table A.17.)

When judged against a background of nineteenth-century population increases, the figures for offenses against property remained fairly steady. (See table A.18.) Between 1875 and 1879 there were 6,799 cases before the lower courts. This increased to 11,555 cases in the next five-year period, the increases beginning around 1881. Over the following fifteen years (1885 to 1899), however, although the overall property cases increased, they did not rise above 13,373 cases in any five-year period. There were no dramatic increases—the overall figure remained at a steady rate over the period, although the rate per 1,000 of population decreased. During 1875–79 there were ten property cases and four convictions for property offenses for ever 1,000 of population. During the 1880s, property cases remained steady at fiftteen per 1,000 while convictions increased slightly from 5.92 to 6.14 per 1,000 of population. During the 1890s there was a decrease in the rate per 1,000 both of total cases and of convictions for property offenses.

These patterns in the statistics must be viewed against the background of economic trends. In classical plantation style, the Trinidad economy experienced periods of boom and bust during the nineteenth century. The economy shuddered from jolts generated by the impact of the Sugar Duties Act between 1846 and 1854. Later, Trinidad's situation as a major importer caused it to respond unfavorably to the impact of the American Civil War between 1860 and 1864. A period of prosperity followed these crises and lasted from 1865 until 1884. After that, a period of depression set in that lasted until the end of the nineteenth century.[1]

The price of sugar on the London wholesale market remained fairly stable between 1866 and 1883. Then it declined swiftly from 20*s.* 11*d.* in 1883 to 12*s.* in 1887. Increased production of the European beet sugar and competition from sugar in Cuba together combined to create this rapid decline in the price of sugar. The effect on wages in Trinidad was immediate and disastrous. One source reported that all estate staff—manager, indentured, and free labor—received a 10 percent cut in wages. The same source also alleged that wages in general fell from sixty cents to approximately thirty-five cents per day in the 1880s and that the indentured Indians received approximately three shillings per week.[2]

The indentured workers on the sugar estates were in serious trouble. Although their wages were stipulated by contract, hard-hit sugar planters were unable to pay. Nevertheless, they refused to release the work force from their contracts to enable them to seek alternative employment. Instead, the planters employed numerous stratagems to avoid paying wages. In some cases the payment of wages was delayed for as much as three months. More importantly, the planters enforced every single clause of the Indentured Immigration Ordinance in order to completely avoid paying wages or to cause the immigrant worker's indentureship to be extended.

Meanwhile, cost of living increased not only because of decreased wages but also because of increased prices for some popular food items. The import duties on bread, crackers, cheese, and flour increased, while salted and dried fish, which were formerly free, became dutiable.[3] Only those who had their own kitchen gardens or plots where they could grow vegetables and ground provisions as an alternative to buying these imported items escaped the effects of the new duties and increased prices.

But the crisis was not island wide, nor did it affect all sectors of the population in the same way. It was essentially a problem for the sugar planters and those directly connected with the sugar industry. Because they dominated the society, however, they projected their sectoral problem as a national problem. As one governor acidly commented, "the sugar planters get more cross every day because the rest of the island won't go into mourning with them."[4] Although he may have exaggerated when he claimed that the island was showing signs of increased wealth, in a sense he was not completely incorrect.

It was only the sugar sector of the export economy that experienced problems. The cocoa industry, although export oriented, grew and exhibited every sign of buoyancy and expansion. The trade in asphalt from the pitch lake increased, and the colony derived £30,000 in annual revenue from this source, so great an amount that the planters attempted to have the export duty collected on asphalt applied to the immigration fund.[5] The government public works program continued to expand and to provide jobs, much to the chagrin of the perennially labor-hungry sugar planters.[6] The opening of the Crown lands in 1869 and the land grants given to immigrants in lieu of a return passage upon the expiration of their indenture facilitated the development of a peasantry producing food crops, including rice, for internal consumption.[7] Although the tonnage of food imported was still high, peasant production contributed to a decreased dependence on the Spanish Main as the sole supplier of provisions.[8] The fruit trade with the United States, which could utilize peasant production, also grew in volume. It was sugar that was in a crisis but ultimately what began as a sectoral problem eventually affected the entire society.

The impact of the sugar crisis was felt first by those laborers who were directly tied to the sugar industry and whose wages were drastically reduced because of decreasing returns from sugar. The indentured workers tied to the estate by contract felt the brunt of it. They had nowhere to run and therefore had to face not only decreased wages but all kinds of stratagems to defraud them of their wages and extract the maximum labor output from them. The nonindentured workers on the sugar estates fared according to the degree of their dependence on employment on the estates. Those who were totally dependent on estate labor were in almost the same position as the indentureds, but they at least had the option of withholding labor or moving to the cocoa estates. Many of them migrated to the urban areas, where it was believed job opportunities existed. Some of them were fortunate, but eventually the migration decreased the opportunities available and in fact created a floating labor force of casual labor. Those who were only partially dependent on estate employment depended on either their peasant holdings, and therefore greater participation in the internal market economy, or employment in cocoa, coconuts, coffee and citrus fruit estates. Meanwhile, despite the crisis, the sugar planters continued to import indentured immigrants and turned a blind eye to their own role in the pauperization and criminalization of large segments of the population.

PAUPERISM AND INDEBTEDNESS

There was no systematic provision other than the hospitals for the relief of persons destitute through want of employment or other causes.[9] Earlier attempts to pass a poor law and establish a board for the relief of indigents met with the usual opposition from the planters and their allies, who foresaw the abuse of the system by a people whom they considered naturally inclined to be lazy. The district wardens supervised the disbursement of a small fund allocated in the annual budget, and this was generally restricted to outdoor medical treatment and the burial of paupers. In fact, because of the system of disbursement, or rather the lack of an efficient system, only those who desperately required medical attention—and one had to be at death's door to qualify as desperate—ever received assistance. Without strict guidelines, the disbursement of relief was influenced by the biased and subjective judgment of the wardens.

The wardens continually complained both of the able-bodied men who were quite capable of working but sought relief and of the overabundance of non-natives on the relief rolls. The warden of Couva and Chaguanas Ward Union situated in the heart of the sugar belt, grudgingly granted 757 certificates in 1886. He recommended that a strictly enforced vagrant law be instituted "by which all idlers in the towns and villages could be taken up and indentured to estates far away from their regular haunts."[10] Nonetheless, the governor complained that the wardens tended to bestow charity somewhat too freely.[11]

Some wardens found it difficult to understand the connection between the economic crisis and the rise in applications for poor relief. Thornton Warner, the warden of Montserrat, noted that applications for pauper relief increased from 80 cases in 1885 to 194 cases in 1886, but he commented that:

"This will, I presume, be attributed entirely to the continued depression in the sugar market; but another undeniable cause there is, that hundreds of vagrants are wandering all over the island living a hand to mouth existence, until sickness, produced by constant exposure of their ill-clad and ill-fed bodies during a heavy rainy season, drives them into hospital; the necessity for a Penitentiary and other such institutions becomes annually more pressing."[12]

It was quite clear that if there were a need, relief was given grudgingly in time of crisis, but that the authorities considered pauperism a crime. Even those who were not desperately ill found the pittance they received barely sufficient to satisfy their needs. Mary Sandy, a thirty-five-year-old widow of Rambert Village, received 12*s*. 6*d*. per month to support herself and her seven children, who ranged in age from twelve to one-and-a-half years. Susan Callender of St. Madeline, a thirty-year-old widow with six children, the eldest ten years, received the same amount.[13] The imagination boggles at the stratagems Mary Sandy and Susan Callender must have been forced to devise in order to survive in an age without state support for children below school age and were work was scarce and the cost of living high.

Not only were the authorities parsimonious about the distribution of relief—only £724 were spent on pauper relief for 4,956 recipients in the northern districts in 1889[14]—but they claimed that the destitute were responsible for their own condition. In testimony before the Royal Commission of Inquiry in 1897, one justice of the court, Justice Nathan, went on record as saying that *thrift* was a word untranslatable in the popularly used French patois.[15] In Nathan's opinion, any problem faced by the Creoles during the period of crisis stemmed from their spendthrift nature.

Nathan merely echoed a popular sentiment about Creole character that was based on biased observations of Creole behavior. Their love of fine clothes and the size and spread of catering for weddings, wakes, and other receptions were taken as sufficient evidence for comments about Creole attitudes toward thrift. The fact that few Creoles had bank accounts led many observers to this erroneous conclusion about Creole behavior. But what Nathan and others did not understand was the deep-rooted mistrust of banks and the existence of alternative saving schemes. Slaves had been encouraged to use the savings bank since the time of the amelioration measures in an attempt to encourage thrift, especially among those who intended to accumulate funds to pay for their manumission. The scheme was not extremely successful then, nor was banking popular in the postemancipation period. The failure of the West India Bank in December 1847, when a number of Creoles lost their savings, further decreased the attractiveness of the Government Savings Bank. In addition, until 1886 there were only two branches, one at Port-of-Spain and one at San Fernando. Many people in the rural areas preferred to save at home rather than take the long journey to the urban centers; in rare cases they made an annual trip to deposit their year's savings.[16]

At any rate, many of the Creoles (and Africans) preferred to save communally by using "the box" or *sou-sou* system, a system of rotating savings that was very popular in West Africa.[17] Since no records exist for these savings schemes, it is unfair to label the Creoles as averse to savings. It is difficult to chart how effective they were during times of economic crisis.

We are on much safer ground with the Friendly Societies. Weekly or monthly contributions to the Friendly Societies proved to have greater attraction than the Savings Bank. Membership in these societies brought with it certain social benefits that were absent in the rather cold and impersonal government banking system. These societies provided financial assistance—for medical bills during times of ill health and to pay for burials at death. They also provided the opportunity for conviviality and camaraderie, for leadership training, and for discharging community responsibilities. Many of them were organized as fraternal groups with membership based on ethnic lines; one such group operated among the Yoruba in a Montserrat squatter element in the early 1860s.[18] Most of them were short-lived: they were organized, flourished, and died. Their life cycle reflected shifting ethnic and residential patterns and fluctuations.

Although it is fairly safe to imagine that the institution had been in existence, in this or some other form, since the slave period,[19] by 1900 the list of *registered* societies indicated that the oldest registered group, the Port-of-Spain Wesleyan, began in 1889.[20] In 1894, there were 61 registered societies with a total membership of 6,384—by 1900 the number of societies had decreased by 4, but total membership increased by 346.[21] Although the savings banks were not popular with the Creoles, government regulations in 1888 demanded that the societies use the banks.[22] In 1890 only 20 societies had their liquid assets deposited in the banks. By 1895 this had increased to 61, and by 1910, 160 societies were listed as depositors.[23] Their assets were modest but significant: the 61 societies in 1894 had $11,209.20 deposited in the bank and had $455.21 in hand and real property to the value of $9,328.76.[24]

These societies and their savings demonstrated the falsehood of the popular charges of spendthriftiness leveled against the black Creoles. Ironically, the success of these societies provided a ready excuse to avoid instituting a well-organized system of relief for indigents. The usefulness of these institutions did not go unnoticed by some authorities. In 1889 one report noted: "individual efforts to grapple with the demoralising taint of pauperism. These may be seen in the activities of various societies for benevolent purposes now established for sick relief and interments of members, their wives, children and dependents; and thus also engendering habits of thrift and laying the basis of an effective substitute for a poor law."[25] Unlike these voluntary organizations, savings banks on the whole did not really enjoy any great popularity: in 1882 only 1 percent of the population had deposits in the bank, and this slowly increased to 4 percent by 1896. The state took great efforts to encourage savings, since in the words of the receiver general savings were a guarantee that the depositor "will be a peaceful and orderly citizen and that greater interest will be taken in promoting the harmony and well being of the state."[26]

Mistrust of banks since the failure of the West Indian Bank in 1847 and the availability of more socially attractive alternative saving schemes kept the Creoles away. But the East Indians became the bank's best customers. Many East Indians, with the drive that characterizes immigrants who intend to be successful in their adopted land, were the chief depositors—in 1895, 40 percent of all depositors were East Indians. Just as the Creoles mistrusted the banks, East Indians were scared of private saving schemes, and with good reason. In 1883, Archdeacon Richards, Rector of the St. Mary's Anglican Church, was unable to account for some £20,000 he had received from East Indians over a twenty-year period.[27] In fact, this episode impoverished many East Indians and increased their general defenselessness during the economic crisis.

Many immigrants cherished the hope of returning to India with their accumulated savings upon the expiration of their contract. Some of them managed to achieve this goal, and this success was used to vindicate the system of indentureship. But as Hugh Tinker acidly commented, those who returned were either "the defeated or the winners, either poor or rich." The spectacular wealth of the few masked the dismal poverty of the many. In 1916, of the 580 immigrants returning from Trinidad, 120 carried *Rs* 150 or more and 192 had *Rs* 1 or more, but 388 had nothing at all but the clothes on their backs.[28] The records do not reveal the length of their indenture and how long and by what means those who saved managed to accumulate. In fact, many of the richer passengers were either sirdars (headmen), shopkeepers, or moneylenders; the latter group in particular accumulated their savings through the extortionate lending rates they demanded from their less fortunate compatriots.[29]

The economic crisis not only affected laborers and resulted in increased pauperism, it also affected the extent of indebtedness. Between 1875 and 1879, there was a moratorium on imprisonment for debt, and Ordinance 2 of 1874, which amended the law of arrest for debt, was opposed by a petition of provision and other merchants on the grounds that the ordinance virtually abolished imprisonment. By 1879, the *Port-of-Spain Gazette,* the traditional mouthpiece of the plantocracy, claimed that the opposition of the mercantile interests to the passage of the ordinance had been well founded, since debtor's summons were useless and shopkeepers were incurring debts and declaring bankruptcy, with impunity. East Indian and Chinese shopkeepers were planters' prime targets, and the *Gazette* editorialized that: "The Asiatic element is so obviously conspicuous in the commercial frauds of the colony as to furnish a sufficient reason why we should be indifferent to the reproach of receding into a barbarous stage, by seeking to re-establish imprisonment for debt."[30] The advocates for imprisonment had their way, and imprisonment for debt was reestablished during the period of crisis. (See table A.19.)

Many of those imprisoned for debt were petty traders and small shopkeepers who sought to escape the domination of the plantation by huckstering and retail trade. They depended on the urban-based import merchants for their stock, which they retailed in small shops throughout the countryside. Earlier, some interest groups had tried to curtail the proliferation of these shops by advocating the imposition of restrictive taxes. Increased import duties on popular items during the crisis of the late 1880s, decreased the sellers' margin of profit. Decreased wages during the depression of the same period reduced their clientele, since many of their customers were not in a position to buy as much as before, or often, even to repay debts incurred before the crisis. These shopkeepers were therefore unable to pay their urban-based suppliers, and many of them risked imprisonment by voluntarily filing for certificates of indebtedness. Both directly and indirectly, the depression in sugar prices slowly reduced the opportunities of large segments of the population for honestly and legally earning a livelihood.

In an agriculture-based economy, as Trinidad was in the nineteenth century, increased rates of praedial larceny are clear indicators of the effect of distress on criminality. Praedial larceny is the theft or illegal removal of any living animal or growing crop, and in an agricultural economy there is a greater tendency for this category of offense to be extremely regular and high. But it is largely an "invisible" crime. The stolen merchandise is either immediately consumed or sold directly to a receiver, who further redistributes the item. In the first case, where the stolen goods are immediately consumed, the amount is usually small, and the incidence is regular and persistent. There is great difficulty either in proving the case in court or, for that matter, in putting an end to the practice without the use of draconian measures.

The theft of plantation crops was a common feature of the slave society. Many slaves supplemented their often meagre diets with items purloined from the plantation. The perpetrators usually excused the theft as being part of their rights as slaves to avail themselves of any part of their owner's property. Usually excused but not openly condoned, it was only punished when it reached alarming proportions. After all, it was better to have a slave who, although a thief (and who by the act confirmed the stereotype), still recognized not only the authority of the master but also the relationship between himself and his owner. In the postemancipation period praedial larceny could not be condoned, for it represented an outright attack on the property of the plantation owner without the consoling benefit of recognition of authority and the reinforcement of hegemony that was inherent in the slave's behavior and his explanation.

During the postemancipation period, the authorities persistently complained of the high level of praedial larceny.

When they needed to increase the penalties for this crime, they argued that in fact their legislation was really an attempt to protect the poor from their less industrious and criminally inclined neighbors. There is no doubt that some of the less scrupulous pilfered from their neighbors. In some cases this pilfering was serious, since it affected some peasants who could ill afford to lose the produce or livestock on which they depended for an independent livelihood. In other cases the items were insignificant, and often the thefts were the pranks of juveniles. Even flowers and orchids did not escape, although the *Port-of-Spain Gazette* was quite right in suggesting that the thieves, if they disposed of their orchids, had a selective, discriminating, and ready market—that is, most likely it was the well-to-do who were the receivers of this stolen property.

But it is difficult to believe that the plantocracy really cared about the larceny of the stocks and crops of the peasantry. In fact, it may not be too cynical to suggest that it may have crossed the minds of some that the peasant ruined by praedial larceny would be forced to return to labor for the plantation owner. At any rate, it was suggested that by his activity, the praedial thief was able to maintain his independence and not be forced into the labor market. It was believed that the Creoles could survive on the barest minimum—one official described their ordinary fare as plantains, cornmeal, salt fish, and rice, washed down with rum—and since in the tropics nature supposedly provided these staples, the Creole was not forced by need to seek work.[31] The praedial pilferer, then, would be even less inclined to seek estate employment, since he supplemented nature's ample providence with the earnings from his own criminal activity. The plantocracy therefore continually complained about stolen crops and campaigned for stiffer penalties.

Not that there was no larceny of their precious canes. This too was persistent—by both juvenile pranksters and adults. But the larceny of cane was not really troublesome, only irritating. After all, there was no real market for stolen cane. It was readily believed that a Creole could survive on a few stalks of cane as a regular meal, and one visitor reported that street vendors sold, among other delicacies, "hunks of sugar-cane, to be gnawed by the dawdlers in mid-street" Port-of-Spain.[32] To be a profitable criminal enterprise, the larceny of cane had to be done in bulk, which raised the problem of disposing of the stolen goods. In fact, individuals found with what the authorities considered suspicious amounts of sugar were immediately accused of larceny, and indentured workers were expressly prohibited from having more than one pound of sugar in their possession. In 1893, an East Indian woman, Ramputtiah, was found with one tin of coconut oil, one oil can, and a tin of sugar in her possession. She was unable to provide the magistrate with a satisfactory explanation of how these items came into her possession and was therefore fined thirty shillings or one month with hard labor.[33]

There was pilfering also of sugar and other by-products of the cane crop. The extended and unpatrolled coastline provided an excellent opportunity for adventurous thieves. At least three-quarters of the island's sugar crop was brought in small boats from inland and southern plantations to the main wharves in Port-of-Spain for transshipment to Europe and America. Between Felicity Hall and Couva and Ariapita Estate in Oropouche there were no less than eighteen shipping places. The produce was taken by small flatboats out to the larger vessels anchored a few miles off the coast. Although patrols on the wharves generally controlled plunder on the land, the operators of these flatboats were able to pilfer rum, molasses, and unrefined sugar, both for their own consumption and for sale.[34]

The growing cocoa industry was another favorite target of the praedial thieves. Ordinance 1 of 1885 was a direct attempt to deal with the increasing incidence of cocoa theft. It was modeled on an 1855 ordinance in Barbados that regulated the sale of sugarcane, the 1881 Agricultural Produce Buyers Law in Jamaica, and similar ordinances in Mauritius and the Seychelles. The ordinance required all dealers in cocoa to be licensed and all cocoa transactions to be conducted during set hours of daylight. It further placed the burden of proof of innocence on the arrested offender, since section 5 implied that small quantities of "cocoa in the pod" found in the possession of the accused could be safely deemed to be stolen produce.[35]

The rising price for cocoa encouraged increased traffic in the stolen product. Thieves reportedly took the stolen pods to rumshops, where they were bartered for a dram of rum or some bread and cheese at the rate of ten or twelve pods for ten cents. In some cases, the thieves opened the pods in the field at night and sold the collected beans at a nominal price. By licensing all cocoa dealers, Ordinance 1 of 1855 aimed at closing off the market for stolen cocoa and making it difficult for rumshops to operate as receivers.

Further changes in the law against praedial larceny came the following year in response to cries for stiffer penalties. Ordinance 22 of 1886 sought to increase the penalties inflicted on those convicted of the offense. Under Ordinance 11 of 1842, punishment for praedial larceny had been "one month's imprisonment with or without hard labor *or* a fine over and above the value of the article stolen not exceeding £1 for a first offence and six months for a second offence." The 1886 ordinance inflicted stiffer penalties.

Initially, it imposed a term of twelve months' imprisonment for a first conviction. The Colonial Office disagreed, however, and suggested instead a maximum of three months, as in Jamaica. The new ordinance took away from the magistrate the option of imposing a fine instead of punishment and now required peremptory imprisonment. The new ordinance of 1886 also prescribed the punishment of whipping for a first offense in the case of males under sixteen years of age, instead of only for a second offense, as in the previous legislation.

The ordinance was ruthlessly applied: in 1897, Daniel Lambert received thirty-six lashes and six months hard labor for the larceny of two goats, and Joseph Branch received twelve lashes and six months hard labor for the unlawful possession of sugarcane.[36] The new ordinance also had its effect on the criminal statistics. The rate of convictions (table A.20) which increased slowly from 49 percent in 1875–79 to 53 percent by the end of the century, testifies to the continued difficulty of establishing proof and securing convictions. Despite the overall increase in the use of fines rather than imprisonment as a means of social control (described earlier), the authorities preferred to opt for imprisonment in the case of praedial larceny. The numbers fined decreased drastically from 50 percent in 1875–79 to 12 percent by 1895–99. But what is particularly interesting is the increased number of orders for whipping, which moved from 2 percent in 1875–79 to 21 percent at the end of the century.

The incidence of praedial larceny is closely related to the fortunes of the peasantry in nineteenth-century Trinidad. The bulk of those who engaged in praedial larceny did so in order to use the items stolen for their own consumption or to exchange them for cash or material goods for their own subsistence. As more land was converted to the production of export crops—sugar, cocoa, coconuts, fruit—there was less land available for the production of food crops for internal consumption. As the cocoa industry replaced sugar as the new income generator, many small-scale cultivators were robbed of their land and many sharecroppers found that their access to land was greatly restricted. In fact, many of those involved in the theft of cocoa were often dissatisfied sharecroppers who sought to increase their share of the cocoa crop by private though illegal transactions. In general, as more people were forced off the land and into the urban areas for whatever reasons, and as food production declined with increased dependence on imported foodstuffs, the occurrence of praedial larceny remained persistent, though not a major proportion of the crimes against property.

The bulk of the cases, convictions, and committals for property offenses came, not from praedial larceny, which was essentially a rural phenomenon, but from larceny and theft, which in nineteenth-century Trinidad was predominantly but not exclusively an urban phenomenon. (See table A.21.) Praedial larceny constituted only 2 percent of total cases in 1875–79 and declined to less than 1 percent of all cases by the end of the century. It never increased above the 1875–79 rate. Praedial convictions were but 7 percent of total convictions in 1875–79. This figure increased to 11 percent by 1885–89, but it declined from that period until the end of the century. Praedial larceny was not even the major property offense. Only 15 percent of all property cases in 1875–79 were praedial; this declined to 4 percent by the end of the century. 18 percent of all convictions for property offenses in 1875–79 were praedial, but this declined to 5 percent in 1899.

These figures should be compared with the incidence of praedial larceny in Barbados. In 1876 this offense accounted for 17 percent of all convictions and 60 percent of all property convictions. Ten years later, it was 20 percent of all convictions and 70 percent of all property convictions—although by the end of the century it had declined to 12 percent of all convictions and slightly less than half of all property convictions.

The difference in patterns is clearly related to the different socioeconomic structures of the two colonies. Barbados remained dominated by sugar monoculture for the better part of the nineteenth century, and its class of peasant proprietors developed rather slowly in the late nineteenth century.[37] Still tied to the plantation, with little alternative but emigration, and with little access to land for internal food production for those who remained in Barbados, the Barbados working class had no choice but to resort to agricultural theft in order to survive. On the other hand, in Trinidad the continued existence of land not used for export-oriented cash-crop production facilitated the existence of a peasantry, albeit small and under attack, engaged in the production of internally oriented food-crop production. Furthermore, the existence of employment opportunities outside of the sugar industry, for example, in public works programs, meant that there was the possibility of earning wages to pay for both locally produced and imported foodstuffs. Property offenses in Trinidad became increasingly an urban phenomenon rather than a rural one in the nineteenth century, as the increasing urban-based population sought ways other than praedial theft by which to survive.

Given the physical conditions of Port-of-Spain and its housing, a steady rate of crimes against property should not be surprising. As the chief of police complained in 1870: "How then can it be otherwise in a town like Port-of-Spain with an area so extended and of which the local features make it so admirably adapted for the commission of crime and the escape of criminals. Badly constructed and worse secured houses, surrounded in many instances by vacant lots and frequently situated in the immediate neighborhood of hovels and yards which would seem to have been copied as to appearances and population from the Rookery of London."[38]

Most houses, although supposedly tightly locked at night, were in fact insecure mainly because of the fragile material used in construction and their delapidated condition. As Fraser complained, "bolts and bars, if used at all, were mere idle precautions as the doors and windows are without shutters and are made in nine cases out of ten of the flimsiest jalousie work."[39] Under such conditions breaking and entering and unlawful entry were purely academic, and many cases were dismissed in the courts because of sheer inability to prove unlawful intent or that the accused had actually broken into a dwelling and not merely walked into a room that had not been previously locked.

In many cases, at least until the late 1870s, the houses of the rich were in no better state. Many of the lower-class tenements were in close proximity to houses of the well-to-do middle class, and until the opening of St. Clair and Woodbrook as exclusive housing areas, they were also in close proximity to the houses of the rich upper classes. Even the large commercial establishments were surrounded by the houses of the poor, with their stores openly accessible to the inhabitants of the surrounding shacks.[40] Very often the owners of these establishments lived upstairs from their business places, but this did not prevent those who felt the need to relieve them of their possessions from doing so almost at will. Before 1880, the physical arrangement of the city lent itself to repeated crimes against property and created constant sources of temptation. The tradition of appropriating the property of the upper classes forged during slavery died hard during postemancipation. Some stole whether they needed to or not, and in times of distress they had even less compunction. But many also stole not only from their betters but also from their neighbors.

Most of the cases of larceny and theft were restricted to small items of little value—some cash, very often no more than a few shillings, or a few articles of clothing—since these thefts were often unpremeditated acts and were merely committed on the spur of the moment to take advantage of an opportunity offered by seemingly convenient circumstances. As a result of this rashness, the identity of the person committing the offense was usually known, and the items were usually recovered. This often resulted in a steady rate of convictions and committals rather than the drastic fluctuations observable in the general crime rate or in the other categories of crime. While it was good for accessibility, proximity had its disadvantages in its potential for discovery. In poor, small communities, sudden changes of fortune are easily noticed and commented on with suspicion that is often tinged with jealousy. The large network of informers maintained by the police thrived on the information often unwittingly divulged by jealous slum dwellers. Even some of the crimes stemmed from this climate of jealousy, which is always present in poor communities. The theft of clothing did not always indicate want; it could also have been a conscious act of leveling applied by a slum dweller to keep another co-misfortunate on the poverty level. The thief in these communities was likely to steal only items that could be immediately consumed and not easily identified or those that he could easily pass on to a receiver.

The incidence of the charge of receiving stolen property is a good indicator of the spread of illegal activities and is indirectly a reflection of the effect of changing economic conditions. At least two people are involved initially, and very often a third person joins the network, since the charge is also applied to any individual who knowingly acquires a stolen object either directly from a thief or from an intermediary. The total complex is an indication that the thief prefers to redeem or exchange the stolen item for cash or perhaps its the equivalent in goods and that the receiver, if he is a professional and not an individual receiving for personal use, has a potential buyer or is aware of a market. Widespread use of this marketing network also speaks volumes about people's attitudes towards property rights and perhaps the relative absence of any stigma applied to this kind of illegal activity. In times of economic distress, the activities of the receiver as middleman would tend to increase, as more suppliers exchanged stolen property for cash or goods, and his market would tend to expand, as there would be a greater demand for goods at the reduced rate at which the receiver would normally sell his illegally acquired goods.

There was a large network for receiving and exchanging stolen merchandise in nineteenth-century Trinidad. Prison committals for receiving stolen property increased from a total of 244 in 1875–79 to 441 at the end of the century, yet these figures do not tell the full story. There were many more cases before the courts and many more were convicted and paid fines than is suggested by the figures for prison committals. Storekeepers—for both rum and ordinary fare—were the major culprits. Their places of business provided ideal venues for the receiving, exchange, and distribution of stolen property. In those establishments few questions were asked and even fewer answered by either the owner or the clientele. Despite the passing of "the sale of cocoa" regulations, many rural shops were notorious as exchange centers for stolen produce. In the urban areas, rumshops shared a reputation with pawnshops as popular establishments for the conversion of stolen items into ready cash. One visitor in the 1850s reported an absence of pawnbrokers; another source claims that the first licensed pawnshop was opened by Joaquim dos Santos in 1881.[41] But there is no doubt there were establishments that operated as pawnshops before 1881, and those were popularly known centers for the redistribution of stolen merchandise. At any rate, the chief of police recommended the passage of Ordinance 22 of 1889 aimed at regulating the business of pawnbrokers, since they had become notorious as receivers of stolen property.

There were not many major robberies involving large sums, but those that did occur were noteworthy for their daring. In 1879, thieves broke into a store in the immediate vicinity of the railway station in Port-of-Spain. Despite an alarm bell on the front door, they entered and removed an iron chest from the store. They took their booty to a spot a mere hundred yards from the store, where they smashed open the lock on the chest. They took the cash, but probably unaware of the value of the paper contents—securities, bills, deeds, and a will—or of a market for its disposition, they made a bonfire of it. This was in the heart of the commercial district, yet during all this commotion they were undisturbed and were able to escape with their loot.[42] Two years later, two other burglars made an attempt to force open the vault of the public treasury with gunpowder. They were not so fortunate and were interrupted by a passing policeman. Nevertheless, they still escaped, and the police offered a reward of £75 for the capture of two Frenchmen, Charles Robert and Antoine Noel, who were suspected of being responsible for the act.[43] This attempt also took place in the heart of the capital city and speaks volumes not only about the daring of the thieves but also about the inadequacy of the police force.

Robbery with violence was relatively infrequent during the

1860s and early 1870s, and the roads were relatively safe from highway robbers. Many people made trips between town and country at night without fear of being robbed, and East Indian women, who were usually heavily bedecked with gold and silver ornaments, seemed not to have been the victims of highway robbery. But this safety may have decreased considerably in the latter years of the century. Total cases for robbery with violence increased; in the 1870s, there were thirty-four cases before the superior courts, in the 1880s there were seventy-two; and in the 1890s this increased to ninety-two. But because of the rather vague way in which the offense could be defined, the increase may really indicate the inclusion by the arresting or prosecuting officer of any crime of theft from the person that involved the slightest degree of force.

The line between pickpocketing and robbery with violence, for example, could be extremely thin and easily crossed by a bungling amateur. The crime of pickpocketing is one of those that usually goes unnoticed and only comes to the attention of the police when the perpetrator is caught in the act. Many of the victims may believe that they might have dropped their money or wallet. If the pickpocket is caught in the act and struggles to complete the theft, this could easily be interpreted as an attempted robbery with violence. On the other hand, if the penalty is less severe in the lower courts and the police are not on one of their regular and publicized campaigns of crime suppression, the charge of larceny may be laid rather than the more severe robbery with violence.

Pickpocketing does not appear as an offense on the list of *committals* before 1895, but in the five years there were eleven people jailed for this offense from 1895 to 1899. It is quite likely that that offense had previously been included in the general category of larceny and theft, and the practice may have been more popular than is suggested by the rate of committals. The *Port-of-Spain Gazette* of 14 January 1897 reported the case of Rebecca Carter, a Barbadian of about fifty, who was sentenced to six months for the larceny of twenty-five shillings from the person of Frances Henry. The report described Rebecca later as an incorrigible pickpocket who had been charged twenty times before with similar offenses. But pickpocketing is so closely related to opportunities afforded by clothing styles that the history and incidence of this particular offense must await a future detailed examination of sartorial styles and changes in nineteenth-century Trinidad.

Highway robbery was not alarmingly high, but remained at a steady rate between 1870 and 1900. Even though the tracks that passed for roads were unprotected, there were relatively few cases of highway robbery before 1870. Many of those both before 1870 and after were directed at payrolls. Plantation payrolls totaling at least $30,000 were carried every Saturday from Port-of-Spain to San Fernando in "canvas bags slung across a saddle bow or deposited at the bottom of a Yankee waggon," but there were few robberies before 1870. Fraser, writing in 1871, claimed that there had been only two attempts in forty years—a successful one at Chaguanas and an abortive robbery in 1865 at Brothers Estate.[44]

In January 1877, a lone gunman attacked the manager of the Phoenix Park Estate on his way from Esperanzo with a payroll of $750. The manager received slugs in his breast and shoulder, and the bandit escaped, but without the payroll. Since there had been a similar attempt four months before in the same district, the *Port-of-Spain Gazette* described the incident as "another of those bloodthirsty and murderous attacks which have lately disgraced our community." Quite possibly the media exaggerated as usual, since Governor Irving just barely remembered another robbery in the same district about a year or two before 1877.[45] A much more suspicious secretary of state at the Colonial Office observed the unwillingness of the residents of the area to assist the police in their investigations and commented that the incident resembled the "agrarian outrages in Ireland," rather than a "simple attempt to rob in an atrocious manner."[46] Since there was persistent unrest on the plantations, it is tempting to make a connection between any payroll robberies and protest on the plantations and therefore to describe the perpetrators as social bandits.[47] But it will be difficult to document these acts as prepolitical or political protests. At any rate, the robberies declined for a while as managers made increased use of an expanded railway system.

There is no doubt, however, that the "malicious injury to property," another category of offenses against property, was in fact a prepolitical protest. Slaves had traditionally damaged plantation property as a means of protesting their conditions and to vent pent-up frustrations. The Creoles in the postemancipation period continued this tradition of protest, and the indentured East Indians, finding themselves in a situation not quite unlike slavery, resorted to the same form of protest.

Changes in the law and the definition of what constituted malicious injury to property also contributed to the increase in *convictions* for this category of offense. The law prior to 1885 only covered those instances where the damage to property was done when the accused were "riotously or tumultously assembled," and convictions could not be made unless the prosecution proved that the damage was committed by an individual during a riotous assembly. But Ordinance 5 of 1885 amended the law in order to provide "for the punishment of individuals maliciously damaging machinery used for any agricultural operation."[48] The convictions for the offense increased from a total of 271 in the period 1871–75 to a total of 419 during the period 1891–95. It was quite obvious that the rate of damage to plantation property and equipment increased, particularly during the period of the sugar crisis, when workers protested not only decreased wages but also the withholding of them altogether.

Arson was one of the major fears of the planter class. In the dry season of 1869, some twenty-seven fires occurred in the St. Ann's Ward Union alone. In a letter to the Colonial Office, one individual charged that "the great majority of those fires are set by negroes or coolies for some reason or other wish for revenge." The governor disagreed and considered the charge a gross exaggeration. Instead, he claimed that the fires due to revenge were comparatively few and that the majority of the fires were caused accidentally either by individuals clearing land of felled wood and rubbish or by the operation of illicit charcoal burners on Crown lands. Whether accidental or deliberate, the fires in 1869 caused extensive damage: in two districts, North and South Naparima, fires destroyed 5,562 acres of standing cane valued at £48,831 and mills and buildings valued at £16,878; in Cedros, 1,725 acres of cane valued at £27,000 were destroyed by fire; and in Couva, a *portion* of the crops destroyed amounted to £11,790.[49] During the slave period, the plantocracy had passed a regulation that prohibited smoking on plantation roads, in order to preempt the use of accident as an excuse for plantation fires; their successors in 1869 passed Ordinance 24, with similar restrictions to prevent accidental fires.

Arson was also a problem in the urban areas. Between 1880 and 1886, there were 123 cases of fire in Port-of-Spain, with as many as 33 in 1882 alone. Fifty-three of these fires were believed to have been purposely set and malicious attempts at destroying property. But detection was extremely difficult, and only eleven persons were ever brought to trial for those acts—in 1882 alone there were 33 fires, of which 15 were believed to have been maliciously set, but only three persons were tried in the courts. Overall, there were seventeen committals for arson during 1880–84 and twenty-one in the period 1890–94.

Some of the fires were accidental, and the extensive damage was really a result of the flimsy wooden construction of most buildings and an inadequate fire brigade. In the 1890s the fire brigade had only eight regulars and depended on a volunteer force, many of whom did not turn out for an alarm.[50] Port-of-Spain was destroyed by fire once in March 1808 and again in 1896. In the former case, it gave the government the opportunity to rebuild the city and to pass a law that prohibited the use of wood in house construction. The second fire completely destroyed the business section of the town and did damage to the extent of half a million pounds. The presence of a British man-of-war whose crew did valuable service in assisting the understaffed, untrained fire brigade prevented much more extensive damage. San Fernando also received severe damage from fire, first in 1818 and again in 1883, and there too an understaffed fire brigade was little help in a city of wooden buildings.

But many of the fires were deliberately set by arsonists. In one case in San Fernando a gang of thieves set fires so that they could rob shops while the police and the crowds were distracted by the fire.[51] Many buildings were set on fire in order to collect insurance. In 1883 the trial of Gomez and Lafont for conspiracy to set fire to a building at the corner of Duke and St. James streets in Port-of-Spain revealed the existence of a ring of professional arsonists hired by property owners to set fire to overinsured wooden buildings. Gomez received one year hard labor and was ordered to pay £200 and costs, while his accomplice, Lafont, received eighteen months hard labor and was fined £100 plus costs. The possibility of extensive damage to the entire city of Port-of-Spain with its numerous old wooden buildings prompted the passage of Ordinance 8 of 1884. The new ordinance increased the severity of punishment in cases where malicious injury to property was occasioned by fire,[52] and thus in 1887, two arsonists, D'Azevedo and Fyfe, were sentenced to life and fourteen years respectively for the arson of the European Hotel in Port-of-Spain. D'Azevedo received the heavier sentence since he owned a dry goods store at the back of the hotel and had planned to set fire to the building in order to obtain the insurance payment.[53]

But arson was not the only fraud perpetrated in nineteenth-century Trinidad. Ordinance 15 of 1877, which amended the law concerning offenses against property, introduced two new sections in order to deal with two practices of fraudulent conversion. Section 3 introduced the English enactment by which bailees who fraudulently converted property entrusted to them were made guilty of larceny. The attorney general had advocated the introduction of this English practice and claimed that the use of fraud by bailees was extremely common in the colony.[54] Committals for fraud as a bailee appeared as a separate category for the first time in 1886: between 1886 and 1890, fifty-three persons were imprisoned for this offense; between 1891 and 1895 there were forty-one committals; and, between 1896 and 1900 sixty-four more committals were made for this offense.

The second new section of Ordinance 15, section 8, was largely an extension of section 3. The attorney general had also complained of the widespread practice of fraud among artisans. It was claimed that these artisans demanded cash advances to purchase material to complete their contracted assignments but instead used the advances for their own purposes and never completed the work. The new ordinance allowed this fraudulent conversion to be prosecuted as larceny.[55] This practice may have been as widespread as the attorney general and the other council members claimed, since many Creoles did set themselves up as artisans in the postemancipation period and hoped to escape plantation labor through the use of their artisan skills. Some of them did have skills, but many of them did not, and some of the unscrupulous who did not found that this was a clever way to amass capital without labor.

There were numerous other cases of fraud by private citizens. Some unscrupulous men toured the countryside and preyed on the superstitions and sensibilities of the gullible. There were those who sold fraudulent religious charms to ever-ready believers or who solicited contributions to nonexisting charities or funds to erect chapels from unsuspecting rural dwellers. In an age of widespread illiteracy, those who had mastered the written word took advantage of their not-so-fortunate compatriots and used their skills to defraud them of their land and money. In a multilingual society where English was pushed as the official language, many dishonest men seized the opportunity to use their knowledge of English to enrich themselves at the expense of the non-English speakers. In a monetary system that for the better part of the nineteenth century was chaotic at best, with numerous kinds of specie used as common currency, the skillful counterfeiter had a field day.

Fraud, embezzlement, and forgery were crimes that were largely the preserve of the literate in the society. This is not to suggest that there were no areas of fraud that were accessible to the nonliterate—in fact, the dishonest person, if he was intelligent, converted any opportunity to his own ends or, as the popular local folklore saying advised, "Where a cow tie is there he must graze." But in a largely illiterate society, the literate became an elite with enormous influence and access to the mechanisms for converting their literate skills into capital. The roll of dishonor of those convicted of "white collar" crimes is replete with the names of some of those who frequently made the society pages of the newspapers. The roll for the last thirty years of the nineteenth century opens with Charles Warner, attorney general for the thirty formative years of the postemancipation society, during whose tenure was laid the legal framework for the anglicization—and by extension "civilization"—of the postemancipation society. He was forced to resign as a result of his inability to deliver and account for inheritances entrusted to his care as the trustee and guardian of a minor.[56] Throughout the century the names of other legal luminaries were added to the list—magistrates, justices of the peace, clerks of court, other lawyers. The list included the ex-chief of police, L. M. Fraser, who embezzled court funds while acting as a magistrate, and C. W. Baker, the inspector-commandant of police, who misused funds from the police canteen.

Literate men staffed the civil service. From this position, they were able to seize opportunities for fraud and embezzlement. Upon assuming that post, Governor Irving quickly discovered that the civil service "was largely composed of incompetent and dishonest men, supported and encouraged by dishonesty outside the service and by an unscrupulous press."[57] In four years, 1875–78, the governor dealt with no less than sixteen public functionaries for all forms of fraud, embezzlement, and forgery—this included wardens who, though parsimonious about distributing pauper relief, were not reluctant to use those funds for their own purposes; clerks in the Crown lands office, who, like some wardens, used their position to illegally acquire land; clerical officers in the customs; and medical officers who overcharged for their services to indentured estate workers.[58]

The statistics on committals for white-collar crime grossly understate the extent of these practices. Many never came to trial—those who held senior positions either were transferred or promoted to other positions outside the colony or they simply absconded, very often with the connivance of the authorities and the assistance of their friends in high places. Many who came to trial were never convicted. They were able to take advantage of a chaotic jury system and of class, race, and color conflicts, or by posing as martyrs, they could take advantage of the growing spirit of Creole nationalistic consciousness and antimetropolitan sentiment and antagonisms. Many of those who were convicted received slaps on the wrists in the forms of fines and very often reduced or commuted sentences; Many of these were junior civil servants, who did not have the friends and connections in the society to protect them altogether from blind justice. Many who were actually imprisoned were in fact on the low rung of the ladder of tricksters and swindlers, those with no connections in the society.

Every unpunished white collar crime glaringly revealed in greater detail the inequalities of a system based on race, class, and color. Every unprosecuted or lightly punished public official made a mockery of the criminal justice system and undermined respect for the rule of law. The criminal activities of the elite of the society, the misdoings of those who flaunted themselves as the paragons of morality and virtue in the society, did not go unnoticed by those who were continually described as inherently immoral and criminal. The failure of the state to prosecute vigorously and punish relentlessly the crimes of one section of the community as it did the others, and the ease with which white-collar criminals escaped justice and displayed their ill-gotten gains, lent credence to Creole rationales for crime. The inability of the law to protect the property of all of the citizens was interpreted as unwillingness when viewed in conjunction with the alacrity displayed by those same agencies in securing the property of certain sections of the community. In fact, this inequality in the services and protection offered by the law contributed to the increasing phenomenon of the poor stealing from the poor. The attitude toward property rights developed and cultivated during slavery was reinforced during the nineteenth century and gave rise to the Creole saying "Tief from tief make God laugh"—which was a callous but revealing commentary.

Therefore, during the period of crisis, many of the Creoles used illegal means to relieve their distress without compunction or second thoughts. There is no doubt that the economic crisis had the greatest impact on those segments of the population that were directly connected to the sugar sector of the plantation economy. The crisis forced a decrease in wages and an increase in food prices. This increased the level of unemployment in the rural areas and triggered an urban drift in search of jobs and relief that served to swell an already rapidly growing casual labor population in the towns. In both the urban and the rural areas, many Creoles were faced with unrelieved pauperism and the choice of using illegal means to relieve their distress. They fell back on or developed systems of support that were both legal and illegal, and very often in their minds there was little distinction between the two. The working class sought alternatives to plantation labor to reduce the extent to which the plantocrats dominated their lives. But for these alternatives, there would have been even greater poverty and more crimes against property. The plantocrats saw these options as threats to their hegemony and moved to reduce them, and in the process they opened wider the floodgates of criminality in nineteenth-century Trinidad.

CHAPTER SIX

Violence and Social Disorder

Trinidad in the late nineteenth century was a violent society, and the statistics on crime testify to a high incidence of crimes against the person and other forms of violence in the society. Crimes against the person ran the gamut from the more serious murder and manslaughter to the exchange of fisticuffs between two individuals. They included attempted murder, cutting and wounding, rape, and riots or battles between groups armed with weapons designed to do grievous bodily harm.

Between 1870 and 1889, crimes against the person constituted between 26 and 28 percent of all the cases before the courts. (See table A.22.) There was a noticeable decrease in the 1890s: as a percentage of all cases, crimes against the person decreased by about 5 percentage points between 1890 and 1899. This pattern of increase between 1870 and 1889, with a peak around 1884 and a decrease in the next decade, coincided with a similar pattern in the crude figures for the total cases and the annual averages for crimes of violence. Between 1870 and 1884, the crude figure for total crimes against the person before the courts, in five-year periods, moved from 18,109 in 1870–74 to 24,119 in the period 1880–84. The annual average increased by 33 percent, moving from 3,622 to 4,824 cases for the same two periods. After 1885 there is a decrease in the crude figures both for total cases and for annual averages: crude totals in the five-year periods decreased by 14 percent between 1885–89 and 1895–99, and the annual average decreased by 11 percent during the same period.

But the criminal statistics were an uneven reflection of the incidence of crimes of violence. The level of forensic ability of the crime detection agency as well as popular attitudes toward the courts and the rule of law reduce the reliability of court statistics as a useful guide to the real incidence of these crimes of violence. The figures for murder and manslaughter—the charges laid when life is lost as a result of an incident involving violence—tended to be much closer to the real incidence than those for charges of fighting or assault and battery. In the case of murder, the existence of a dead body found under particular circumstances is a clear indication that a crime of violence had been committed, whether or not the perpetrator is known. But the figures from the courts (see table A.23) reflect *only* those cases where suspects had been caught by the police and brought to trial and did not include instances in which the police had been unable to make an arrest. The police in the nineteenth century claimed it was easier to apprehend a suspect in those cases where the victim was female than where there was a male victim. Fortunately for nineteenth century police, however, most homicides occurred in circumstances where the perpetrator was well known at least to the community and the victims' friends and family.

In the case of assault and battery, attitudes toward the justice system and the rule of law had their effect on the number of cases brought before the courts. The charge of assault and battery was usually laid by one private citizen against another. But many assaults occurred in which the assaulted persons declined to prosecute, either because they may have judged the incident too minor to be prosecuted or because it would have been too difficult to secure a conviction in the courts or because they preferred to seek private revenge and to bypass the courts.[1] Fluctuations in this category tell more about the extent of general confidence in the justice system and the rule of law than they do about the recurring incidences of the offense.

The level of legal skill as well as popular attitudes toward the court also affected the rate of convictions, and the statistics on convictions were not completely reliable indicators of the rate and nature of violence. (See table A.24.) At no time between 1875 and 1899 did more than 45 percent of the cases tried in the lower courts result in convictions for crimes against the person: the rate of conviction increased slowly from 32 percent in 1875–79 to 45 percent at the end of the period. The number of cases dismissed on their own merits remained between 20 and 25 percent. The cases discharged—that is, dismissed because of lack of evidence or unwillingness on the part of complainants to prosecute—decreased from 43 percent in 1875–79 to 32 percent by 1899.

The pattern in the superior courts is reversed. (See table A.25.) Convictions decreased from 70 percent in 1875–79 to 60 percent by 1895–99. Acquittals—that is, cases dismissed on their own merits—fluctuated from 24 percent to 25 percent. But the percentage of cases that fell through—that is, where the case did not proceed because either evidence or witnesses had been compromised—moved from 5 percent in 1875–79 to 14 percent in 1895–99.

These statistics reveal a great deal about the level of competency in the courts and about the extent of confidence in the justice system. The highest rate for discharges was for cases for assaults tried in the lower courts. The usual complaint was that the charges of assault were frivolous and that complainants compromised the case before trial, hence the high rate of discharges. The police claimed that in those cases where the police prosecuted, there was a return of 75 percent convictions, while in those cases where private citizens prosecuted, the conviction rate was less than 50 percent.[2] It is debatable whether the charges of assaults were indeed frivolous, but it is quite certain that private citizens sought justice and revenge outside of the courts rather than prosecuting within the court system. Many of them reported incidents of physical violence but registered either their distrust of the efficiency of the system or its ability to exact the extent of revenge that would satisfy their sense of justice by seeking satisfaction outside of the courts. But when they took the law into their own hands, they set in motion a cycle of self-perpetuating violence.

The rate of convictions and the disposition of these convictions had an important impact on the development of attitudes towards violence in the society. It was obvious that the possibility of convictions was higher in the superior courts, even though over the period 1875 to 1899 the number of cases in which convictions were secured decreased from 70 percent to just slightly above 60 percent. In the superior courts it was easier to undermine the system of justice by buying witnesses or unduly influencing the jury, but overall those who were accused of a crime of violence had a much better chance of escaping a conviction before a magistrate than before a judge and jury.

Even if convicted, the perpetrator of a crime of violence found that the pattern of punishment was not totally unbearable. Those convicted in the lower courts were more often fined than imprisoned. (See table A.26.) In the 1870s, the magistrates fined 56 percent of those convicted, imprisoned 28 percent, and bound over the remainder. In the 1890s, the percentage fined decreased to 46 percent and the number imprisoned decreased to 20 percent, but the number bound over more than doubled, to 35 percent. Among those imprisoned, the number who were imprisoned in default of fines increased from 9 percent to about 14 percent from 1875–79 to 1895–99, while those who had been peremptorily imprisoned decreased from 19 to 6 percent of the total imprisoned.

Imprisonment was decreasingly used as a method of punishment for those convicted of crimes of violence. Significantly, the whip, which was used liberally for those convicted of practicing Obeah and praedial larceny or for the unemployed convicted of being incorrigible rogues or vagabonds, was rarely used during the earlier periods in cases involving violence against the person.

Between 1870 and 1899, there were only seventeen cases, all of which occurred between 1884 and 1899, in which the magistrates ordered flogging for those convicted of crimes against the person. The harshest punishment for the lower classes came for those who dared to interfere with property or for those who, by their attitude, showed a disinclination to work, but not for those who did bodily harm to their fellow sufferers.

The attitudes of the courts and the pattern of conviction and punishment were merely facilitating factors, however, and they do not fully explain the pattern of violence in the society. The fundamental causes of this high incidence of violence can be traced to the nature of the society and its social organization. The society bred a pattern of violence that was both impulsive and implosive: that is, it manifested itself as the violent actions of irrational men wreaking havoc on themselves rather than on the source of their frustrations and oppression. Slavery, the basis of the development of the island as a plantation society, was violent, and the extent of systematic physical violence inherent in slavery has been well documented elsewhere. More importantly, colonialism, the social and political framework in which both slavery and indentureship operated, was a violent system. Crucial to the success of colonialism was the notion of racial inferiority and the separation and treatment of people based on the immutable fact of the color of their skin or their racial origin. The colonial society based on the psychological violence that was racism denied the individual his right to self, to individuality, in effect his right to life. This disrespect for life created a climate in the society in which other forms of physical and psychological violence could thrive. For it was this racist disrespect for the lives of those who were nonwhite that permitted the existence of atrocious living conditions that affected the quality of life available to the masses and promoted a climate in which violence and aggression became prominent features.[3]

Just as slavery was violent, so too its successor, indentureship, was a system that demanded physical violence and was replete with cases of cruel coercion. The whip was as commonly used as a mechanism for labor persuasion as it had been in the worst days of slavery. In a number of cases, a severe whipping resulted in death, yet the perpetrators managed to escape on technicalities and often as a result of blatant miscarriages of justice. Few members of the elite noticed, and even fewer cared. Indentured laborers could be whipped and coerced with impunity, and all kinds of violence was used against the bodies of those who found themselves bound to labor on the plantations.

The examples are numerous. Charles Forget, the owner of an estate in Naparima had a quarrel with Soudar Singh, an indentured laborer, over wages. Forget claimed that during the quarrel Singh made "impertinent" remarks about Forget's mother and sister, threatened to break Forget's bones, and boasted about his role in the Indian Mutiny. Forget and seven Creole laborers, after beating Singh, tied him down in a cart and drove him seven miles to a police station, where Singh was imprisoned for four days and then released without an inquiry. Singh took the matter to the courts, but Forget and his associates were found not guilty.[4]

In 1871, Mr. Ache, the manager of the Bronte Estate in Victoria, was fined a total of Six pounds sterling for assaulting two East Indian women: in one case he was fined one pound, and in the other, where the assault had resulted in the death of the woman, he was fined five pounds sterling. Ache claimed that he horsewhipped the deceased Labjadee because she refused to obey his orders to clean the yard of the estate house. But before her death Labjadee reported a different story. She claimed that she was whipped because she complained about her weekly rations, which were guaranteed under the indenture contract. Prior to the whipping she had been hospitalized for rheumatism, but Ache ordered her discharged then whipped her on three consecutive days, each whipping accompanied by kicks to her body. She was rehospitalized and died forty-four days after the incident. In Ache's defense, Dr. Hammond, the medical examiner, claimed that Labjadee's death was the result of diarrhea, dysentery, and debility and was not attributable to Ache's assault. Ache was therefore fined five pounds for assault and was not charged with manslaughter.[5]

In another case, Sahti, indentured to the Perseverance Estate in Chaguanas, was admitted to the hospital suffering from the effects of a beating she had received from F. Henderson, the son of the estate proprietor. Sahti died fourteen days after the assault, and the postmortem examination revealed cerebral hemorrhage and apoplexy caused by a rupture of one of the branches of an anterior or middle cerebral artery. Yet the coroner's verdict was death from natural causes, and the charge of manslaughter against Henderson was withdrawn.[6]

The cases cited above underscored for the East Indian community that the authorities considered East Indian life to be cheap. East Indians could be whipped, kicked, and beaten to death with impunity. There was no recourse to the law, since the courts invariably released the aggressor with ridiculous fines or warnings. Each miscarriage of justice reinforced in the minds of the East Indian community their lowly status and their peculiar position of servitude in a free society. It built up a distrust of the law, especially in those instances where their rights had to be protected against the rapacious exploitation of owners, managers, and overseers. Since the official avenues of redress were blocked, some of the East Indians vented their pent-up aggression and frustrations against the weaker members of their own community; others occasionally attacked the perceived sources of their oppression.

Sometimes the indentured workers retaliated against the violence perpetrated on them and attacked owners and managers. In the closing years of the 1860s, there were so many of these incidents that the 1869 Report on Immigration commented with relief that "whether due to the increased supply of food or to other causes distinct or collateral, one of the marked features of the year 1869 has been an almost complete freedom from those crimes of violence against managers or superintendents, whose frequency during the two preceding years had caused no small uneasiness to the proprietary body of this colony, and more than one formal representation to the Government."[7]

There were also many attacks against some of the lower-level management figures: that is, the foremen or drivers, many of whom were Afro-Trinidadians. In 1870, Seepaul and Ackbarli, two indentured East Indians, were convicted in the Supreme Court of the murder of Babb, an African, who had been employed as a foreman on the Macoya Estate. During a dispute, Babb was struck on the head with a hoe, which fractured the skull. The court sentenced the two workers to death. Fortunately for them, however, the governor commuted the sentence to life imprisonment and argued that there was no common design or premeditated murder, but rather a case of impulsive wounding with intent to do grievous bodily harm.[8]

This kind of impulsive violence against middle-level authority figures was common, and although more often than not victim and accused were of different racial groups, the violence never really exploded into large-scale racial war, though it no doubt fueled animosity between the two racial groups. In some of these instances, the foremen were East Indians. These sirdars, as they were called, were often as vicious in the execution of their duties as their African counterparts and often imitated the oppressive behavior of the European managers and owners; they therefore often received their just due at the hands of East Indian workers. In one case, on the Ste. Marie Estate, eleven workers attacked the sirdar during a dispute over wages and beat him to death.[9] In many instances, the viciousness of these sirdars may have introduced a sense of class consciousness that blunted the edge of a potential racial conflict.

Although the continued importation of indentured East Indians during the post-1884 sugar crisis contributed to increasing unemployment and depressed wages, there is little evidence of widespread Afro-Asian conflict. No doubt there were incidents between individuals of different races and some of them between groups divided by race, but these were rarely motivated by intense racial hatred nor were they widespread enough to be considered seriously as race riots. In those instances when an Afro-Trinidadian was before the courts for murder or violence to the person of an East Indian, it was more often than not a felony committed in the course of another crime, like robbery.[10] There were numerous comments about the antagonism between the races, and each race had its stockpile of derogatory stereotypes about the other. But for the most part, during the nineteenth century residential patterns, occupational specialization, and the powerlessness of both groups kept the races apart, and minimal contact reduced the possibility of interracial strife.[11]

If anything, the antagonism seems to have been reserved for the immigrants from the other West Indian islands, in particular those from Barbados. It would appear that Afro-Trinidadians accepted the myth that plantation labor was now the preserve of the East Indians; they assumed, however, that the middle-level positions and the skilled jobs were theirs by right of some postslavery inheritance. But West Indian immigration, especially during the post-1884 crisis, threatened these nonpraedial jobs they considered to be their birthright. The West Indian Creoles were as eligible for those jobs as their Trinidadian cousins. They therefore competed not only competed for estate jobs but also for jobs in the public sector and in the nonagricultural private sector and for the independent enterprises possible in the urban area, and thus contributed to the depression in wages. Since few East Indians were in competition for these nonagricultural jobs, the Afro-Trinidadians came into direct conflict with the West Indian immigrants. The antagonism between the two groups and the contempt in which Trinidadians held Barbadians—the latter already over-represented in the detested police force—is clearly revealed in the calypsos that have survived from the 1890s.

There was a high rate of violence against the person, but it is incorrect to assume, as Dr. Bakewell complained to the Colonial Office in 1871, that there was "insecurity of life in Trinidad" and that crimes of violence were committed with impunity.[12] This was a gross exaggeration. During the sixteen months between January 1870 and April 1871 there were 445 cases of assaults against the person in Port-of-Spain, the urban center. But 3 of these were "by and between resident gentlemen," *none* were "between resident gentlemen and the lower orders," and 442 were "by and between" the lower orders. Furthermore, 395 of these cases took place in private places—that is, homes and barrack yards—and only 50 in public places.[13] If life was insecure and violent, certainly it was not so for "resident gentlemen." Trapped in their vicious and pitiful circle of existence, the lower orders attacked each other more often than they attacked their social superiors. The violence that was perpetrated on them, both consciously and unconsciously by the very condition of their lives, they turned inward upon themselves. It is no surprise that death or grievous bodily harm came as the result of most of these altercations. In some cases the rudimentary medical services available failed to save the lives of many of those involved in incidents of violence. But it is significant that the availability of lethal weapons for use in altercations increased the possibility of grievous bodily harm or death. In an agricultural society, the cutlass, the common agricultural tool, became a lethal weapon in the hands of those bent on violence. It was because of this accessibility that Chief Justice Gorrie ruled that "if a man used his cutlass with the intention to punish but with no intention to kill, and death resulted from the use of the cutlass, that was manslaughter and not murder."[14]

An attempt was made to control the possession of guns. After the use of guns in attacks on two plantation managers in

1877, and the refusal of the Couva community to give any assistance to the police or to reveal who owned guns, a number of influential estate proprietors and managers petitioned to have a gun license ordinance that required the registration of guns and the payment of a tax of five pounds sterling. Captain Baker, the chief of police, supported the suggestion of gun registration, since it had worked well with "Kaffir tribes in South Africa." At first the governor was reluctant, but he later relented in the face of arguments that suggested the tax would check "the prevalent and growing practice of carrying arms upon the roads and in other public places by an idle, dissolute and drunken class of people without regular occupation and this frequently resulted in injuries immediately occasioned by carelessness or sudden anger."[15] The ordinance was therefore passed without a dissenting voice by the members of the council.

But there was dissent outside the council. The major of Port-of-Spain, some merchants, and others connected with the cocoa interest claimed that the ordinance pressed with undue hardship upon peasant proprietors who needed guns to protect their cocoa crops from animals. The Chief Justice, who was a nonresident proprietor of a cocoa estate, categorically denied the existence of such a necessity, however, and the objection was overruled. The ordinance may really not have affected many peasant proprietors, since in the year of the ordinance 168 licenses were granted in Toco, a district almost exclusively inhabited by peasant proprietors.[16] The rest of the island also increasingly complied with the law: 606 licences were granted in 1880, 791 in 1882, and 1,000 in 1900.[17]

Given the cost of a gun, their possession was the preserve of a small group who could afford them. Although Governor MacLeod complained in 1845 that because of the doings of the Anti-Slavery Society, "everyone who is not actually a field laborer considers himself a gentleman, and it is no uncommon thing to find them going through the forms of duel with firearms,"[18] possession of guns was not widespread. They were not the favorite weapon used by those involved in cases of violence. (See table A.27.) Many other kinds of weapons were used: stones easily available in the unpaved streets of Port-of-Spain, hunting lances, pointed rods used to pick cocoa pods, razors, and sticks. Whatever was at hand was used, since most of the cases of violence tended to be impulsive rather than premeditated.

But poor medical facilities and the ready availability of lethal weapons aside, some of the incidents that resulted in death seem to have stemmed from such simple immediate causes that the apparently irrational behavior demands explanation. For example, in June 1871 a man was stabbed in a cookshop on Coffee Street in San Fernando. There was apparently no motive. On investigation, it was revealed that the deceased had offered the murderer breakfast. The latter refused, whereupon the victim jokingly threatened to beat the accused if he did not eat with him. In a fit of rage the suspect seized a knife and stabbed the deceased.[19]

The murder in the same year of John Cumberbatch, second cornet player in the police band, is another example. Benjamin Callendar, a colored Barbadian like Cumberbatch, was a recent immigrant from Barbados. Both men lived in one of the notorious barrack yards on Duke Street in Port-of-Spain. During the night Cumberbatch complained about noises coming from Callendar's room. A fight ensued, and Cumberbatch received a fatal eight-inch cut with a razor, popularly known as "the Barbadian weapon." In sentencing Callendar to death, the chief justice, commented on "the revolting barbarity" with which Callendar committed the act.[20]

A final example from 1872 further demonstrates the bizarre and almost irrational nature of some of these crimes of violence. In that year, an East Indian called Ramlal was tried and convicted for the murder of another East Indian called Ramdial, but even the chief justice recommended that the death sentence be commuted to life, since there was "no malice aforethought." For although it was quite clear that Ramlal intended to take a life, he apparently did not care whose life he took. Before killing Ramdial, he first wounded, without prior provocation, a woman called Lucy. He then threatened Elias Ward, a constable.[21] It would appear that "something snapped," but there was no evidence in the record of the immediate predisposing factor that sent Ramlal on his rampage.

Ramlal and Callendar, East Indian and Barbadian immigrants respectively, and the suspect in San Fernando, presumably a Creole—all formed part of a pattern of implosive and impulsive violence that was characteristic of nineteenth-century Trinidad. When such behavior is isolated, the social psychologist is quite correct in demanding that any explanation of it must be restricted to an examination of the psychohistory of the individual. But when these are no longer singular incidents but form a persistent pattern, then wide social causes should be sought rather than narrow, individual, idiosyncratic explanations. Contemporaries quickly gave racist explanations. The agent general of immigration was convinced in 1872 that violence among East Indians occurred only in the early stages of indenture, when "their habits and prejudices have been but little modified by a sojourn among strangers." He was willing to argue further that "the *few* hours of work and the amount of personal freedom, together with higher wages and a free indulgence in rum and bhang" encouraged an aptitude for violence.[22] But these racist explanations are also inadequate. Violence could erupt long after "the first stages of indenture"; not *all* Indians erupted in this impulsive violence; and not *only* Indians were part of this pattern of violence.

Ramlal and Callendar and others had one thing in common—they were all victims of the same system of oppression. They may have felt its effects in different ways, but the plantation system and colonialism—the framework within which it operated—affected all of them.

POPULATION AND THE QUALITY OF LIFE

Both directly and indirectly, the plantation system contributed to this high incidence of violence in nineteenth-century colonial society. Its dependence on a system of labor that required coercion for its success created an oppressive system that generated violence. Its mad search for labor created a rural laboring population, the majority of whom were imprisoned on the plantation in unnatural female-deficient communities. Its manipulation of the labor market contributed to the creation of an urban-based population of unabsorbed migrants and unassimilated immigrants who fought for living space in an overcrowded urban center. Colonial disrespect for the person of non-Europeans facilitated not only connivance at atrocious living conditions but a disinclination to improve medical services or any social services but the prisons, police, and courts. The result was a life that, in Hobbes's description, was nasty, brutish, and short. Some sought escape from these conditions by recourse to intoxicants, a few were driven insane, and violence became a way of life for many.

The population of Trinidad grew rapidly in the nineteenth century. (See table A.28.) At emancipation the population was approximately 36,655, and six years later, the census of 1844 gave the population at 59,815. There was a further increase of 8,785 in the seven years between the census of 1844 and the first decennial census of 1851, which recorded the total population at 68,600. In the next twenty years, 1852 to 1871, the census returns indicated that another 41,038 had been added to the population. Between 1851 and 1861 the population increased at an average of 1,580 per year, and during the next decade the increase averaged 2,520 annually. During the next thirty years another 145,510 persons were added to the population, an average increase of 4,850 persons each year: in the first decade, 1871–81, the increase averaged 4,350 per year; in the second decade it averaged 4,700 per year, and the highest point came between 1891 and 1901, when the increase averaged 5,500 annually.

At no time before the decade 1901–11 did natural growth contribute more than 35 percent to the overall population increase. The increment from natural causes was small between 1844 and 1871, but tripled between 1871 and 1901. In the decade 1871–81, only 10 percent of the total increase came from natural causes; in the following decade, 1881–91, this figure rose to 23 percent; and in the last decade of the century it was 34 percent. These increases represented a decrease in the overall death rate, particularly in the area of infant mortality.

The death rate was extremely high throughout the nineteenth century. In 1880 the death rate was 28 per 1,000 of the population. Death came chiefly as a result of problems of the digestive system, cutaneous ailments, respiratory diseases, and—particularly among the East Indians—anklytomasis. In 1890, 13 percent of the registered deaths were from diarrheal diseases, 10 percent from phthisis, 10 percent from respiratory problems, 6 percent from diseases of the nervous system, 5 percent from debility, 4 percent from diseases of the nervous system, and 4 percent from anemia. Interestingly enough, according to that register only 3 percent died from old age and 1 percent from violent causes.[23]

Many of these deaths stemmed either directly or indirectly from the conditions of work, especially work on the plantations. The protector of immigrants in 1881 reported that "ulcers" increased among the immigrants during the wet season, but that since the introduction of a clause in the Indentured Immigration Ordinance that forced planters to provide immigrant workers with adequate food rations, the indentured workers suffered less from ulcers, at least during their first year.[24] The surgeon general also pinpointed the working conditions of plantation labor as being favorable for the development of skin ulcers. He cited the prevalence of malaria, employment during the wet season in damp localities, and an impoverished diet as the major causes of the problem.[25] In 1875, 206 of the 833 cases treated at the San Fernando Hospital (which was located in the urban center nearest to the southern sugar belt) were cutaneous, that is, skin diseases that the nineteenth-century medical terminology called ulcers, which were incurred while on the job.[26]

The primitive condition of the hospital services was also a major contributing factor to the high death rate. Between 1870 and 1880, a total of 30,108 patients (some of whom were multiple admissions) were admitted to the two hospitals of Port-of-Spain and San Fernando, and 3,441 of these admissions died. This death rate of 12 percent was a marked improvement over the 20 percent figure for the 1860s. It represented, of course, only those who died in the two institutions, since many never reached the hospital and died at home without the benefit of hospital care. Twenty percent of those who died in 1890 died under medical care, but many more died without any sort of medical advice or assistance. Many, of course, refused to go to the hospital until the last minute, since they had little trust in the efficacy of the medical services.

But more importantly the centralization of these services put medical advice out of the reach of many. As one report indicated:

> This heavy proportional mortality will undoubtedly be considerably reduced when your Excellency's scheme for District Hospitals, on the cottage system has been fairly carried into effect. There can be no doubt that the peasantry in general are greatly averse to leaving the neighbourhood in which they and their friends reside, and repair to the Colonial Hospitals of Port-of-Spain and San Fernando, for medical treatment or advice, until their maladies have reached a stage, in many cases beyond the skill of the Physician, or necessitating a long and painful course of treatment. The injury caused by exhaustion incident on a journey of ten or twelve miles to the hospital, probably taxes the vitality of the sufferer as much or more than the disease itself.[27]

But even the introduction of district hospitals did not bring relief; they tended to be poorhouses occupied by those who were destitute and required food and shelter more than they required medical treatment. No important surgery was undertaken during 1881, owing to the continued overcrowding of the two major hospitals.[28] In 1896, all of Trinidad had a total of

1,035 hospital beds to serve its population of roughly 227,588. The major hospitals at Port-of-Spain and San Fernando together had 817 of these beds, and the remaining 218 beds were to be found in the seven district hospitals.

The natural increase in the population was modified not only by a high death rate but also by an even higher rate of infant mortality.[29] In 1910 the child mortality rate was 155 per 1,000 live births. This was an improvement over the situation in the 1890s, when it averaged 170 per 1,000 live births. Nine hundred and eight-four infants born in 1885 failed to attain the age of one year. In 1894, 21.5 percent of the total deaths were of infants under one year of age, and in 1897 one-fourth of the total number of deaths occurred among children two years and under. Surviving the first year was only one stage of the battle: in that same year, 1897, there were also 567 deaths within the group from one to five years of age.[30]

A combination of factors was responsible for this situation. Most births took place at home under insanitary conditions and with unqualified midwives. The Port-of-Spain hospital registered only 130 births in 1891, although the total births in that year may have been nearer 1,209. Although the surgeon general reported that the hospital trained twelve midwives per year in the 1890s, the many available but unqualified midwives were more often employed, since the trained midwives charged prohibitive fees.[31] The inadequate hospital services also took their toll. The case of Mary Alexander—who in 1879 at age eighteen, had to walk from Mayaro to Port-of-Spain, a distance of approximately thirty miles over unfavorable terrain, during the ninth month of her pregnancy—may not have been an uncommon one among pregnant women.[32] And finally, the fact that many expectant mothers were forced, out of necessity, to work at arduous tasks, on and off the plantations, until the final stage of their pregnancy and to return to those tasks after the barest minimum of postnatal recuperation is of crucial importance in understanding this high rate of infant mortality.

The population expansion of the nineteenth century in Trinidad did not come from natural increases but was a result of massive immigration. One major source of immigrants was the nearby British West Indian islands. Net immigration from the West Indies for the period 1871–1911 was approximately 65,000. During the earlier period, 1844–70, many of the immigrants had tended to be transients. They came, worked during the crop season, and then returned to their families with their accumulated savings. In fact the population listed as British West Indian declined from 12,000 in the census of 1844 to 10,000 in the census of 1851. But in 1861, it increased again to 11,000, and it reached 13,000 in 1871, 24,000 in 1881, 33,000 ten years later, and was listed at over 46,000 in the census of 1901. The cessation of subsidized British West Indian immigration in favor of East Indian immigration had been responsible for the earlier period of decrease, but the opening up of the Crown lands in 1869 and the sugar crisis of the late nineteenth century drove many more West Indians to seek refuge in Trinidad.

East Indians formed the bulk of the immigrant flood, however. Between 1845 and 1917, with only a short two-year break in 1848–49 they came in a steady stream, to a total of 143,339. Although the mortality rate among them was extremely high in the early years of the scheme, and although others returned to India or emigrated to other areas, this source of immigration made an indelible impact on the demographic and sociocultural profile of Trinidad. There were few years in which less than 1,500 East Indians landed in Trinidad; more often than not, the figure was in the vicinity of 3,000 per year, and in some years it was as high as 4,000.[33]

Since this incoming population was intended as labor for the plantations, it meant that the population expansion was skewed towards the rural areas. The population of the four major sugar-producing wards—Tacarigua, Chaguanas, Couva, and Naparima—increased by at least 85 percent between the censuses of 1871 and 1891. In 1871 the combined population of the four districts was 39,343; in 1881 this increased to 55,876; and in 1891 the population was 72,668.

Montserrat, another rural district and the center of the Crown-land distribution program, also experienced a remarkable increase in population. The census return for 1871 showed that Montserrat had 3,388 inhabitants; ten years later the population had more than doubled to 7,354. Since Montserrat and the sugar-producing wards were the recipients of the immigrants, the population profile also showed a preponderance of East Indians in those areas. In 1871 Montserrat returned a population of 21 percent East Indians; ten years later the East Indian segment formed 38 percent of the Montserrat population. The same pattern is repeated in the four main sugar wards: 42 percent East Indian in 1871, 52 percent in 1881, and almost 60 percent in 1891.

The urban areas also grew, although at a much slower rate than the rural districts. After the first rush into Port-of-Spain in the years immediately after emancipation, the urban drift stabilized and was affected only by seasonal fluctuations. But in the last decades of the century, especially after 1880, migration increased again. The population of Port-of-Spain increased from 18,980 in 1861, to 23,561 in 1871, 31,858 in 1881, and 33,782 in 1891.[34]

The population increase, especially in the last decades, came from the combination of increased migration of Afro-Trinidadians away from the rural areas and the influx of newly arrived West Indian immigrants. This pattern reflected the social and economic dislocations partially caused by the continued immigration of East Indian labor to the rural districts even during the sugar crisis. The Borough of Port-of-Spain returned 3,254 residents in 1851 who stated one of the other West Indian colonies as their place of birth; in 1861 this figure was 3,823, in 1871 it was 4,947, in 1881 it was 9,777, and it reached 10,565 in 1891.

Because of the source of the population increase (namely, immigration) and the purpose of this immigration (namely plantation labor), the demographic profile reflected a young and male bias. The plantation required workers, but preferably young and male. During the slave period it had sought to fill its labor needs with the young males of Africa, and after emancipation it again tried to impose its preferences on its labor supply.

According to the census of 1844 the total number of females in Trinidad was nearly equal to the number of males: the males were 51 percent of a population of 59,815, and the 29,102 females formed 49 percent of that population. But the male complement continued to increase until by the census of 1871 it formed 55 percent of the population. Massive immigration between 1851 and 1871 was the major cause of this male predominance.[35] In 1871 there were 82 females to each 100 males, and twenty years later, in 1891, the ratio was still only 84 females to each 100 males.[36]

The population was also incredibly young. Between 1871 and 1891, the group from twenty to forty years of age formed roughly 40 percent of the population of Trinidad. At least three-quarters of the population were below the age of forty. In 1881, when 78 percent of the population were forty and under, 40 percent were between the ages of twenty and forty, 18 percent between ten and twenty, and 20 percent of the population under the age of ten.

But two important exceptions within this general profile of a population that tended toward the young and male have serious implications for crimes of violence. In the first place, the male bias is a condition chiefly of the immigrant groups. In 1891, when females were 46 percent of the overall population, they constituted 39 percent of the East Indian population and 46 percent of the British West Indians, but among the Creole population the female complement was slightly above 50 percent. Second, the bulk of the urban population was female. (See table A.29.) The population of Port-of-Spain in 1881 was 31,858, and approximately 52 percent of that number were females. Most females (except East Indians) were attracted to the urban centers and the possibility of jobs as domestics, seamstresses or laundresses. In 1891, 60 percent of the female population in Port-of-Spain gave their place of birth as Trinidad and 31 percent as a West Indian colony; age, in terms of 23 percent were listed as between ten and twenty years old, and 35 percent were between the ages of twenty and forty.

The plantation system created a peculiar residential pattern based on occupational specialization and structured along age and sex lines. It forced a male-dominated labor force to live on or around plantations, in the rural areas, during the prime years of their lives—that is, between fifteen and thirty-five—and in female-deficient communities. It simultaneously created a situation where the urban population was predominantly female, most in the prime years of their lives, and dependent for their livelihood on marginal occupations. This residential pattern also followed ethnic lines, that is, the urban-based, female-biased population was predomoninantly Creoles of African descent and the bulk of the male-biased East Indian population lived in the rural plantation areas. The frustration and tensions generated by this situation contributed to the pattern of impulsive and implosive violence that was a noted feature of the society.

Those who resided on the plantation lived in a rigidly controlled and supervised semimilitary situation. Every aspect of their lives was controlled by the workings of the Indentured Immigration Ordinance and its amendments, which virtually imprisoned them on the plantations. The ordinance provided the legal framework that governed every activity of the working day, and like the slave laws of the previous system, it dictated what the Indians did from dusk to dawn and how and where they lived.

The bulk of them lived in barrack ranges—some recently evacuated by the former slaves and many in various stages of delapidation. As many as four single adults or a married couple and all their children occupied the roughly 1,200 cubic feet of space that was the size of the rooms in the ranges. Everything was done in these little boxes, and since adjoining rooms were separated only by partitions that never reached the roofs, there was no privacy either within the individual cubicle or between cubicles.[37]

Living conditions for the urban population were no better than those of their rural compatriots. They lived in the wretched and notorious barrack yards that could be found all over Port-of-Spain. Typically, these yards consisted of:

> a narrow gateway leading into a fairly big yard, on either side of which run along low buildings, consisting of anything from four to eighteen rooms, each about twelve feet square.
>
> The space between the roof and door is so small that the wire netting placed there for ventilation is practically useless. The low partition which divides one room from another is made up for by bars about four feet long by three inches wide, set about three inches apart, thereby enabling the carbonic acid gas from one room to pass to another and be breathed again.[38]

The facilities available were shared in common by the inhabitants of these yards: a water closet, unmistakable by smell if not by sight and responsible for the cholera epidemics of the nineteenth century; a structure that masqueraded as a bathroom and that made ablutions a public spectacle rather than a private ritual; very often a single water tap for cooking and laundry; and a mound of stones for bleaching clothes with crisscrossed lines for hanging the laundry to dry. These shared facilities often gave rise to numerous conflicts; for example, women whose livelihood depended on doing laundry for the middle class often came into conflict with other women, some of them also laundresses, over the use of the common laundry facilities.

These hovels may have provided urban accommodation that was barely adequate even in the early nineteenth century, but they quickly turned into slums under the pressure of an increasing urban population swelled by migrants from the rural areas and immigrants from the islands. The passage of the Building Ordinance of 1868, which prohibited the erection of new wooden buildings in the city,[39] only exacerbated the situation, as the increasing urban population found difficulty in locating alternative accommodation. Furthermore, unscrupulous landlords, although quick to collect rents, were conspicuously slow to repair damages and generally maintained their property in a condition unsuitable for human habitation. The reluctance of the authorities to handle the situation is no doubt related to the underlying need to coerce the surplus urban population back to the plantations. At any rate, there was endless conflict between landlords and tenants over the collection of rents and the "illegal" occupation of premises.[40] If the East Indians were forced to remain in the plantation ranges because of the stipulations of the Indentured Immigration Ordinance, the urban dweller, though not legally restricted by an ordinance, had little choice in alternative accommodation and remained imprisoned in the wretched barrack yards.

These plantation cubicles and barrack rooms became breeding grounds for disease and violence. Superheated by day (because of the corrugated iron roofing) and overcrowded at night, they facilitated the spread of contaminative diseases of the lungs.[41] Many people tried to escape the barrack yard and spent most of their waking hours on the streets. Especially for the unemployed, the freedom of the streets, both by day and night, was preferable to the confinement of the barrack room. Hence the numerous comments by locals and visitors alike about the "numbers of young and able bodied men . . . who lounge about the streets in utter idleness, save when engaged in gambling, fighting, or even more questionable pursuits."[42] Very often, therefore, the interpersonal conflicts and tensions that were heightened by the lack of privacy and close living in the barrack yard and that resulted in violent clashes were transferred to the streets.

THE MECHANISMS OF ESCAPE

The street was only one way of escaping the brutal conditions of their lives. Some succumbed to the pressures and tensions of society and took their own lives. The figures for suicide in the nineteenth century are not easily available, but the few fragments suggest that suicides were not infrequent. There were sixteen reported suicides in 1894,[43] but in many years the incidence was probably underreported or not reported at all. The phenomenon seemed to be more predominant among the immigrants than among the creoles. Those East Indians who took their own lives generally did so after having committed some other felony: wife murder, for example. The Portuguese were noted for their susceptibility to bouts of mental depression that often ended in suicide. This state of mental depression was particularly noticeable among Portuguese prisoners, who were reported "to waste away under the depressing influences of prison life, without any disease other than the mental prostration being apparent."[44] Some of the Chinese immigrants—who, like the East Indian and Portuguese immigrants, found themselves in a strange land, subject to strange customs and stringent regulations—also took their own lives in order to escape the oppression of the colonial plantation world.[45]

Others fled into the "otherworld" of the insane. In 1870, Dr. Murray, the surgeon general, complained about the steady increase in criminal insanity. He reported an insanity ratio of 1 in 1,500 of the population in 1863, 1 in 1,300 in 1868, and 1 in 1,000 in 1870.[46] But these figures do not tell the full story. The Lunatic Asylum was opened in 1858 at Belmont Circular Road with accommodations for 48 patients.[47] Prior to this, criminal lunatics were housed in the prison, while those who were not considered seriously ill or dangerous were not institutionalized. Even after the opening of the asylum, excess male lunatics were still sent to the prisons. By 1870 the new asylum was overcrowded. It then held 102 patients, some of whom had to be housed in tents on the grounds of the asylum.[48] The residential capacity was expanded in the 1870s, and again in the 1890s, and a system of accommodation in private homes was suggested, though not implemented, to cope with the increased numbers of admissions.[49] By 1900, when the asylum was removed to larger premises at St. Ann's, the number of patients in daily residence had risen to over 400.

The insane population reflected the overall demographic profile of the society. Between 1858 and 1911, slightly more than 5,000 patients were admitted to the mental asylum.[50] Males constituted 56 percent of these admissions, although in some years females tended to be about half of the resident patient population. The patients also tended to be young, with the bulk of them between the ages of twenty and forty. In 1890, 134 patients were admitted to the asylum. Sixty-four patients, or 48 percent of the total admitted, were between the ages of twenty and forty. The mean age of the males was thirty-eight and the mean age of the females was thirty-five. Unmarried individuals formed the biggest group, 67 in all, or 50 percent; but the martial status of 32 patients, or 24 percent of the group, was listed as unknown. Occupational status showed a predominance of laborers, 80 of them, or 60 percent of the group. According to the place of birth given, 32 percent were born in Trinidad, 27 percent in the British West Indian colonies, and 25 percent in India.[51]

The lunatics admitted were described according to their diagnosed state of lunacy. The categories used were maniacal and dangerous, quiet chronic, melancholy and suicidal, and finally, a category that included the idiotic, paralytic, and epileptic. In 1875, for example, among the 120 patients in the asylum, there were "24 cases of acute and unremitting insanity, who are at all times more or less wild, intractable and occasionally dangerous"; 86 were considered quiet, chronic of long standing—harmless but incurable; and 10 were epileptics.[52] The categories used reveal the concern of the authorities with their ability to impose control on those admitted for treatment. In the four-year period 1879–82, 50 percent of the 1,032 patients admitted to the asylum were listed as maniacal and dangerous. Whether they were, in fact, dangerous is debatable. But the categories are nonscientific and do not permit us to really understand the extent, nature, or causes of lunacy in nineteenth-century Trinidad.

The explanations offered about the causes of and the increase in lunacy are a combination of unveiled racist notions and pseudoscientific speculation of the nineteenth century. Dr. A. A. De Verteuil's explanation in 1858 was typical: "The slow but continued action of moral causes, and habitual drunkenness, seems to be the determining causes of lunacy. I have remarked, in the case of females, that jealousy and religious enthusiasm are the predisposing agents towards this terrible malady; in many instances, it terminates in confirmed idiocy, as if the cerebral organ had given way and broken down, under the pressure of too powerful a stimulus."[53]

The Colonial Office, curious about the number of female lunatics, claimed that in warm climates lunacy among European females could be traced to sexual causes and wondered whether this was also the case in Trinidad.[54] The surgeon general, in keeping with his profession, tended to be more scientific. He declared that female lunacy could be traced to the working conditions of the women. In 1869 he reported:

> amongst the native general population here, the women are really the working and industrious class; and although this, purely in itself would, I think, tell favourably for them, yet it must be borne in mind, that as washers and hucksters, market women and cigar makers, etc. they are necessarily much exposed, not only to weather and fatigue, but unfortunately to trials of temper, to which their greater natural susceptibility makes them prone to yield, as well as to the endless small, but by them made serious, troubles daily arising, and assailing them in their contact with the rough every day battle of life.
>
> The exciting causes are either physical or moral, or, more

> frequently, both combined. Of these I find intemperance, associated with vice and idleness, the most prolific in the male; and uterine, including puerperal disease in the female. After these come strong passions and violent tempers in the latter, loss of property and domestic affairs in the former; next in both sexes, epilepsy and diseases affecting the brain.[55]

The Colonial Office, as guardians of the dispossessed and disenfranchised masses and their protectors against possible exploitation by the plantocrats, should have the last say. In 1871 one official declared that the increase in lunacy in Trinidad was due "to the increase of industry and cultivation which has brought to the country many thousands of strange immigrants of bad habits, and a great increase of shipping and in consequence discards of all kinds."[56] This was his considered opinion thirty-three years after the Colonial Office had agreed to a policy of subsidized immigration to meet the labor demands of the plantocrats, and forty-eight years before it would put an end to the scheme.

The reasons given for lunacy mirrored the general racist attitudes of the time as well as the paucity of the state of knowledge on insanity. Unscientific notions on the inherent criminality and disposition to deviancy of non-Europeans often masqueraded as scientific judgment. East Indians, for example, were accused of feigning insanity in order to be institutionalized until the expiration of their indenture.[57] No doubt some of the more adventurous East Indians found that a temporary sojourn at the lunatic asylum provided a well-needed respite from the rigors of plantation life. But it is difficult to believe that many of the 163 East Indians who formed 34 percent of the inmates in 1900 feigned insanity.

The authorities at the asylum was in no position to give reliable data on either the "predisposing or exciting" causes of lunacy. They did not begin keeping systematic records of the previous history of patients until the twentieth century. Patients were generally sent to the asylum accompanied by a policeman, who at most could give only the patient's name, age, and sex.[58] Hence, in many years between 35 and 40 percent of the cases were registered as lunacy induced by causes unknown, and where a cause is listed in the other 60 percent of the cases, it tended to be more guesswork than scientific diagnosis. Yet there were numerous reasons given for the lunacy of the annual admissions. Among the reasons given were heredity, epilepsy, childbearing, Obeah or witchcraft, wounds and head injuries, excitement or violent temper, loss of property, grief and depressing passions, chronic physical diseases, religious excitement, and intemperance. The latter was a popular diagnosis—intemperance in sex (satyriasis among males and wanton lust among females excited the Victorian mind) and intemperance in the use of opium, ganja, and alcohol.

There is no doubt that alcohol was a precipitating factor in a number of situations that resulted in violence, if not in lunacy. Working-class Trinidadians consistently resorted to alcohol and other stimulants to escape from the drudgery of their working conditions and their everyday lives. They used alcohol for the reasons humans have historically used or misused these stimulants: to provide Dutch courage for the coward, to serve as a lubricant in social intercourse for the inhibited, to furnish some with the mechanism for creating a fantasy world into which, for a brief moment, they could escape from the realities of living in the colonial world. In nineteenth-century Trinidad—where thousands of recently arrived and unassimilated immigrants, live in atrocious housing conditions that which gave rise to daily frustrations and tensions—alcohol became a fuse to a powder keg of violence.

The widespread use and abuse of alcohol was a prominent feature of life of Trinidad, and like so many other aspects of life in that society, it had deep historical roots. During slavery it had been the common practice of the planter class to issue portions of rum as part of the regular rations and this continued even after slavery. During the first few years after emancipation many of the magistrates blamed the numerous brawls, fights, and assaults on the excessive use of alcohol. Though it was not the root or the sole cause of this tendency towards violence, alcohol did facilitate an excessive resort to violence to settle disputes. This widespread use of alcohol was exacerbated by the pernicious practice of planter-employers supplementing wages with the rum allowance. The magistrates in the rural areas foresaw no end to the inebriety of the working class and its connection with crimes against the person until the planters discontinued the rum allowance. But the employers then substituted wine and malt liquor, and it took another three years before they made any serious effort to stop the practice.[59]

Trinidadians continued to drink excessively, and the results were quite evident. The numerous comments by visitors and local residents about the scenes of drunken orgies and the numerous idlers dissipating their lives in alcohol were largely exaggerated, but they most certainly contained more than a grain of truth. One of the most popular pieces of advice given to most Englishmen before immigrating to Trinidad was a warning against rum and its effects on Englishmen in the tropics. And Europeans did seem to suffer the most from the excessive use of alcohol. We have already mentioned the cases of the magistrate committed to a mental asylum with an attack of delirium tremens and the Irish policeman who died of alcoholic poisoning within one year of his arrival in Trinidad. To these examples could be added that of the head of a civil service department so addicted to drink "that after breakfast he was unable to discharge his duties,"[60] and the deaths from alcohol within the space of twelve months of ten soldiers of the Forty-First Regiment.[61] These were by no means extreme cases, but point to the persistent and widespread pattern of alcohol abuse. They come to our attention because of the prominent positions these victims held in the society. The victims we do not as readily see are those of the working class and the lower orders who had their health damaged, their sense of judgment impaired, and their families destroyed because of the excessive use of alcohol. These cases mainly come to our attention as casualties of the legal system.

Committals for drunkenness and for drunk and disorderly behavior are not the best guide to the extent of alcohol consumption. The statistics for these offenses fluctuated regularly throughout the nineteenth century. During the period 1848–54, the number of annual committals for drunkenness declined dramatically from 128 to 20. But in the 1860s, committals averaged in the fifties annually. There was an increase in the 1870s to 130 per annum, then a decrease to 120 during the 1880s, and a further decrease to an average of 100 per year during the 1890s. This pattern does not mean that the society experienced periods of sobriety followed by alcoholic binges. Since these are figures for committals and not convictions, they mask the real extent of alcoholism. In fact, committals depended largely on the attitudes of arresting officers, the whims of prosecuting magistrates, and the ability of the accused to pay the imposed fines. Both arresting officer and prosecuting magistrate were often influenced by the intensity of public outcries about inebriety, so that these fluctuations in committals are more an indication of the interest in policing and punishing the phenomenon than in alcohol consumption itself.

Those arrested, convicted, and imprisoned were individuals whom the police and the magistrates judged unable to control themselves as a result of alcohol. But the statistics do not refer to those individuals who while intoxicated went beyond merely disturbing the peace with loud and boisterous behavior and who either damaged property or committed some act of violence against a person. They give us no idea of how many situations occurred in which acts of violence were committed by intoxicated individuals, or in which alcohol or other stimulants had impaired the judgment of individuals and made them willing to resort to violence to settle disputes. There is no doubt, however, that in many of the incidents that were recorded as crimes of violence against the person, the convicted or his victim or both had had his judgment impaired by the previous use of alcohol.

Opium was also linked to lunacy, although it was rarely suggested that it figured prominently in crimes of violence. The use of opium was restricted largely to the Chinese community. But some non-Chinese Trinidadians were also reported to be habitués of the opium dens of Port-of-Spain.[62] In fact, although the Chinese community was listed as only 1,400 strong in the census of 1871, more than 36,464 pounds of opium were imported into Trinidad between 1864 and 1878.[63] Some of this may have been medical opium, since some medicines of the time contained opium, and it is also quite likely that some of the nonmedical opium may have been used by some non-Chinese. But the latter group may have been small and not significant enough to cause alarm or to change the identification of the Chinese community with the use of the drug.

The Chinese community was small and insignificant from the perspective of plantation interests. According to the 1871 census, the population born in China was 1,400. In 1881 it was 1,266, and the 1891 census lists 1,006 in this segment of the population. Orginally, the Chinese had been brought as plantation labor long before the end of the nineteenth century, but they had deserted the plantation for other occupations. In 1881, 26 percent of them lived in the urban center of Port-of-Spain, and the 1891 census indicated that 65 percent of them were involved in shopkeeping and huckstering. By and large, they were a law-abiding group: between 1877 and 1899 only 235 of them had been imprisoned for any offenses. They were identified, not with crimes against property or the person, but more with social economy offenses; that is, gambling, indebtedness, and breaches of the opium ordinance. But there were many references to Chinese who had been sent to the mental asylum and whose lunacy had been attributed to the use of opium. But opium users were rarely connected with crimes of violence, except when they took their own lives, and they were allowed to use the drug, regardless of the long-term effect on their health, until the end of the century, when opium was illegalized.

Ganja, however, presented numerous problems to the authorities. The medical profession was divided in its opinion about the relationship between ganja and lunacy, but most professionals and laymen tended to believe that there was a definite connection between ganja and crimes of violence. The acting attorney-general, M. Maxwell-Phillip, claimed that ganja was the cause of many of the crimes committed by the East Indian population, and since there were already other available intoxicants, the cultivation of the *Cannabis sativa* should be suppressed.[64] The surgeon general considered ganja an important factor in inducing insanity among East Indian immigrants.[65] The acting surgeon general, Dr. C. B. Pasley, argued that the habitual use of the drug was very debilitating and often produced homicidal mania and other forms of madness.[66]

But there were dissenting voices. In 1899, although twelve district medical officers argued for strict prohibition of ganja, there were at least nine other medical officers who could find no compelling medical reasons to argue for prohibition.[67] In fact it was emphasized that the Indian Hemp Drugs Commission in 1894 had pointed to its use by Indian doctors in bowel complaints, as appetizers, as nervous stimulants, and as a source of great staying power under severe exertion, exposure, or fatigue.[68] If the medical qualities that East Indian doctors ascribed to the plant were indeed correct, and if the East Indians in Trinidad used the plant for those reasons, then the popularity of hemp constituted a telling indictment of conditions in Trinidad.

The control of alcohol, ganja, and opium were thorny problems for the authorities, and the campaigns to suppress them were conducted with ambivalence and revealed how private interests could influence campaigns supposedly conducted to enforce public morality. Despite all the attendant problems that were loudly trumpeted by the moralists, rum was a major by-product of the chief staple of the island. Its manufacture and sale was an intimate part of the economic life of the society. Any campaign to beat the problem of alcoholism and its attendant evils had to be conducted with this in mind. There could be no prohibition; only a control of the market: illegal rum distillers were hounded down, since their stills could be detected and raided; the proliferation of retailers was controlled by prohibitive licensing policies; and illegal sellers were policed. Opium was an imported item, the market was supposedly small, and there were no interest groups fighting for control of the retail trade and therefore there was no real concern about prohibition. But ganja was a problem of a different order. Not only was the market large, but its use was popular among an important segment of the population, namely, the East Indian labor force that had been imported from so far and at such great expense. Furthermore, the cultivation of the plant was much more difficult to control than the manufacture of rum and the importation of opium. It could be grown profusely in the countryside and required no capital investment. Despite attempts to regulate, control, and eventually prohibit access to the drug, the use of ganja continued to be popular and to be identified as a responsible agent in crimes of violence committed by East Indians in the nineteenth century.

The lower class of Trinidad used alcohol, ganja, and opium extensively as a mechanism of escape from the brutalizing conditions of their lives. These conditions were a natural result of the nature and structure of the society and its particular way of organizing life and labor. Since the structure of society did not change, the need for intoxicants continued to exist. It was a need that was satisfied whether the intoxicants were legally available or not. The use of these drugs facilitated the recourse to violence that was common in the society, but they were used as means of escape and as responses to oppressive conditions just as much as violence itself was a means of escape and a response to the conditions of the times.

THE PATTERN OF VIOLENCE

The brutal conditions of life made mere existence a daily struggle and forced many into using intoxicants to escape from the reality of their lives. But this escape route had its price—for the excessive use of intoxicants disrupted the mental balance of some, endangered the health of many, and often led to violence. Fighting was a major "pastime" of the population of nineteenth-century Trinidad. (See table A.30.) Each year between 1875 and 1899 there was an average of 240 committals for fighting and disturbing the peace; there were many more convictions, since many of the combatants escaped with fines; and there were even many more cases that were compromised before trial, as many of the belligerents sought justice and revenge outside of the law.

Much of this fighting was done by groups called bands. In the opinion of the authorities, these bands were organized only for the purpose of dancing, drinking, fighting, gambling, and sex. The attorney general noted in 1879 that "these bands consist for the most part of persons without any settled occupations, subsisting by theft or by the favor of prostitutes whose wages they share. They have no charitable, political or other definite object, are called into operation only for the purpose of fighting with other bands or otherwise creating disturbances."[69]

The public behavior of these bands lent credence to this description. When they congregated in the barrack yards or on the streets, their meetings appeared to the eye of the unsympathetic, Victorian-biased observer to be nothing less than bachanalian orgies—the liberal use of alcohol, loud singing, and suggestive dancing into the wee hours of the morning seemed to confirm these accusations. But more importantly, the individual members of these bands were continually before the courts for fighting, disturbing the peace, causing affrays and rioting. At any time in the year, but particularly around the pre-Lenten annual carnival, they were involved in some kind of physical violence.

But the group violence that formed a principal item on their agenda is easily explainable in the context of the social disorder engendered by the population expansion of the nineteenth century. The numerous groups of immigrants—both West Indian and East Indian—found themselves in a new society where there was a need to establish networks and linkages in order to cope with the uncertainties of life. Similarly, in the urban areas the migrants from the country districts needed to establish networks in the city to ease the trauma of settlement. These bands, therefore, were not purposeless groupings given only to senseless violence, as the attorney general and others described them, but were fraternities or sororities that acted as oases of friendship for newcomers to strange and alienating situations.

There are no extant records of bank memberships, but the social conditions of the nineteenth century suggest ways in which members may have been recruited originally to these bands. Recruitment may have been based on ethnic origin, island of birth, previous association on old plantations, and residence in new neighborhoods. The youthfulness and the general diverse origins of the population facilitated this tendency to gregariousness. Among the East Indians in the rural areas there were strong loyalties to plantations, but it is quite possible that there may have been other criteria—like place of origin in India, time of arrival in Trinidad, caste membership, or religion—on which group affiliations were also based. In the urban areas, where gangs made up of those of African descent were quite prominent, the social melee of urban Port-of-Spain provided numerous bases for band membership. There were known associations of Congos, Dahomeans, and Yorubas. Some of the bands were of Creole migrants who may have lived in the same rural districts prior to migration, and previous residence may have been a basis for association. Other bands were composed of immigrants from particular West Indian colonies—Barbados, for example. But increasingly, residence in a particular locale transcended these original patterns of association, and residence in a particular street or neighborhood became the common bond.

Many of these band members were unemployed or marginally employed, and during the period of the sugar crisis there was increased animosity between Creoles and immigrants, as the latter were singled out as the cause of the depression of wages. This may have been at the root of a number of clashes during the closing decades of the century. But it was not the sole cause, nor does it fully explain the persistence of the group violence throughout the century. Unemployed youths in their prime, condemned to a life of marginality because of the color of their skin and their refusal to be subjected to unrewarding employment on the plantation, were the major perpetrators of this violence. They used their untapped energies and endless time to focus on what they considered to be invasions of their territory, insults to their manhood, and alienation from the favors of their women by those whom they designated as rivals. Minor insults became major reasons for strife. They found many areas of activity in which they competed, and this rivalry resulted in numerous violent clashes. More often than not, they refused to allow the courts of the land to be the final arbiter in their disputes, and in seeking revenge outside of the courts, they set in motion never-ending cycles of violence and counterviolence.

The pattern of violence among the East Indian community was a clear reflection of the combined effects of demographic pressures, sexual imbalance, social and cultural changes wrought by emigration, and the brutalizing effects of an all-pervasive system of labor. Between 1872 and 1880, 27 percent of all the murders committed were by East Indian immigrants; in the next period, 1881–89, East Indians committed 60 percent of the murders; and between 1890 and 1899, the same ethnic group committed 70 percent of the sixty murders reported for that period.

The agent general of immigration was convinced in 1872 that "these cases of violence here have for the most part occurred among coolies in the earlier stages of the indenture, when their habits and prejudices have been but little modified by a soujourn among strangers; they enjoy too, apart from the hours of work, an amount of personal freedom apt to turn into license when in the receipt of higher wages, and of a freer indulgence in rum, bhang (ganja) and other stimulants than was their want [*sic*] in India."[70] Despite this unfounded, racist, but optimistic comment, however, homicide increased among the East Indians, and the pattern of violence was clearly related to the condition of their servitude.

The bulk of these homicides were the murders of women who were either wives, concubines, or fianceés. (See table A.31.) In 1872–80 all the victims of the twenty-two murders by East Indians were women, and they were all wives; in the next period, 1881–89, 60 percent of the forty-five murder victims in the East Indian immigrant community were women, and 89 percent of these twenty-seven women were wives; and between 1890 and 1899 there were forty-nine murders reported among East Indian immigrants—73 percent of the victims were women and 55 percent of these thirty-six victims were wives.

This particular pattern of violence stemmed from the sexual imbalance of the East Indian population. (See table A.32.) Although the overall population showed a male bias in its demographic profile, that bias was most acute among the East Indian community. The planter class were biased traditionally towards the importation of male labor and only reluctantly recruited females. The value of imported females in a labor-short society only slowly entered the one-track mind of the plantocrats. This attitude, combined with the traditional reluctance of single females to emigrate, made the East Indian community one that was dominated by young males. Between

1871 and 1891, 49,855 East Indians were introduced as immigrants to Trinidad, and of that group 70 percent were males. In the period 1881–91 approximately 25,037 East Indians landed in Trinidad. In that group of immigrants 85 percent, or 21,220, were listed as adults, that is, above the age of fifteen; 11 percent were children, and infants constituted the remaining 4 percent. Among the adults, 70 percent were males and among the children, males again predominated to a total of 57 percent.

Since there was also a traditional bias on the part of the planters against the recruitment of males above the age of thirty-five, the immigrant male population tended to be young, single, and in the prime of their lives. The scarcity of women increased the competition among single male East Indians for spouses. Although single East Indian males used the services of Afro-Trinidadian prostitutes and had sexual liaisons with Creoles, they were reluctant on the whole to either marry or set up nonlegal relationships with non-East Indian women. The available women therefore became valuable and the source of numerous jealousies and quarrels that ended in violent conflict. Those males who were married either before coming to Trinidad or while in Trinidad guarded their wives as if they were prized pieces of property.[71]

There were many temptations to marital infidelity for the East Indians. Not the least of these temptations was the advantages available and the prerequisites accruable to those who had relationships with the holders and brokers of power in the plantation world, namely, the owners, managers, and overseers. It was within the power of these men to make or break the life of any immigrant—male or female. They could affect the quality of life and the quantity of necessities available for survival by their control over the distribution of rations and the size of the work load. And because of the influence they had on the justice system, they could convince magistrates that some unfortunate immigrant had contravened one of the innumerable regulations of the Indentured Immigration Ordinance and therefore was liable to imprisonment. Many of them behaved like feudal lords or old slave masters and imposed a sexual droit du signeur that affected the lives of East Indians and precipitated the use of violence by the males affected.

It is this situation that lay behind the indictment of Louis Thomas, an East Indian, for the murder of his wife, Romain, and his subsequent conviction for manslaughter in 1873. The deceased Romain "had for sometime left her husband and formed a connection with Nivet, the manager of an estate adjoining that on which Louis Thomas lived." Relationships between managers and East Indian women were so common that the chief justice in a letter to the agent general of immigrants thought that it was his "duty to reprobate in the strongest terms the practice on the part of managers and overseers of cohabiting with female coolies, and to point out that amongst a jealous and susceptible people it sometimes led directly to the murder of the woman."[72]

Because of the inequality of the relationship, East Indian women got the worst of the situation. The chief justice took the opportunity during the Louis Thomas case to repeat the popular denigration of these women. He expressed comments on "the very loose character of the majority of coolie women, and the temptations to which men in the position of managers and overseers are subjected."[73] It was a classic case of blaming the victims. The benefits of liaisons with these managers tended to be illusory, temporary, and fraught with danger. The women were frequently sexually used and then abandoned, sometimes with an offspring, since these liaisons rarely ended in marriage. Single women faced ostracization from an unsympathetic community or death from a jealous East Indian suitor who felt rejected, and married women faced death from a cuckolded husband.

Unfortunately for these East Indian women, they were part of a male-biased culture in which perceived slights to male pride had to be avenged. In a misguided manner, but dictated by East Indian tradition, it was the wife who paid with her life for daring to cause the East Indian male to lose face and suffer dishonor among the community and his peers. It did not matter if some of these women sought to ease the conditions of their own lives and their husbands' by succumbing to the temptations offered by the managers or overseers. The penalty for transgressions was instant death.

The situation in the new society in Trinidad undermined many traditional values of the East Indian community, in particular, the male-female relationship. Males pressured by sexual hunger in a female-scarce situation abandoned traditional respect for marital ties and seduced wives away from their spouses. The fact that marriages performed with Indian religious rites, either in India or Trinidad, were not recognized by the law in Trinidad only served to compound the problem.

The traditional dependence of East Indian women was undermined by the liberty that came from the ability to sign individual indenture contracts and become independent breadwinners. Rations, wages, land, and money in lieu of return passages were all given to women as independent agents, without reference to traditional patterns of female dependency. This contributed to the sense of freedom that some East Indian women developed in their new homeland. Sensing their strength because of their scarcity, some of the single female immigrants exploited the situation, challenged traditional values of dependency and subservience, and made free and frequent choices of their paramours. For many of them this bid for independence ended in death at the hands of rejected lovers: this was the situation that resulted in the murder of Rookmania in 1872. The unfortunate woman rejected her lover, Darsan, another East Indian immigrant, in order to live with the East Indian overseer. The fact that Rookmania chose to live with her new lover on the same estate as her last may have only hastened her demise. Three weeks after her rejection of her first paramour she paid with her life for the bold act.[74]

Even some callous parents exploited the female-scarce situation. The tradition of arranged marriages, where females of tender ages were betrothed and pledged to a male suitor on the payment of a dowry, lent itself to ready exploitation. Those parents with girl children who were callous enough maneuvered between multiple suitors, manipulated the hopefuls, exacted dowries from some and tribute in the form of services from others. That too was a dangerous game that sometimes ended in death. In October 1878, for example, Jhuly, an East-Indian immigrant, killed the ten-year-old Chetapeah and her mother, Palowa. The homicide took place during a dispute over either the return of a $400 dowry or the hand of Chetapeah in marriage, as had been promised by Palowa.[75] Starting very early, East Indian female children were exposed to a system in which their bodies were items of property and men often died for the possession of them.

Most Trinidadians received early lessons in violence, since corporal punishment was an essential part of socialization and child training. For Afro-Trinidadians in particular, attitudes developed in slavery died hard. Parents sought to protect their children from the many dangers and pitfalls that could result from the pranks and misdemeanours of a child unaware of the restrictions placed on childhood by the life of slavery. They often used excessive force to punish their children and restrained them from potential conflict with the ruling class by curbing youthful exuberances.[76] Some parents may also have unwittingly taken out the tensions and frustrations inherent in their condition of servitude by too severe chastisements. But although overt oppression ended with emancipation, the end of slavery did not put an end to tensions and frustrations for both Afro- and Indo-Trinidadians. Parents continued to try to protect their children from the physical and psychological violence that characterized the colonial society—and to unconsciously take out their personal frustrations on their defenseless children.[77]

East-Indian parents were particularly worried that, in the new land, their children would be seduced by the scandalous life-style of the Creoles and therefore abandon the customs and traditions of the old country. They thus became more vigilant as they observed, with horror, traditional parental and family relationships of authority undermined by the demands of the conditions of indentureship. The parent who worked long hours under oppressive conditions on the plantation was hardly in the best condition, either physically or psychologically, to deal with the myriad problems of parenthood and childrearing in a strange land. The tendency was to demand strict and blind obedience and too often to resort to harsh punishments.

And yet this harsh punishment was often accompanied by displays of excessive love. Afro-Trinidadian parents, in particular, were noted for the way in which they sometimes overindulged their children. This seeming ambivalence created confusion in the minds of children. Its worst effect was to encourage the belief that violence or hurt could be easily redeemed or recompensed and that damage done to another could be compensated for with signs of remorse and forgiveness. Many of the cases settled out of court may in fact have been prompted by this vacillation between the need to demand immediate punishment and subsequent remorse.

The violence gleaned at home was reinforced by a system of education that emphasized violence. Corporal punishment was a stable in the pedagogical diet of the Trinidad school system, as it was in the British school system on which it was modeled. The teaching of the largely irrelevant curriculum to uninterested and very often underfed pupils in overcrowded schools could be accomplished only with large doses of corporal punishment by the untrained and underpaid teachers.[78] The use of the strap or the rod became an absolute essential. Atrocious physical facilities and too many pupils forced many teachers to abandon any pretense at developing young minds and to concentrate instead on simply maintaining discipline. Their attitude toward their charges came to resemble that of lion tamers, and many of them felt beleaguered by the children of people whom the authorities labeled as savage, barbaric, and uneducable. Many of the teachers, both black and colored, who had unconsciously imbibed and internalized all the feelings of inferiority and self-hatred that came as a result of living in a racist colonial society, may have seen in their pupils a constant reminder of their own inferior positions and may have chastised those pupils in fits of unconscious self-hatred.

This is not to detract from those nineteenth-century teachers who were dedicated and deeply concerned professionals. They saw the acquisition of education, or to be more precise book learning, as being absolutely essential not only for social mobility but also for racial vindication. And it is precisely for this reason that they too were inclined to quickly resort to the whip. Fired by this need to vindicate the race, to provide the passport for social mobility, they did not spare the rod as they tried to drag their charges into the "civilized" world. For whatever reason, whether unconscious self-hatred or conscious racial pride, those teachers used force as a pedagogical tool and in so doing cultivated and gave legitimacy to violence in the society. The whip, which was the badge of authority during slavery, was no less important during the postemancipation period as the badge of authority of the pedagogue.[79]

The nineteenth-century child was the recipient of excessive punishment at home and the victim of an education system where the strap was standard fare. His education in violence was reinforced by constant exposure to the violent treatment of women both at home and in the community, where he witnessed the male exercising an almost undisputed right to the body of women. It was a right of lordship that was reflected in the community-sanctioned right of the male to use corporal punishment to effect domestic law and order. It was taken for granted that males had the right to use violence to punish real or imagined transgressions of their domestic rules or to revenge real or imagined slights to their ego.

The phenomenon of battered wives was a public matter, since the spatial arrangements of the plantation range or the urban barrack yard made privacy virtually impossible, so that domestic disputes were conducted in full view of the community. Although sometimes some of the onlookers became participants and took sides in the dispute, generally there was little intervention. The idea that "a little blows" was an indication of love was prevalent, and the folly of interfering in "husband and wife business" was well known.

Many of these domestic disputes were settled out of court, so that the statistical evidence is not a reliable guide.[80] Although on the spur of the moment the woman may have reported the incident to the police or lodged a complaint at the court, more often than not, after passions cooled, she compromised the matter and did not pursue the case. Legally sanctioned spouses were less prone to report disputes and to follow the matter through the courts. Unless the violence did extensive physical damage, they considered the abuse part and parcel of the respectability that came with marriage. Common-law wives, the predominant union, made a decision to pursue the matter based on their interpretation of the purpose of the chastisement. They reported the matter initially in order to save face, and if they read the beating as a notice of the termination of the relationship, then they would most likely proceed with the court case. But if the beating was interpreted as merely the exercise of conjugal rights, then convention ruled, and the matter never reached the courts. Since many of these wives, whether married or common law, were either unemployed or marginally employed, they often preferred to suffer brutalization in silence rather than face a life of poverty without the financial support of some man.

The crime of rape was the classic example of the oppression of women in the society. Given the understandable reluctance of women to report incidents of rape, the number of reported cases is noteworthy. There were 206 cases tried before the superior courts between 1870 and 1899. In the first two five-year periods, 1870–79, there were 17 rape cases; this number increased to 26 in the next five-year period, 1880–84. The number of rape cases continued to increase, and it peaked at 56 in the period 1885–89, but it then decreased to 50 and then to 40 in the succeeding five-year periods.

This decrease in the number of cases *before* the courts is no indication of any real decrease in the incidence of rape. It is more likely that fewer cases were being reported and tried before the courts. Curiously enough, the decrease coincided with the decrease in the rate of convictions. The rate of acquittals for rape offenses increased over the period 1870–99. During that thirty-year period, of the 206 cases before the courts, 59 percent ended in conviction, 27 percent of the accused were acquitted, and 14 percent of the cases fell through, that is, were returned nolle prosequi. In the period 1875–79, of the 16 cases tried, 81 percent ended in convictions and 13 percent in acquittals, and 6 percent fell through. But in the period 1895–99 this situation changed. During that seven-year period there were 40 cases, of which 52 percent ended in conviction, 33 percent resulted in acquittals, and 15 percent of the cases were aborted before the completion of prosecution.

It is quite possible that there may have been serious travesties of justice in the earlier part of the century and innocent men fell victim to a court willing to believe the accusations of women. After all, judge and jury were quite aware of the scarcity of women among the immigrant population, and therefore they would have been quite willing to believe that some men driven by sexual hunger would resort to rape to satisfy their needs. Furthermore, in the minds of many, rape by an accused man of African or Indian descent was not inconceivable, since many believed those races were likely to rape, given the scarcely bridled passions that were supposedly part of their racial heritage. It is also quite possible that, in the interim, legal defense improved in quality, hence the increasing rate of acquittals. Furthermore, there is no doubt that the outcome of the acquittals and cases that fell through were a result of the bribery of jury, witnesses, and sometimes even the complainant.[81] Therefore, the increasing number of aborted cases may well indicate the increasing reluctance of female accusers to proceed with rape charges, since they were aware of the likelihood of their success.

The racist and sexist traditions of the society had its impact on the legal system and discouraged many more women from bringing rape cases to the courts and completing the process of prosecution. The stereotypes and the characterizations of all non-European women as being of loose character and questionable morals constituted a major problem of proving rape and was a favorite defense in the courts. The idea that all these women of non-European stock were sexually promiscuous, inveterate liars, and devoid of what Fraser called any "womanly sense of shame"[82] dominated the thinking of the nineteenth century. Accusations of gross immorality and promiscuity against the *jamettes,* as the female gang members and inhabitants of the barrack yards were called, accompanied the vigorous campaigns to stamp out the bands in the 1880s and 1890s. Any working-class complainant in a rape case had to fight against these racist and sexist stereotypes.

The argument of one defense attorney in a rape case in 1869 was typical of the defenses used in rape trials. The defense attorney claimed that the prosecutrix had previously had sexual intercourse with the accused and others and suggested that there was a possibility of consent. He cited British cases as precedent and argued that "the more deeply steeped in looseness of character a woman may be, the more stringent may be the evidence required by a jury to satisfy them that there has been no consent, and if she has been repeatedly unchaste, unless there be satisfactory evidence to the contrary, *consent may be reasonably presumed*" [emphasis mine]. This line of defense prompted a response from the chief justice that constituted one of the few glorious moments in nineteenth-century jurisprudence in Trinidad; he declared "that even the greatest strumpet has a right to assert an assumed chastity against a trespasser to her will."[83]

A low age of consent provided an exploitable line of defense for those accused of the rape of girls of tender ages. Ordinance

1 of 1889 lowered the age of consent from sixteen years to thirteen years. One of the reasons advanced for this reduction was that under the Immigrant Marriage and Divorce Ordinance of 1881, the large East Indian population was at liberty to marry at the age of thirteen, although the age of consent for the general population was sixteen. The proponents for reduction claimed that this created a number of legal problems. The nonofficial members of the Legislative Council, who represented the interests of the plantocrats, also argued that "girls developed more rapidly in tropical climates and sooner attained the age of puberty."[84]

This latter piece of pseudoscientific nonsense was advanced to hide the reason why they advocated a lower age of consent. The plantocrats, who were always concerned about their supply of labor, knew that a lowered age of consent would increase the number of people who could legally sign contracts of indenture or seek employment and would therefore expand the pool of possible labor. Two years later, when Ordinance 20 of 1891 sought to fix the age of consent for all purposes at sixteen, the planting interest unanimously expressed their dissent and walked out of the council chamber to prevent the passage of the bill. They refused to accept the observations of some magistrates and the police that a higher age of consent was valuable in policing the brothels and checking the growth of prostitution among female juveniles. The official members of the Legislative Council, representing the governor and the Colonial Office, were forced to compromise, and the plantocrats accepted fourteen as the age of consent. The interests of the plantation therefore triumphed and served to perpetuate a situation that facilitated the exploitation of women.[85]

The brutality of slavery and its perpetuation in the conditions of the colonial plantation society facilitated the development of women who were as violent as their male counterparts. The violent society bred violent women who returned violence in like measure as they received it. The slave records are replete with women who responded to the violence of slavery with as much violence as both their physical capacity and their position in the social structure permitted. This pattern did not disappear in the postemancipation period: during the first generation after slavery, 1838–69, women could be found in the forefront of every affray and riot, which were very common in the era of transition. Their participation in the violence that characterized the late nineteenth century, 1870–1900, was no less noticeable and earned them frequent comments from a shocked elite.

They played both a supportive and an active role in all the violent activity of the society. The police reported that it was the women who encouraged the men to riot during the massive demonstration that marked the departure of Chief Justice Gorrie, a hero of the lower classes, from Trinidad; they had done the same during the riot in 1849, which was in part prompted by an attempt to shave the heads of female prisoners.[86] In both cases they taunted the men for their lack of aggression. They were the *chantwells,* who sang the fighting songs that served to intoxicate the male stick fighters as they prepared to do battle on carnival and other days.[87] The singing of the East Indian women served a similar function for the *gatka-wallahs,* the East Indian stick fighters, as they re-created the battle of Kerbala at the annual Hosein celebrations.[88]

Bands of women were also among the many fighting bands that existed in Port-of-Spain. Clementia Mills was one of twenty women charged with causing an affray in the public streets of Port-of-Spain in June 1864 and "being unlawfully assembled and arrayed in warlike manner." Clementia, armed with a horsewhip, led a band of women, numbers of the "Mourcelines," to do battle with another group called the "Don't care dams," which was led by a flag-bearing woman. The women of both groups were armed with stones in their aprons and with knives and razors, and with their frocks tucked up, they battled each other in a fight that spread from George Street to an open field on the banks of the Dry River.[89]

Annie Coals, Myrtle the Turtle, Alice Sugar, Alice's younger sister Piti Belle Lily, and Boadicea are some of the more notorious fighting women of the time. Their exploits earned them places in the archives of the oppressed, the calypso. Boadicea fought Alice Sugar for over an hour for the right to the sexual favors of a well-known stick fighter called Cutaway Rimbeau. The fight formed grist for the calypsonian's ready mill. In an ironical twist, Boadicea subsequently whipped Rimbeau with his own stave for having dared to extend his sexual services to the defeated Alice's sister, Piti Belle Lily.[90] Just as the scarcity of females prompted violence in the urban community, it often led the unemployed or marginally employed women to resort to violence to secure and maintain the companionship of males.

The tendency to violence in the society was honed by certain recreational activities that promoted and contributed to the glorification of violence. Cockfighting, although illegal after 1868, was a popular sport, and the lower classes enjoyed seeing the animals engaged in bloody combat as they placed wagers on the winner. Many children, and adults too, got vicarious pleasure from the beating of an effigy of Judas Iscariot through the streets on the Easter weekend, a custom reputedly introduced by Portuguese immigrants. The stick fighters were celebrated in song for their agility and the skill they displayed as they used their deadly staves to smash in the heads of their opponents. Those who were famed for their mastery in sticks, knives, or fists were able to take advantage of the companionship of the female population. It became a vicious cycle of existence as violence bred further violence and aggression became a necessary mechanism for survival in nineteenth-century Trinidad.

CHAPTER SEVEN

The Mechanisms of Labor Control

There is one major characteristic in the plantation system that is crucial to its existence: it requires a large, continuous supply of menial labor, generally unskilled—a virtual army of workers that can be moved or removed at will to satisfy the demands of the process of production. It must therefore be in a position to use political power to secure the legal right to control and when necessary to coerce this labor. This authority is used not only to control the labor at its disposal, but also to maintain an army of reserve labor and to ensure that no other sector of the economy could compete for "its" labor. It is these interrelated factors that propel the plantocracy to seek to establish hegemony over and total society. They need to ensure that all institutions are geared towards the plantation dynamic, namely, the production of an agricultural staple for export.

In territories like Barbados and Antigua, where preemancipation development had secured for the plantocracy the monopoly of arable land and where the land-labor ratio was such that it precluded any alternatives to plantation domination for the recently emancipated, the system reinforced itself during the transition from slave labor to wage labor. In other societies, like Trinidad and British Guiana, there was a lower ratio of population to available arable land, and this tended to increase the available options for those formerly enslaved. Although the results were the same, the transition was more complex. It required far more activity on the part of the plantation interests to reestablish control over the society.[1] In Trinidad the importation of labor became the major mechanism used to redress the balance of power that was upset by emancipation. An estimated minimum of 40,000 immigrants came to Trinidad in the years between 1839 and 1861; thousands more were to come in the remaining years of the century. Their arrival had serious implications for the socioeconomic structure of nineteenth-century Trinidad, and quite apart from the obvious demographic impact, the new immigrants brought changes to the pattern of crime in the postemancipation society.

Importing labor did not automatically mean the control of that labor, as the planters soon learned to their dismay. The labor force continued to disappear. In the main, the West Indian immigrants were seasonal and tended to return home soon after harvesting the crop. Those who remained began to follow the example of the Creoles and settled either in the towns or in squatter communities. The Africans also quickly left the plantations to form separate communities of squatters, since to some extent it was difficult for them to blend into the Trinidad Creole community as easily as the other West Indians. Furthermore, the chaotic conditions of nineteenth-century Trinidad reinforced any initial desire on their part to resist integration into the wider community.

The Portuguese workers soon found that labor on the West Indian plantations differed in significant ways from that in the Madeira wine industry. Wracked by illness as they adjusted to a new climatic and disease environment, and subject to bouts of melancholia that encouraged suicide attempts, they very quickly rejected the plantation. Fortunately for them, they were able to establish themselves as shopkeepers, an occupation they dominated until challenged by the Chinese in the second half of the nineteenth century. The Chinese were the most intractable of the lot. Although they worked quite willingly and efficiently on their own garden plots, they seemed to have had no intention of working for planters.

The East Indians also immediately reacted to the conditions of plantation life and visibly registered their objection by deserting the plantation. Equally subject to adjustments to a new disease environment, and badly treated on the estates, the East Indians' lot was an unhappy one in those early years of immigration. They, too, fled the plantation. The planters therefore soon found it necessary to introduce legislation to give them total and effective control over the labor force they had gone to such lengths to import from so far away.

THE DIRECT CONTROL OF LABOR

At first the planters were loud and magnanimous in their praise of the East Indian and his suitability to replace the African as the principal labor force for the estates. The proprietor of the Union Hall Estate in South Naparima, who had been a commandant of the quarter during slavery, compared them to the bondsmen under his previous jurisdiction: he found them "more intelligent, more apt, more docile, more civil, more obliging, and more obedient, less easily offended, devoid of the savage disposition of the African." Ten other planters continued in the same vein. But one planter hinted at the problem of "maronage" that had slowly begun to plague the planters, as it had done their predecessors during slavery. The manager of the Union Estate in Couva, who agreed that the East Indians were "docile, obedient and of a cheerful disposition," also remarked that they needed a "judicious but adequately stringent superintendence restricting them in the ruinous habit of wandering through the country."[2]

The manager's comment was directed at the increasing number of East Indians who deserted the plantations in reaction against the harsh conditions of plantation life and the attitudes of plantation proprietors and managers, which had hardly changed since the end of slavery. Since there was little government provision for them and as they were alien newcomers in a strange land and initially without ethnic community support, they were often found wandering on the rural roads or in the city—ill-clad, hungry, and destitute. The less fortunate were picked up dead at the roadside.

It is this that prompted the passage of regulations in 1846 that, on the pretext of concern for his health, in fact bound the East Indian to the plantation. Two sections in particular raised the ire of the Anti-Slavery Society and forced the colonial secretary to overrule the regulations. Section 6 made provisions for the strict surveillance of the East Indian while at work and was justified on the grounds of the supposed proverbial propensity of the East Indian "to lie down and smoke while at work, and to seize every available opening for evading it." Section 9 required every East Indian not on the plantation to have in his possession a ticket of leave that specified name, period of leave, plantation to which he was attached, and locality he was given permission to visit. Another section confined the indentured to the estate hospital without wages if he was on the sick list. The regulations were designed to combat the growing defection of the imported labor force; but in typical fashion, moral and humanitarian reasons were given, and racist characterizations were used as added justification. In defending the stringency of the regulations Lord Harris argued that "the coolies are placed here under peculiar circumstances, as utter strangers in a foreign land, and therefore requiring the zealous and increasing care of Government; that they are also far from being the best class of the Indian labouring population, are naturally dissolute, and depraved in their habits, if left to themselves, and much inclined to fall into the habits of drinking, and of wandering about idle about the country, and therefore require the close supervision of Government, in order to correct if possible, but at all events to prevent, any evident and public cases of vagabondage and licentiousness."[3] But behind this curious admixture of humanitarian concern and racist slurs lay the stark economic reality of a disappearing labor force that had to be strictly policed.[4]

Despite Lord Harris's brave attempt to rationalize these draconian regulations, the Colonial Office—urged on by a still vigilant antislavery committee—promptly disallowed the regulations.[5] Yet, despite its withdrawal, succeeding ordinances passed between 1847 and 1854 retained at least the spirit if not the letter of the disallowed regulations of 1846. The Colonial Office disallowed some of these ordinances, for example, Ordinance 3 of 1847, but the local government eventually introduced many of the prohibitions that made the East Indian the substitute for the African bondsman on the plantations. Ordinance 5 of 1850, for example, set the penalty for unauthorized absence from work at 6*d.* per day and authorized the arrest without warrant of any immigrant found more than two miles from his/her contractual estate without a pass during the week. Another ordinance in 1852 substituted a fourteen-day imprisonment instead of a fine for breach of contract and desertion. Ordinance 24 of 1854 codified all the existing ordinances pertaining to immigration. The local legislature continued to pass other ordinances that increased the web of entrapment that governed the lives of indentured workers until they consolidated all of these ordinances in 1899. This final consolidating act remained in force until the end of indentureship in 1917.

From very early, the workings of the immigration ordinance(s) brought East Indians into contact with the law enforcement agencies. Between 1849 and 1854, some 967 workers were imprisoned for breach of contract—some of them Africans, the bulk of them East Indians. Another 282 were imprisoned between 1852 and 1854 for specific breaches of the Immigration Ordinance of 1852. After the passage of Immigration Ordinance 24 of 1854 the flood increased: of 8,000 East Indians under indenture in 1858, there were at least 400 imprisonments for breach of contract. Between 1871 and 1874, there were 12,198 cases for infractions of the 1854 Ordinance, 5,214 convictions, and 3,856 committals to prison.

This pattern continued throughout the nineteenth century as the law enforcement agencies were used as the major mechanism for labor control. (See table A.33.) During the period 1875–79, 20 percent of all the cases before the courts were concerned with infractions of the two major ordinances covering labor; namely, the Master and Servants Ordinance of 1846 and the Indentured Immigration Ordinance of 1854. This figure declined, but only slowly, to 16 percent of all cases by 1911 and in the last six years of the labor scheme declined to 10 percent of all court cases. The convictions under these ordinances remained roughly at 23 percent of all convictions between 1875 and 1899, although there was a slight decrease to 19 percent in the period 1895–99 that coincided with a decrease in total cases. But the conviction rate climbed back to 21 percent in 1900–1905/06 and only slowly declined to 12 percent of all convictions by the cessation of indentured immigration in 1917. Except during the period 1885–89, the labor ordinances contributed no less than 20 percent to the total number imprisoned; in fact, in the period 1900–1905/06, 32 percent of all the prison committals were for offenses committed under the labor ordinances.

The pattern of cases, convictions, and committals for the period 1895–1905/06 requires some speculative explanation. The number of cases dropped three percentage points as well as declining, in real numbers after 1894, but it increased in both percentage points and real figures in the period 1900–1905/06. Similarly, convictions decreased in both indicators only to show a subsequent increase. It is only the committal rate that continued a steady increase, from 18 percent in the 1885–89 period to as high as 32 percent by 1900–1905/06—with the greatest single increase during the latter period. These fluctuations occurred during the period of the sugar crisis, when the planters—faced with a decline in sugar prices and a professed inability to pay wages—struggled to extract the maximum labor from their indentured work force. The presence of the royal commission of inquiry that took evidence into the extent of distress caused by the crises may have inhibited the planters and their magistrate allies in 1896 and 1897. The negative publicity engendered by a growing antiimmigration lobby may well have forced many planters to be slightly less persistent in the prosecution of offenses. But following the publication of the report and the return to some measure of normalcy (although still plagued by adverse market conditions), the planters and their allies were back to their usual legal machinations.

It is interesting to note that committals continued to be returned at a high rate and even increased during the period 1895–1905/06. (See table A.34.) It is quite clear that prison continued to be the most favored method of disciplining recalcitrant labor even when the overall national figures show a shift to the use of fines rather than imprisonment as punishment! The number of those who were imprisoned upon conviction moved from 38 percent in 1875–79 to 52 percent in 1900–05/06. While nonindentured labor was forced to pay for its breaches of the law, not with incarceration, but with a monetary imposition—thereby forcing the individual to seek employment in order to pay the fine—indentured labor, already obliged to labor under penalty of law, was imprisoned. This may have been intentional and connected with the seasonal requirements of the plantation. The planter most likely found it convenient to insist on imprisonment during the off-season of the sugar crop, since it removed surplus workers and temporarily suspended the planters' obligations to them—and therefore decreased the wage bill. The time spent in prison was not to be used in rehabilitating exercises: the planters objected to the use of "their" labor on normal prison projects—for example, the tending of the botanic gardens on the government grounds. Even more important, the time spent in prison was counted as lost days and was eventually regained by extending the period of indenture.[6]

It was this use of the criminal justice system to satisfy the labor demands of the plantation that was in large measure responsible for a number of other aberrations in the annual statistics. The number of cases discharged was no less than 20 percent at any time between 1885 and 1906: it averaged 27 percent between 1875 and 1884 and 22 percent between 1885 and 1899 before dropping to 20 percent by 1906. Yet the figure for discharged cases did not really represent the discriminating wheels of blind justice separating the innocent from the guilty. Instead, it reflected yet another aspect of the misuse of the system of justice in the pursuit of plantation aims. In many instances summonses to attend court (which are entered in the court docket as a case) were used by planters to coerce workers. Very often they had no intention of prosecuting the case, but the threat of a summons before the magistrate was often enough to bring a worker back into line. In fact, either the threatened worker was forced to pay the cost of the summons immediately or it was deducted from his future pay.[7] The planter argued that prosecuting these cases during crop time resulted in a loss of labor and unrecoverable time lost in court.

Many of the indentured who acquiesced to this system of coercion and badgering were fully aware of their chances before the courts. They knew full well that magistrates openly connived with planters. Without a good working knowledge of English they were at the mercy of unscrupulous interpreters who often misrepresented their pleas. The chances of being convicted for a labor offense were much higher than for any other crime: in 1875–79 only 48 out of every 100 cases resulted in convictions, but during the same period 54 out of every 100 labor cases tried before the magistrates ended up in convictions; and when in 1895–99 the overall conviction rate was 62 out of every 100, labor cases averaged 73 convictions in every 100 cases. The chances of a case being dismissed on its merits were conversely low: in 1875–79, 18 percent of the cases were dismissed, but this figure dropped to 4 percent by 1880 and remained there for the rest of the century. While in the statistics for *all* cases before the courts, dismissals on merits averaged 20 percent, only 4 out of every 100 labor cases were dismissed on their merits.

The result of a conviction was also certain: imprisonment, fine, or bound over—and normally in that order. The percentage of those convicted who received prison terms *increased* from 38 percent in 1875–79 to 52 percent in 1900–1905/06; the percentage of those fined *decreased* from 39 percent to 24 percent during the same period; and those who were bound over increased from 23 percent in 1875–79 to 40 percent in 1885–89 but then decreased back to 23 percent by the end of the period. Those who were bound over ultimately faced the same fate as those who were either imprisoned or fined, for being bound over meant that the decision was entered as a conviction and that the convicted had his indenture endorsed with the equivalent number of days added on to his term of indenture. Sometimes a magnanimous planter paid his fine, but usually this amount was then deducted from his next pay.

Life for the indentured worker was a hazardous existence. The law made a nine-hour day mandatory, and failure to answer the early-morning roll call usually meant endorsation and/or loss of pay. Those who were absent from work or absent from the plantation for three days without leave merited a £5 fine. Those who dared to face their bleak existence fortified with the comfort provided by alcohol found that on their return to sobriety they faced the reality of fourteen days in jail or a £1 fine. Being drunk on the job for the worker was like being drunk on duty for the soldier. Like his predecessor, the slave, the indentured worker did not dare leave the plantation wihout a pass and likewise the nonindentured East Indian, just like the free black of the slave era, had to be always preprepared to prove his status: for refusal to produce documentary identification was punishable by a fine of £1 or a term of fourteen days.

The indentured worker was completely controlled, and on and off the estate his every action was always in jeopardy of contravening some regulation. (See table A.35.) Even to be sick was hazardous. Any worker who reported on the sick list had to remain in the hospital under penalty of fine or imprisonment. Many tried to "escape," not only because of the unsanitary conditions of the cowsheds that passed for estate hospitals but because hospitalization meant lost wages and the probability of the inevitable endorsation.[8] The list of pitfalls was endless: aiding immigrants to leave the colony; using false passports; enticing away a female immigrant; threatening *his* wife who, since she was indentured, was the "property" of the estate owner; and of course the trademark of societies based on coercion and forced labor—disobeying or threatening one in authority.

The indentured worker was in an anomalous position: he could not withhold his labor, for that meant not merely the loss of wages but the possibility of a prison term. Nor could he complain about wages, since this could set off a series of events that usually culminated in his imprisonment. In 1880, for example, workers on the Dinsley Estate complained about not receiving the full amount of their wages. They did not receive satisfactory replies, and after beating the overseers, 44 of them proceeded to Port-of-Spain to lodge a complaint with the protector of immigrants. On their way, they were arrested as vagrants. The following morning the police arrested 100 more and charged them with rioting. During the day 40 wives who came to inquire about their husbands were also arrested by the police. The entire 184 were charged with vagrancy, breaches of the Immigration Ordinance, and the civil charge of rioting.[9] Another group of southern workers found themselves in similar problems in 1900. Sixty-four of them left Harmony Hall Estate in Naparima to go to San Fernando to complain about discrepancies in their wages. Leaving the estate without permission was in contravention of clause 139 of the Immigration Ordinance, however, and they were held and sentenced to twenty-one days hard labor.[10]

The planters, who seized every opportunity to enforce the

Immigration Ordinances, blatantly contravened many of the regulations that were designed at least theoretically to protect the indentured worker. Few of them were ever brought before the courts for their failure to pay correct wages or to pay them on time or to provide the adequate housing and medical facilities required by the law. Those who were summoned knew that the cases against them would be dismissed by magistrates who sympathized with them and that the staff of the Immigration Department was often reluctant to prosecute plantation owners and managers. The complaints of East Indians were viewed as evidence of their litigious nature and the behavior of complaining children. Small wonder, then, that the protector of immigrants could report that in 1894 at least 50 percent of the estates were in contravention of section 66 of Ordinance 12 of 1870, but that they were not prosecuted, since so many estates were affected that to enforce the law would practically stop immigration.[11] Yet the manager of the Colonial Estates in 1896 advocated the reduction of wages and the application of even more stringent laws and heavy punishment for the work force, and some planters could successfully advocate for the removal of a magistrate whom they found too lenient in his dealings with immigrants.[12]

The system of indentureship made workers' rights a criminal matter. It was the perfect replacement for the system of slavery for it was all-encompassing and put every aspect of the workers' rights under the jurisdiction of the employer. It was conflict-prone and therefore could not help but inflate the statistics of cases before the courts, the number of convictions, and the number of those imprisoned each year. Like slavery, it was a distinctive mechanism of labor recruitment and control. For just as color of skin and ethnic origin made the helot class distinguishable and therefore easily controlled in the slave society, so too, the existence of a labor force that was almost exclusively East Indian, of distinguishable ethnic origin, made the control of the labor force decidedly easier in postemancipation Trinidad. The pass law that tied the worker to the plantation, for example, was enforced not only by the estate police and by the regular police, but also by those Creoles who viewed the East Indians as their replacement on the estates.[13]

The criminal statistics testify to the persistent conflict between planter and worker as the former sought to extract the maximum output from his indentured labor and the latter sought to protect his rights and prevent his complete exploitation. Unfortunately, the statistics really represent only the unfortunates—those who were caught and those who were imprisoned. Every year some 30 percent of the indentured labor force—which was roughly 67 percent of the agricultural labor force—were before the courts for labor offenses; annually no less than 20 percent of the indentured workers were convicted for offenses under the Immigration Ordinances. Some of those who did not end up on the court or prison rolls were found in the hospitals and asylums as casualties of the plantation system. There were numerous strikes, go-slows, etc., but since the policy was to single out only the ringleaders for punishment, many of the other participants escaped punishment or, at any rate, did not appear in the criminal statistics. Many workers used the secondary forms of resistance—destruction of property, for example—reminiscent of the slave period.

Many accommodated to the system and in so doing made it difficult to wage successful collective resistance. But it is precisely because indentureship, unlike slavery, had built into it the promise of eventual freedom—a return back to India, passage paid and rich, which is the usual hope of every immigrant—that it was so much easier for many of the East Indians to endure the hardships of indentureship. Present suffering could always be excused and rationalized as the price one pays for future comfort. The daily slights and insults, the numerous restrictions on freedom, the insulting incursions into the private arenas of life—all these and more could be suffered in silence and viewed as temporary inconveniences. After all, although the reality of indentureship was far removed from the promises of the recruiters, the indentured had volunteered for their term. Furthermore, there was always the comforting thought that one's progeny did not inherit the status and that the sacrifices of the present were necessary to provide the legacy that the children could possibly inherit. The possibility of commuting the return passage for a land grant only made the reward for suffering much more attractive and only served to dull the mind to the injustices of life. For in the final analysis, the half-free nature of indentureship, the twilight zone of existence that made the indentured worker neither a slave nor really free, the certainty of freedom if one survived, became the system's most effective and vicious mechanism for control.[14]

THE CONTROL OF NONPLANTATION LABOR

The control of indentured immigrants was only one aspect of the attempts to control all labor in the nineteenth century. The planters also devised other mechanisms for both the direct and the indirect control of those who labored independently of the plantation and those who dared to commit the cardinal sin for West Indian plantocrats in the heyday of Victorianism: that is, not to work. Immediately after emancipation, as many of the former bondsmen moved quickly into activities that gave them the opportunity to exercise control over their labor power and independence from the plantation, so too the planters moved quickly to ensure that they had control over a labor force for their labor-intensive sugar industry. Indentured immigration was only one such method. They also used the law to block, or to make inconvenient, nonplantation activities developed by the Creoles. Laws were passed to police artisans and domestics, to prevent the development of an independent peasantry, to harass all forms of nonplantation labor, and to inconvenience the lives of those who were described as vagrants and idlers.

The chief ordinance for prosecuting nonindentured labor

was Ordinance 6 of 1846—the Masters and Servants Ordinance. In the years after emancipation, the planter class found great difficulty in extracting from the artisans, craftsmen, and other skilled workers the same quantity and, as they claimed, quality of work as during the period of slavery. Artisans took advantage of a scarce labor market and demanded increased wages, and there was constant conflict between employers and skilled workers over job descriptions and task definitions. Domestic servants, freed from the restrictions of slavery but realizing how much the traditions of slavery had created habits of dependence in their employers, were not slow to take advantage of the new situation. They too redefined what constituted domestic service and attempted to prevent their new wage-labor positions from being reduced to the old slavery. Under Ordinance 6 of 1846 a series of punishments—fine and/or imprisonment—were provided for those who broke their contracts, or were guilty of misconduct or ill behavior while on the job.

Another of the definite responses made by the ex-bondsman during the postemancipation period was to take advantage of the unalienated land available on the sugar frontier. They settled either on unused Crown lands, then abundant in Trinidad, or on abandoned estates, of which there was a growing number, especially after the crisis of 1846–47. The availability of land permitted some of the squatters to become independent peasants growing crops both for their own consumption and for selling the surplus on the market. Others grew subsistence crops and supplemented this with part-time work on the estates.

Although squatting was viewed as

> an evil of much detriment, inasmuch as it exercises the most baneful influence on the morality of the people and the interests of the country, for a squatter is a man who violates the rights of property, and to a certain extent, frees himself from the obligations which are imposed on the other members of the community. . . . For not only is squatting an usurpation

> of the rights of property, but it evidently tends to create in individuals a disposition to insubordination, and to the nurture of savage dispositions; and it may be affirmed, with certainty, that in all countries where squatting prevails, squatters form a dangerous class.[15]

The squatter-peasantry continued to increase between emancipation in 1838 and 1868, and they continued to use the land to grow ground provisions, some of it for the internal market. The planters' alarm grew, since "not only peons or individuals of mixed blood, not only Creoles and Africans, have squatted on Crown lands but lately also a few Chinese and Coolies."[16] The recently imported labor force had also taken to the woods, and by 1862 few estates in Trinidad retained a fraction of their original allotments: that is, few retained those who had completed their indenture.[17] Many planters realized that with the uncertainty of fresh arrivals and the existence of land as an alternative for the time-expired immigrants, the repatriation of the East Indian immigrants added another dimension to their labor problem. The solution to their problem was partially bound up in the solution to the squatter problem and the development of the plantation's archenemy, the peasantry. It was also bound up in the fortunes and development of the French Creole elite of the plantocracy.

The Crown Lands Ordinance of 1868 regularized the sale and distribution of Crown lands. As early as 1836, the secretary of state instructed the colonial governors not only to prevent squatting on Crown lands but "to fix such a price upon all Crown lands as may place them out of the reach of persons without capital." The minimum lot to be sold was fixed at 340 acres, and this figure was raised to 680 acres in 1841.[18] The high cost of land, the minimum amount available to be sold, and the bureaucratic inconveniences caused by all sales having to be finalized in Port-of-Spain created serious hindrances to ex-bondsmen and encouraged squatting. But while these regulations were useful for preventing the legal development of an independent peasantry, they also prevented the French Creole elite from taking advantage of available land. The French Creole planters needed the land for expansion, since many of them had been ruined or prevented from expanding by a new class of aggressive English planters and their London-based allies, who were supported by an equally aggressive program of anglicization. Since the Creole elite had been ousted from sugar, they were concentrating on cocoa production as the new money-spinner and replacement for sugar. But the best available lands for cocoa were in the slightly sloping hills of the Montserrat district, a Crown-land reserve occupied by illegal squatters. The French Creoles were therefore extremely active in the movement to open up the Crown lands for purchase.

The 1868 ordinance reduced the cost of the land and simplified the procedure for acquiring lands. Those who had illegally settled on Crown lands were given time to purchase their settlements and have them registered at the Crown Lands Office. In the Montserrat Ward, in the district known as Congo Wood, some 200 squatters paid up for their lands, and in other parts of the island illegal squatters slowly sought to regularize their position.[19] Those who refused to take advantage of the new ordinance were brought before the courts: in Tortuga, the stipendiary magistrate tried twenty-eight cases for squattering—he fined eighteen of those convicted, imprisoned four, and ordered the ejection of six; one of the ejectees who insisted on returning to his plot was arrested for trespass, convicted, and imprisoned for two months.[20]

The cooperation of the planters, reduced costs, and less cumbersome bureaucratic procedures combined with an expanded police force to make the antisquatting thrusts of the Crown Lands Ordinance a success. The Subintendant of Crown lands reported in 1870 that 508 grants of land had been issued from the Crown Lands Office: "In a financial point of view this result is sufficiently satisfactory, but the chief value is in the conversion of the roving squatters into peasant cultivators. Heretofore living in a state of semi-barbarous isolation, shifting capriciously from spot to spot, wasting the finest trees, ruining the best land by a temporary clearing succeeded only by denser bush, and inaccessible to Police, Schools, and the influence of society—the squatters were worse than useless; but now, fairly fixed in their holdings they will be gradually brought under the dominion of law and civilization."[21]

By 1897, it was generally agreed that squatting was virtually a thing of the past, although new land surveys would occasionally reveal a few cases of illegal encroachments.[22] This, of course, did not mean that there were no squatters. All it meant is that the state no longer considered it a major problem and therefore no longer expended the time and energy of its law enforcement agencies in this direction. There were still squatters, especially on the fringes of the urban area, but since their labor was not urgently required and they were not on potentially exploitable land, this was not viewed as a problem. But as these new squatter settlements developed and their population was fed by the increasing urban drift of the late nineteenth century and the illegal West Indian immigrants of the early twentieth century, the law enforcement agencies once again found squatting a problem, and these settlements were viewed as dens of criminals.

The employers of indentured immigrants also welcomed the passage of the Crown Lands Ordinance, for it assisted them with their labor problem. The planters were alarmed at the growing number of East Indians who joined the squatters on the completion of their term. Since the East Indians were entitled to a return passage upon the completion of their term of industrial residence, the planters complained about the loss of their "seasoned" labor. The solution was to find a way to have the "seasoned" East Indians, even after indenture, readily accessible for plantation labor. The planters' prayers were answered in 1869, when Governor Gordon agreed to the proposal of twenty-five Indians who were eligible for their return passage, but opted to remain in Trinidad if they were given grants of land in exchange for the passage. The governor therefore began a scheme of commuting return passages for land grants for East Indians and encouraging them to purchase Crown lands.

At first the distribution was slow, but the pace soon picked up: between 1870 and 1879, 75,164 acres were granted and sold; during the next decade, another 75,317; and during the nineties, a further 71,612 acres were alienated. Most of the plots were under 100 acres. Between 1873 and 1882 a total of 70,806 were granted and/or sold: of these 61,059 acres, or 86 percent, were divided between 5,869 recipients in plots averaging 12 acres; another 7,444 acres (10 percent) were divided among 44 recipients; and there were 8 recipients of the remaining 2,303 acres. Much of this land went to East Indians. In the first seven years of the program, 1,722 East Indians received a total of 13,250 acres in lieu of their return passage—there were 928 10-acre plots and 794 5-acre plots.[23] For example in 1875, 4,104 of the 9,854 acres in plots of under 100 acres were purchased, and 5,750 went to East Indians in lieu of their return passage, and in 1877, 2,617 of the 4,317 acres alienated, were purchased, and 1,700 acres were granted to East Indians.

But it is quite clear that these Indian settlements were little more than labor pools for the estates. In his first report on East Indian land purchases, the commissioner of Crown lands claimed that the applicants evinced a strong desire to form themselves into small communities within easy distance of some sugar estate and that they generally preferred already worked land rather than difficult virgin soil. But the pattern of settlement was too suspiciously convenient to the planters' needs for it to be considered largely accidental. In Couva there were settlements immediately behind the Caracas and Bivulet estates and in Pointe a Pierre and North Naparima, the East Indian settlements were situated in the immediate vicinity of the Bonne Aventure, Ben Lomond, and Santa Margarita estates. The East Indian settlements had become mere labor pools situated for the convenience of the planters.

The East Indians soon started making a contribution to the production of food crops for themselves and the internal market. They also pioneered the planting of rice and later emerged as major cane-farmers.[24] But despite this, there were still voices that complained against the growth of the East Indian land settlement program. Henry C. Warner, the assistant warden of Savanna Grande, complained that the district was rapidly acquiring the appearance of a "coolie settlement," since "a large proportion of the lands lately sold in this district have been, I am sorry to say, purchased by coolies." His complaints came in the midst of the sugar crisis, and he saw the land settlement program as "alienation of a good deal of most valuable labour." In his opinion the land could not stand "the constant crops of rice and corn, with constant burnings and hoeing, the coolie system of cultivation." East Indians, he advised, should only be sold land in blocks only large enough to grow provisions for subsistence, and this land should be within easy reach of an estate.[25] This belief about the East Indian and what his role and position in the society should be—that is, that his lot in life was to labor on sugar plantations—influenced the attitudes and behavior of many of the wardens and their subordinates when they collected taxes and ward rates and policed the East Indian peasantry.

The squatters now turned legal peasants soon found themselves in other kinds of legal problems. Many of them became cocoa farmers, an activity that was well suited to their small plots. Cocoa farming was now a booming industry, and with prices rising on the world market, 1870–1920 were the golden decades of cocoa.[26] The cocoa industry was a mixture of large estates and land held by small peasant proprietors. The larger estates were owned principally by the leading French Creole families, who had used the capital derived from the sale of their sugar estates to the large metropolitan companies to buy Crown land in the Montserrat district to develop as cocoa estates. These large estates were worked either by East Indian indentured labor or by the use of contract labor. Under the "contract" system a proprietor employed a laborer, or contractor, to cultivate six to ten acres of forest with cocoa seedlings. The contractor lived on the land rent free and during the gestation period of the cocoa grew provisions both for his subsistence and for the market. During this five-year period, the proprietor paid the taxes, and the contractor was responsible for planting cocoa trees and keeping the estate free from underbrush. At the end of the period the proprietor resumed occupation of the land and paid the contractor roughly one shilling for each thriving tree on the land.[27]

The system was rife with exploitation and led to numerous complaints. Frequently, there were no written contracts; in fact, these arrangements were neither contracts of labor nor contracts of lease, nor could they be considered partnerships.[28] Furthermore, they were defective in essential particulars. Occasionally, the agreement stated that the proprietor would only pay for bearing trees. Thus, since cocoa trees first bear fruit in five years, the contractor was, in fact, only paid for the first year of his work, and his labor in planting and nurturing trees in the second, third, fourth, and fifth years (which would bear in the succeeding seventh, eighth, ninth, and tenth years) was, in fact, given free. There was no payment even for the young plants in their fourth year, since these were still not considered bearing plants. Many contractors found themselves cheated of their payments on minor technicalities. Some of the proprietors refused to pay and claimed that their contract stipulated that all the land should have been kept clean and free of weeds. They argued that on their inspection—which often included the contractor's provision grounds—they found that the contractor had not kept his part of the bargain. Many contractors were not only cheated but often found themselves before the courts for breach of contract.

Not only were contractors cheated, but many small peasants lost their lands. The existence of a defective mortgage law permitted the existence of a system akin to the sharecropping in the post-Reconstruction American South and restricted the development of an independent peasantry. Many of the small cocoa cultivators mortgaged their properties to merchants in Port-of-Spain as security for advances to develop their plots. Generally, the terms of the mortgage obliged the mortgagor to purchase all agricultural implements and supplies from the merchant-mortgagee. They took these supplies from the merchant at his own price and were obliged to deliver their produce to the merchant, who either purchased the crop at a price set by himself or sold it on commission as the cultivator's factor.

Many small farmers soon found themselves in debt to these urban merchants and found their property on the auction block, since the mortgage law empowered the sale of the peasant's property to pay off the debts to the merchants. The non-English speaking proprietors became the victims of unscrupulous merchants who advertised the properties of defaulters, as the law demanded, but without prior warning to their debtors and in English newspapers that many of their debtors did not or could not read. The sale took place by private auction among other mechants, and the property was sold for the sum of debt owed and therefore at a price without any relation to its real value. Since the merchant could not be both seller and buyer, he generally used a third party, who bought the property and, in a subsequent fraudulent transaction, resold it to the merchant.[29] In the 1880s the boom in the cocoa market attracted many merchants who exploited the deficiencies in the mortgage law. Merchants and firms accumulated estates of considerable value and size by this means and at the expense of many unfortunate small proprietors. The sale of Crown lands from 1868 in Montserrat made that area originally a district dominated by small peasants. By the end of the century this pattern was reversed, and the area was dominated by large cocoa estates, which came, not from the purchase or grants of Crown land, but by the amalgamation of smaller estates.[30]

The attacks against the peasantry and other forms of independent labor in both the urban and rural areas are concealed in the criminal statistics especially under the heading "social economy" in the statistics for convictions. (See table A.36.)

The convictions for "social economy offenses," after remaining at 4 percent of total convictions for fifteen years from 1875, increased by 1 percent in the period 1890–94, and more than tripled to 18 percent of total convictions in the period 1895–99 (table A.37). But only a minority—not less than 10 percent and not more than 20 percent in 1885–89—of these convictions led to imprisonment. The bulk of the convictions—not less than 63 percent in 1885–89 and no more than 81 percent in 1880–84—were fined. In fact, the state found that fining convicted offenders was surely more lucrative than imprisonment. In the fiscal year 1909/10 the state collected £2850 from the prosecution of 4,598 social economy cases. More than half of this sum, £1587, came from the prosecution of three types of social economy cases: furious riding and driving on the road, nonpayment of licenses, and the weight and measures ordinance.

The category *social economy* touched all the nonplantation labor in the society. In the rural areas it affected those peasants who hunted and did not license their dogs or guns, those who burnt trees on Crown lands to sell as charcoal without a government license, those who made and sold alcohol without a license, those who cultivated and sold ganja, those who cut wood to be sold or used as firewood without a license, or those who did not pay the ward rates and taxes assessed on their land and crops. In the urban areas the net was equally wide: it included in its sweep market vendors for transgressing market bylaws; cabmen and carters for furious riding and driving, leaving the cart unattended, riding on the shaft, or obstructing the street with their carts; and porters for plying their trade without a license.

The rationalization for the series of laws under which nonplantation labor was convicted was admirable—they were justified by the need either to impose health and sanitary standards, or to control congestion in the urban areas, or to protect the consumer by imposing standards of quality, or to protect society from the accidents caused by ill-disciplined hunters and charcoal burners. But in the hands of a belligerent police force, or before courts adjudicated by magistrates who were allies of the planters, or applied by wardens who saw the growth of the peasantry as tantamount to the alienation of valuable labor, they became tools of oppression. Nonplantation workers were badgered, coerced, and harassed in both the rural and the urban areas. Since they were fined rather than imprisoned, it meant that the social economy convictions were a useful mechanism for controlling the growth of nonplantation labor not only by making their working lives miserable but by continually diminishing their capital and profits with court costs.

The full wrath of the planter-dominated state, however, was reserved for those who did not work. For like their class allies in Victorian England, the Trinidadian elite detested with a passion those who refused to work and considered this a cardinal sin in a labor-hungry economy. L. M. Fraser declared with unconcealed exasperation in 1874 that

> The real bane of our society is idleness and all its attendant vices, drunkenness, gambling and immorality of the grossest and most degrading kind, which latter entails two serious physical evils, the deterioration of our population and a check on its natural increase.
>
> The first thing that strikes a stranger arriving in Trinidad is the great number of able bodied men and women who spend their time lounging about the streets literally doing nothing; and after a very short residence here the fact becomes evident that the same people are always thus spending their time, so that it is not merely an accidental holiday or occasional want of work that keeps them doing nothing, but habitual and systematic idleness.
>
> This is the more remarkable in a colony the magnificent resources of which cannot be fully developed from want of

> labour, and to which for the last thirty years labourers have been brought from the East at an immense cost.[31]

The nineteenth-century mind connected idleness with crime and saw regular, systematic labor as the only preventative for moral degeneration. Patrick Keenan, a visiting educator, diagnosed laziness as the chronic disorder of the lower classes in Trinidad and urged measures "to nip such a disorder in the bud, to intercept vagabond and pilfering youths in their descent to crime and wretchedness."[32] Another writer, Charles Kingsley, noted that "The first thing notable on landing in Port-of-Spain at the low quay which has been just reclaimed from the mud of the gulf, is the multitude of people who are doing nothing. It is not that they have taken an hour's holiday to see the packet come in. You will find them, or their brown duplicates, in the same places tomorrow and the next day. They stand idle in the market place, not because they have not been hired, but because they do not want to be hired."[33]

The influential *Port-of-Spain Gazette* echoed similar sentiments and concern about the contradiction between idlers and an imported labor force: "It is a common thing now to see robust men and tall youths playing marbles in the public thoroughfares of Port-of-Spain in the middle of the day, and it is a reflection upon us as a community that such wilful idleness should exist when there is ample employment of every kind to be found and when, to supply our labour market, we have to send thousands of miles for coolies."[34]

The attitude toward idleness was dictated by two considerations and presuppositions of the nineteenth-century mind. In the first place there was the racist stereotypes that non-Anglo-Saxons were inherently inclined to be lazy and that the descendants of the slaves would use every opportunity to avoid work; and second, life in the tropics was so bountiful that not only could the labor force live on the barest minimum but many of them would find work unnecessary. Just as the fear of slave revolt was a persistent preoccupation of the users of slave labor, so too, during the era of free labor, these fears of chronic idleness haunted the thoughts of the postemancipation employers. They therefore took measures to ensure that their labor force did not succumb either to their natural inclination or to the largess of mother nature and rob them of a work force for their labor-intensive enterprise.

The idea of the congenital laziness of the African and those of African descent was one of the major pillars of the justifications of slavery and died hard in the nineteenth century. Equally long-lived was the notion that the West Indies was plentiful in life-supporting flora and fauna and that the inhabitants not only needed little to live on but could actually live on the barest minimum. Locals and visitors alike continually articulated those notions and encouraged stringent measures to coerce the Creoles to work. On a visit in 1869, Charles Kingsley remarked that the idlers in Port-of-Spain "will eat as much and more than a European, if they can get it, they can do well without food; and feed, as do the Lazzaroni, on mere heat and light."[35] Sixteen years later, another visitor commented that "all that is absolutely necessary to life comes ready to hand, one or two shillings a week would be sufficient to support these labourers; and they could easily clothe themselves for a pound or two a year."[36] The warden of the St. Ann's–Diego Martin district complained in 1887 that "the majority of the Carenage and Diego Martin Village people are a lazy and indolent lot, as long as they can catch sufficient fish to keep them going the height of their ambition is gratified."[37]

In the midst of the sugar crisis, two plantation managers, in evidence before the Royal Commission of Inquiry (1897), urged a reduction in wages, since able-bodied men could live on five or six cents per day.[38] Earlier, the Inspector of Prisons L. M. Fraser had explained that in Trinidad:

> Where the first shed or gallery serves for a shelter, where clothing except for the sake of decency is almost a superfluity, and where fuel is only required for cooking, there is

> no such outward pressure brought to bear upon those who are not naturally inclined to work; and what is the result?
>
> They do not starve, for they are to be seen daily in the full enjoyment of the most exuberant health, they do not beg, and most assuredly they do not work.[39]

Before emancipation the plantocracy had anticipated a problem with labor and had therefore quickly moved to prevent the widespread opting out of the labor force. One month after emancipation, they passed Ordinance 12 of 1838 "to consolidate and amend the laws relative to Vagrants, Rogues and Vagabonds, and incorrigible rogues; and to assimilate the same, so far as may be, to the laws of England in like cases." The ordinance defined an idle and disorderly person as:

> Any person being able to wholly or in part to maintain himself or herself, or his or her family, by work or by other means, and wilfully refusing or neglecting to do so, by which refusal or neglect he or she or any of his or her family whom he or she may be legally bound to maintain, shall have been altogether or in part destitute of the means of support, or chargeable on any district, town or place in the said colony; every common prostitute wandering in the public streets or public highways, or in any place of public resort, and behaving in a riotous or indecent manner; and every person wandering abroad, or placing himself or herself in any public place, street, highway, court, or passage, to beg or gather alms, or causing or procuring or encouraging any child or children so to do.[40]

But it is in section 3 of the ordinance that the farmers exposed their real intention, for it defined a rogue and vagabond so broadly and vaguely that the only individuals who were *excluded* were those who were at work, preferably on a plantation. It included:

> Every suspected person or reputed thief frequenting any river, canal, or navigable stream, or any embarcadaire, ferry, wharf,

> store or quay, near or adjoining thereto, or any street, highway, or avenue leading thereto, or any place of public resort, or any street or avenue leading thereto, or any street, highway or place adjacent, *without* intent to commit felony; every person wandering abroad and lurking, hovering or lodging in or about the works or other buildings, or in or about the negro houses of any plantation or estate, without the permission of the owner thereof, or in any deserted or unoccupied building, or in the open air, or in a tent, or in any cart, waggon, or other vehicle, not having any visible means of subsistence and not giving a good account of himself or herself.[41]

It also included fortune-tellers, mendicants, Obeah practioners, those accused of indecent behavior, and gamblers.

Not only was the net wide enough to cover every conceivable action that suggested alternative means of support, but the other measures in the ordinance were equally draconian: the burden of proof lay on the accused; the effects found on vagrants were to be sold and applied towards expenses; and it was lawful to make citizen's arrests under the provisions of the ordinance. Even the Colonial Office—under the direction of James Stephen, a member of the Anti-Slavery Society—balked at this ordinance: they disallowed it, since they found it repugnant to and superseded by an order-in-council for the prevention and punishment of vagrancy that was issued on the seventh of September 1838. But although the ordinance was disallowed, and the order-in-council seemed less draconian and more influenced by the humanitarian ideals of James Stephen, the same antilabor spirit prevailed, since the order-in-council was itself influenced by the Victorian detestation of vagrancy and idleness. But more importantly, the application of the order-in-council and subsequent ordinances was influenced in labor-hungry Trinidad not only by a similar Victorian spirit but by a spirit that was given additional viciousness because of the need of the plantation economy to be always in complete control of all labor.

The campaign against vagrants was a persistent theme throughout the nineteenth century, but the introduction of indentured immigrants, which brought a new labor force, meant that it was not absolutely necessary to vigorously prosecute all Creole vagrants as a means of coercing them back into the labor market. Instead, the provisions of the 1854 Immigration Ordinance made it possible to prosecute East Indians, many of whom were technically vagrants, for being away from the plantation without a pass or for being unable to produce satisfactory identification.

During the crises of the late 1880s, the cries against vagrancy that had been slightly subdued during the 1860s and early 1870s began to be heard again, and there was a campaign from some quarters that urged increased policing and stiffer penalties. The *Port-of-Spain Gazette* editorialized in 1871 that a vagrant law was needed in order to compel strong and active men to account for themselves or to work, and the wardens for both Savanna Grande and Toco advocated the establishment of a penitentiary for vagrants. But during the period of crisis in the 1880s, many of these vagrants were, in fact, time-expired East Indians, some of whom were weakly and sick and had been weeded out from estate pay lists. Some of them had forfeited their return passage earlier for a cash payment of £10, under a scheme that had been inaugurated in 1851, and were now destitute.

The campaign against vagrants was also connected to the campaign against mendicity. In the absence of a well-organized pauper-relief system, during the times of crisis many more people were forced to apply for relief. But there was a belief that mendicants were merely able-bodied persons who were shirking work, and therefore many people were prosecuted for begging alms. East Indians were particularly suspect. The immigration report for 1870 complained about "thirteen sturdy beggars who had earned by residence a right to return were also embarked and were found on the following day among the best dressed of the party."[42] The East Indians were always accused of living off the charitable public, and since it was assumed that it took so little to survive in the tropics, it was thought that the Creoles, too, could easily live on a few cents gained from begging alms rather than attempt to find jobs.

This concentrated attack on labor—prosecutions for squatting, vagrancy, begging alms—which had as its intention the coercion of those segments of the labor force that were not indentured and refused to bend to the demands of the plantation, reached its culmination with the passage of the Habitual Idlers Ordinance in 1918. A habitual idler was originally defined under the proposed ordinance as "any person who during the seven days preceding the laying of a complaint against him for being an habitual idler has not worked for a period of four hours during each of three such days or for a period of fourteen hours during such seven days" and was without visible means of subsistence.[43] But this definition was dropped from the ordinance, and the labeling of the habitual idler was left to the discretion of the magistrate.

The ordinance was supposedly designed to combat the growth of the casual labor population in the urban areas, which, according to one stipendiary magistrate, was composed of a large number of drifters from the rural districts who had been attracted by the glitter of the town. Many of them, he claimed, resorted to begging and stealing to support themselves, and slept in the numerous balconies and deep-arched gateways of Port-of-Spain at night. Again, many of those who were convicted summarily for "sleeping out" as common vagrants were East Indians. The cessation of indentured immigration from India in 1916 had once more posed a serious problem of labor recruitment and control for the plantocracy. It was no longer possible to recruit labor from abroad with state subsidies, and other means had to be found to continue control of the labor force already on the island. The Habitual

Idlers Ordinance of 1918 was one way of stopping the urban drift of East Indians and at the same time dealing with two other urban problems—gambling and prostitution.

Throughout the nineteenth century the police and others complained that many of the idlers were supported by gambling and that they lived off the earnings of prostitutes. They therefore advocated and conducted a relentless campaign against prostitution and gambling. The campaign was, of course, accompanied by loud cries of concern for the health of the individuals involved as well as the society in particular, and women were prosecuted under the Contagious Diseases Ordinance of 1869. There were also shouts of moral indignation and condemnation at the number of young girls of tender ages who were considered prostitutes. The attacks against the prostitutes were viewed as necessary in order to deprive those who did not work from their supposed source of support. But the whole question of prostitution—the labeling of what constituted prostitution and its allied activities and the attitudes to as well as the incidence of prostitution—was also part of the larger question of cultural conflict and the struggle for cultural hegemony in nineteenth-century Trinidad. Similarly, the attack against gambling can also be viewed as one of the numerous mechanisms used to restrict the development of sources of support outside of plantation labor. But these issues are better understood when viewed in the light of the persistent conflict over the cultural definition and structuring of the society, of which tne nature of time and its use was one battleground.

CHAPTER EIGHT

The Struggle for Cultural Hegemony

CRIME, THE MULTICULTURAL SOCIETY AND THE RULE OF LAW

In the criminal statistics the category "Social Order" was the largest in the total cases before the courts, convictions by the courts, and committals to prison. In the statistics on total cases, the compilers in the nineteenth century usually recorded crimes against the social order together with offenses against the social-economy ordinances. The offenses in the latter category, social economy, have been discussed in the previous chapter as attempts to control those forms of independent labor not covered by either the Masters and Servants Ordinance or the Indentured Immigrant regulations. But in the statistics on convictions and committals, it is possible to separate social-economy offenses from those acts against the social order that were labeled criminal. Social-order offenses constituted between 48 and 41 percent of all convictions between 1875 and 1899 and between 49 and 32 percent of all committals to prison during the same period. (See table A.38.) The offenses prosecuted in this category of crime were a consequence of the struggle for cultural hegemony in nineteenth-century Trinidad.[1]

The struggle for cultural dominance was articulated in moral terms, and the attack on non-European and Creole institutions was rationalized as necessary in the campaign to bring moral upliftment to the society. The Masters and Servants Ordinance and the Immigration Ordinances represented the crude and direct efforts to control labor, while the social-economy ordinances were aimed at the "subtle" coercion of non-plantation labor. The social-order offenses were the more sophisticated methods of educating the society into the acceptance of the dominance of a way of life and thought conducive to the perpetuation of the plantation society and consented to by all sections of the population. It meant the criminalization of certain patterns of aesthetic, religious, and ethical behavior and the substitution of a value system that in the words of one scholar: "stressed the importance of Christianity, of education, respect for the law, 'good' as opposed to 'rough' or 'bad' behaviour, the need for moral upliftment, and the importance of using proper language; all factors which emphasized not only the de facto power of the Europeans but also the superiority of English culture."[2]

But the possibility of creating a tropical society, disciplined to the demands of the plantation economy and shaped by the imported values of metropolitan Victorianism, was limited by the persistence of seemingly unchangeable non-European cultural traditions. The presence of these traditions was linked to the labor demands of the plantation economy and its willingness to search worldwide for its labor force. The dependence on an imported labor force of Africans had set the stage for cultural conflict very early. The late development of Trinidad and the rapid buildup of the slave community ensured that a number of traditions and institutions, drawn from various African societies, survived with a high degree of faithfulness to the originals. The continued importation of Africans in the period 1838–69 facilitated the survival of African traditions and revitalized the African heritage in Trinidad. The imposition of the hegemony of the European-oriented ruling class depended, therefore, on the elite's ability to de-Africanize the society. It also depended on their ability to prevent the growth and spread of the cultural traditions of the indentured East Indian community, who, although partially isolated on plantations and on adjacent settlements, were not immune to the process of creolization. And finally, it necessitated the retardation of the growth and development of Creole cultural institutions that could challenge the imported value system for hegemony. The law became the preferred way to impose this value system because of the inability of the church and school to effectively socialize the non-European population.

Education—that is, organized indoctrination through a formal system of instruction—is the principal avenue through which any society socializes its youth into acceptance of the validity of its social and political organization. Primary education in nineteenth-century Trinidad faced serious problems that limited its effectiveness as a mechanism for introducing youths to the virtues of European civilization. Its major limitation was the intransigence of some sections of the local elite, who, even though they paid lip service to its civilizing values, were adamant in their view that the children of the working class required only the barest minimum of education, since anything above this destroyed their usefulness for field labor. This attitude was, of course, reflected in their parsimonious attitude toward funding primary education in any way—either school construction and maintenance, provision of school supplies, or salaries for staff.[3]

The Latrobe Report of 1838 declared that the planters were fully and unhesitatingly supportive of education measures. This seemed to augur well for the future; but the Keenan Report of 1869 painted a dismal picture that stood as an indictment of education in the postemancipation period.[4] The report of the inspector of schools for 1877 adequately summarized the condition of the education system in 1868:

> In 1868 there was scarcely a school in the island with anything like proper furniture: some indeed were almost devoid of the commonest necessaries in this way. Most of the school buildings were unsuitable and many were in extremely bad order. Pens, ink and paper were apparently considered superfluous, for they were scarcely to be found in any school. Slates were provided by the pupils whenever they thought it necessary or convenient to do so. Timetables were only known by tradition. The monitorial system, which was a part of Lord Harris's scheme had gradually disappeared. Teaching was limited to the instruction of one or two pupils at a time, in a perfunctionary manner void of anything like system and the majority of the pupils were at all times openly doing nothing or else idling under the name of "preparing lessons."[5]

Many of the adults who lived in the pre-1868 period had been schooled under these conditions; many youths who lived in the post-1869 period were schooled in a system and under conditions that closely resembled that described for 1868.

Many escaped the system altogether, for school attendance and enrollment was generally low. In 1889, Governor Robinson estimated that about 17,000 of a possible school population of 36,000 received no education at all.[6] In 1874 there were 67 schools with 6,191 scholars listed on the rolls; of these, 53 were government-assisted public primary schools with a roll of 5,688 students and an average attendance of 3,424 students. In 1895, at the close of the century, the number of schools had risen to 187, the student body had increased to 21,895, and the average attendance was 13,895. Attendance averaged 63 percent over the last three decades of the century. But even these figures were not completely accurate: the roll was called once per day, usually before noon; therefore, statistics did not reflect those students who did not return after lunch, and this was a common practice.[7]

There were numerous reasons for this low rate of attendance, and chief among them was economic considerations.

Some parents could not afford to pay school fees, especially those families with more than one child of school age. In most cases, therefore, only one child from a large family was sent to school. Even when there were reduced rates for the second and third child, some parents found it difficult to support more than one child at a time in school. The weekly school fee was not prorated, so that most parents did not send the child back to school if they missed the first day of the week. Advance quarterly payments were introduced in order to encourage parents to secure as much attendance as possible, since they had already paid the fee. But even this measure, in operation during the last two decades of the century, did not appreciably increase the rate of attendance. In many cases, parents kept their children away from school to help them in their gardens during the crop season, or to assist them on market days, or to assist with younger children at home.[8]

There were other reasons for the low rate of attendance that were not necessarily connected with the lack of money or other kinds of economic pressure. Attendance fluctuated according to the seasons: it was lowest during the rainy season, and the most favorable period was between February and May, during the dry season. Leaking school roofs and unusable roads contributed to low school attendance during the rainy months. Some parents saw no value in formal education and just simply refused to send their children to school. The Yoruba felt secure in their ability to provide their offspring with all the education they thought necessary. They refused to send their children either to church or to school unless they were reimbursed for what they considered lost time.[9] One report indicated that the East Indians recognized the advantages to be gained by education but refused to go to the same school with non–East Indians. The report claimed that there was reciprocal dislike between Afro-Trinidadians and East Indians and that the latter refused "to subject their children to the companionship of the less intelligent but hardier pupils of that race and the possible favoritism of their creole masters."[10] But even when the Canadian Mission established schools that catered only to the East Indian community, the rate of attendance was low: in 1880 the total enrollment in twenty-three Canadian Mission schools was 874, and the daily attendance was only 572; and in 1900 there were forty-eight Canadian Mission schools, with a total enrollment of 4,139 and an average attendance of 2,400. The 1891 census gave the total Indian population of school age as 12,643, but only 3,525, or roughly 28 percent, attended *any* school.

Both enrollment and attendance were lowest among the female population of both races, particularly among East Indians. In 1891, there were 5,701 East Indian females of school age, but only 1,003—or roughly 17 percent—attended any school; on the other hand, 36 percent of the East Indian males of school age attended any school. Cultural attitudes among both Afro-Trinidadians and East Indians emphasized the uselessness of education for females and stressed their role in the home. East Indian parents in particular sought to protect their girls from what they considered to be contaminative exposure to the Creoles. But there were other important reasons for keeping the girls at home. There were complaints about the sexual harassment of female pupils by male teachers, and in some cases, these incidents resulted in charges of rape against male teachers. This was a hazard in a school system dominated by male teachers. In 1868 there were no females employed in teaching positions in any of the public schools except the Girls' Model School in Port-of-Spain. Ten years later there were sixty female teachers in the public schools, but only five of these were certified; the others were assistant teachers and monitors. Not until the turn of the twentieth century did teaching become a profession dominated in the lower ranks by females, and the female component of the school population then increased in proportion to their numbers in the school-age group.

Those students who did attend school were tutored by a faculty that was unprofessional, usually untrained, and poorly paid. Dedicated and efficient teachers were few. The Keenan Report of 1869 complained that: "In the primary schools there is little or nothing to be met with to indicate that school organization has become a science, or that eminent teachers in various parts of the world have written manuals and treatises upon the subject. The art of efficiently handling, with a limited teaching power, a large number of scholars is unknown to the masters of the Trinidad schools."[11] Twenty years later, a minority report prepared by Judge Lumb echoed the same complaints: "The teachers, as a body, are devoid of some or all of the better qualifications of their profession—accurate knowledge of the subjects of instruction, capacity to impart knowledge, maintenance of discipline, sympathy with their pupils, and interest in their work. Consequently, the Educational standards and deportment of their pupils are unsatisfactory, and, in some cases, deplorable. It is difficult to say which is the worst, the teacher or the taught."[12]

Yet despite this state of the teaching service, some influential members of the elite argued that it was unsuitable to have "over-educated" primary school teachers, since they would encourage their pupils to abandon unskilled work in the fields.[13] The paucity of the education system resulted in widespread illiteracy whether Trinidadians remained on the plantations or flocked to the urban areas. Between 1882 and 1885 barely 50 percent of the participants in 2,616 marriages could sign their names in the register. In 1882 alone, 56 percent of the participants in the 632 marriages were unable to sign the register.[14] In 1891, about a decade later, 884 (90 percent) of the participants in 986 marriages, were unable to sign the register: 381 (43 percent) of them were grooms, and 503 (57 percent) brides.[15] Since marriages tended to be popular only among the upper and middle classes or the socially mobile of the lower classes, the level of illiteracy is significant. Illiteracy among prisoners, who were predominantly from the lower classes, was equally high. Between 1886 and 1890, 20 percent of the 13,877 committals could read and write; 8 percent could read only; and 72 percent could do neither. In the single year 1886, 17 percent of the 3,423 prisoners could both read and write; 7 percent could read only; and 76 percent were illiterate.[16]

The important point is not how many children received formal education—or for that matter, whether the education they received was relevant—since there is no causal relationship between crime and education. The lack of literacy acted as a limitation on the range of illegal activity available to some, while literacy opened the more lucrative areas of "white collar" crime to others. The fact that the level of illiteracy was high among prisoners was only an indication that more illiterates than literates were caught, convicted, and imprisoned for their offenses.

The high illiteracy rates indicated how many young Creoles were never in school or were not in school long enough to pick up the basic skills of literacy. But more important, the educative process also did not have the opportunity to develop in them, in that slow and subtle way, a respect for authority and habits of work discipline. In most cases the system was too chaotic, and even at its best the authority in the school was a replica of the authority system in the wider society. The harsh taskmasters whose reputations and bonuses depended on examination results educated, not by consent and earned respect, but by fear and coercion. At its worst, the system—with its overcrowded classrooms, its dilapidated buildings, and its scarcity of teaching tools—was too chaotic to inculcate habits of discipline. But even when it was at its best, it induced boredom and alienation with its irrelevant lessons learned by repetition. In the nineteenth century neither state-run nor church-controlled schools were able to effectively socialize the young, despite the heavy emphasis on religious instruction in the curriculum.

Christianization was the other preferred way of "civilizing" the non-European masses and inculcating in them the desired virtues and discipline. Although some missionaries and some lay members of the elite believed that the Christianization of non-Europeans was a hopeless task, they nonetheless proceeded with indefatigable zeal. One missionary declared that Trinidad required an evangelist rather than a theologian to combat the preponderance of Roman Catholic sentiments and the indifference of the people. His assessment claimed that: "The Blacks have always been accustomed to be driven and they require the same treatment today. Although the 1st August, 1888 is the Emancipation Jubilee—my father often said he was a nigger driver. His experience was that the moment he ceased driving they grew indifferent not to say careless. He said one requires an eternal scold with whip always in hand."[17]

His sentiments may have been shared by many of the missionaries from the nonestablished sects. The numerous Christian groups fought each other for command of the religious allegiance of the population. Roman Catholicism was the dominant variant of Christianity, but Anglicanism, as its major challenger, made steady inroads throughout the nineteenth century. The other Christian groups—Wesleyans, Presbyterians, Baptists, Moravians—trailed behind in number of adherents and complained unceasingly about the moral laxity of the Catholic clergy and the unequal distribution of state funds for religious work. Neither complaint was entirely without foundation.

The census returns, which were used as evidence of the size of their congregations or the weakness of their religious foes, became a battleground—so much so, that no religious census was taken in 1881 for fear of what the registrar general called recrimination and altercation. But the religious census was an unreliable guide to either the extent of attendance and affiliation or the impact of Christianity. The census return of 1891, for example, is highly suspect. It listed a population of 2,055 whose birthplace was given as Africa—the descendants of African-born slaves and those African immigrants who came between 1838 and 1869. But 2,041 of this group were listed as Christian (almost 100 percent), and 70 percent of them were listed as Catholic. Despite what would appear to be a rapid conversion to Christianity by these Africans, however, there were complaints about the prevalence of African religious rites throughout the nineteenth century.

The census returns did not include such African interpretations of Christianity as the Spiritual Baptists. The Baptists listed in the returns referred to the Baptist Missionary Society headquartered in London, not the variant introduced by Afro-Americans early in the nineteenth century with its obvious "African" features, such as, "shouting," "mourning," "speaking in tongues," and "spirit possession."[18] The census reluctantly acknowledged the existence of the religious persuasions of the East Indian community; they were first listed as heathen, and then towards the end of the century they were recognized as Hindus and Mohammedans. But nowhere in the census returns was the existence and membership mentioned of Rada and Shango, the two popular African-based religious complexes.[19] Rada was the religious rites of the Dahomean community in Trinidad, and Shango, originally Yoruba, eventually expanded and became a Pan-African belief system that many Afro-Trinidadians found much more facilitative of their needs than Christianity.

But even if the authorities had requested information about membership, it would have been difficult to arrive at reliable data. There was no actual central authority equivalent to, say, an archbishop, but Shango was in fact a number of centers of worshippers with different religious heads, each with its core membership and a number of floating adherents. At any rate, the census takers most likely asked only about membership in the established religions. Since many of the worshippers held dual religious affiliations without any real sense of theological conflict, they would have answered in the affirmative to the question asked without volunteering information about their other religious affiliation. Those Afro-Trinidadians who had been affected by the campaign of de-Africanization and had succumbed to the stigma attached to their religious practices may well have found it convenient to avoid revealing their membership in a Shango group and have claimed to be Christian. The fervor with which these Christian sects battled for the souls of the population made religious affiliation a flag to be waved rather than a faith to be lived. The relationship of church affiliation to social mobility and acceptance was not lost on many of the non-European population. But Christianity's inability to satisfy both religious and secular needs made these African-based religions far more attractive and popular than any census revealed.

The African conception of religion, a conception shared by many Creoles, included a use of religious ritual that was extremely pragmatic and that sought to use supernatural aid in the manipulation of natural forces for the solution of immediate everyday problems. The Afro-Trinidadian lived a life of marginality and required the use of all kinds of devices to assist him in coping with the harassments of daily living. Religion was one way of coping with these problems and the uncertainties of life in the colonial society. One aspect of religion was Obeah—the religious-magical complex that sought to put to practical and everyday use a knowledge of the natural world combined with a manipulation of the supernatural world.[20] The authorities in the nineteenth century made little distinction between formal African religion and Obeah when trying to eradicate the latter. In the process, they criminalized and undermined all African religious practices.

The argument used by the authorities was that although Obeah by itself was harmless and, as a mere superstition, was not the subject for legislation, yet it was the cause of numerous crimes. Governor Arthur Gordon believed that an immense amount of perjury and intimidation resulted from Obeah, and it was "the fruitful parent of the darkest crimes."[21] The anti-Obeah lobby argued that Obeah preyed on superstitious Trinidadians and was a system of religious fraud. The law defined Obeah as "every pretended assumption of supernatural power of knowledge whatever, for fraudulent or illicit purposes or for gain or for the injury of any person."[22]

The penalty was also clearly defined—on conviction before a magistrate, the practitioner was "to be imprisoned with or without hard labor for any term not exceeding six months, and if a male, may be sentenced to undergo corporal punishment, and, if a female, may during such imprisonment, be kept in solitary confinement not exceeding three days at any one time and not exceeding one month on the whole."[23] During the period July 1868 to December 1871, there were fourteen prison committals for Obeah, including two women. The prison terms ranged from one month to as many as six months, and some received as many as thirty-six lashes.[24] In the period 1875–1899, another thirty-nine persons were imprisoned for practising Obeah (table A.39). In order to counteract the difficulty of securing witnesses or the reluctance of complainants to report cases, the authorities relied on entrapment by police officers and the possession of certain articles as proof of involvement in Obeah. This often led to miscarriages of justice and the unnecessary harassment of citizens by overzealous policemen.

The case brought against John Cooper for practicing Obeah highlighted some of the salient features of the campaign to suppress Obeah and the administration of justice in nineteenth-century Trinidad.[25] Cooper, an African immigrant, had arrived in Trinidad with his father in 1860, eleven years before his arrest, and had been assigned to an estate in the St. Joseph district. At the time of his arrest, he was a laborer in Laventille, a settlement on the outskirts of central Port-of-Spain. The court interpreter described him as a Yoruba, but in fact Cooper's real name was Hon Quervee, and he was the brother of Papa Nannee, the leader of the Dahomean Rada community.[26] On 25 November 1871, Constable Leacock arrested Cooper at the toll-gate entrance to Port-of-Spain on suspicion of fowl stealing. Cooper had a bag with two fowls, and Leacock believed that these had been stolen from some person or persons unknown. But the constable withdrew this charge of theft and instead Sergeant-Major Michael Fitzpatrick charged Cooper with practicing Obeah.

Justice came swiftly for Cooper. Constable Leacock arrested him about six o'clock on the Saturday morning at the Eastern Main Road toll entrance to the city, he was taken to the lockup house, detained until 10 o'clock, and then brought before the courts. Magistrate Lovesy sentenced him to six months hard labor and twenty strokes of the cat-o'-nine tails. He was taken to the Royal Jail on Saturday morning, spent the weekend there, and sometime between eight and ten o'clock on Monday morning, an official of the jail administered the twenty strokes ordered by the magistrate. There was no time for appeal, even though this was his right under the provisions of Ordinance 17 of 1869, nor was there any opportunity of communicating with friends or of obtaining legal advice. Some time later, he was able to organize an appeal that eventually reached the appeal court, where the magistrate's conviction was quashed on a technicality.

It is not easy to differentiate between fact and fiction in the case. But the case offers useful insights into the struggle for cultural hegemony in Trinidad and the problems of enforcing the law. The arresting officer first charged Cooper with possession of stolen property, and since the suspected stolen items were fowls, the charge may have been praedial larceny. But his superior officer used the same items to charge Cooper with Obeah. Cooper had in his possession at the time of his arrest two bottles (one of rum and one of sweet oil), two fowls (one dead and one alive), a piece of bone, some powder, and some shells. This was considered to be the paraphernalia of an Obeah man. The police claimed that the dead fowl was used in the performance of his rituals and that the bone was used to puncture a vein and bleed the fowl to death so that some of the blood could be used in a ceremony. There were no witnesses at the trial or at Cooper's interrogation. The police claimed that Cooper voluntarily and repeatedly confessed that his father practised Obeah and that he was himself a practitioner and was looked upon by his countrymen as an Obeah man. He also supposedly told the police that the money found in his possession was part of a payment received from two individuals for Obeah services to ensure their positions as overseers. These two were never called to trial even as witnesses to support the Crown's case. Nor were they charged with aiding and abetting Cooper, since the law prosecuted only the Obeah man and not those who used his services.

The practice of Obeah was indeed widespread and was not restricted to the working class or only to citizens of African descent. The old slave owners were not only well aware of the ability of some Africans to prepare and administer poisons to their enemies but were also aware of the healing capabilities of some of these herbalists. They often used their services themselves, despite their prohibitions against Obeah. Governor Harris believed that members of the upper class also used the services of Obeah men in the postemancipation period.[27] Some of these upper-class clients required not only medical assistance but aid in romantic affairs or legal matters. In 1870, a planter, Nicholas Brunton, and two accomplices were accused of the murder of Abbé Jouin, the Catholic priest of Diego Martin. Brunton was acquitted, and his victory was attributed "to the efficient obeah of the notorious Ojab Papa who during the trials stood outside the Courthouse looking up at the sun."[28] As late as 1936 the *Trinidad Constabulary Manual* reported that "superstition in spite of the advance of education, is still very prevalent in the colony, and is not as might be thought by some confined entirely to the lower and more ignorant classes."[29] But even if some members of the upper classes believed in Obeah and used Obeah specialists, it was the lower classes who had the most use for the system.

The inadequate and chaotic state of the medical services forced many Trinidadians to resort to the use of the Obeah men for medical assistance. The Obeah specialist included in his stock of knowledge not only those herbs that could poison, the aspect of his trade most feared and publicized, but also a wealth of knowledge of curative herbal medicines. The rural masses, in particular, needed the Obeah man—there were no doctors within ten to fifteen miles of rural areas like Moruga, LaBrea, and Toco. There were no government health services in these areas, since the health centers outside of Port-of-Spain tended to be located only in those areas where there was a heavy concentration of indentured East Indian labor.[30] One government official declared that "the African portion of the population can take care of themselves when left alone in the woods."[31] Private practitioners, who saw no great chance of large fees, avoided the rural areas and concentrated in the urban centers. In 1889, the surgeon general proposed an expansion of the medical service. The unofficial members of council blocked the ordinance and complained about "the pauperising effect of the multiplication of hospitals." They feared that the bulk of the population was "state aided from cradle to grave" and that this had a negative effect on individual effort and reduced the inducement to enter the labor market.[32] It is against this background of disregard that many citizens were forced to rely on the medical services provided by the Obeah practitioners. Those who were close to the Shango or Rada religions appealed to those African deities associated with medicine. During the numerous epidemics that visited Trinidad in the nineteenth century, Sakpana, the Yoruba deity associated with smallpox, may have been very popular.

The argument against Obeah stressed the fact that the practice was fraudulent and hid and encouraged further crime. But Charles Kingsley unwittingly hinted at the more important reason behind the campaign against Obeah when he argued that it exercised "no small political authority, which has been ere now, and may be again, dangerous to society."[33] For it was precisely because religion represented the potential for an organized challenge to the hegemony of the ruling class that it was found necessary to campaign against it and to discredit the Obeah man.

Attempts were made during slavery to combat Obeah. But this was not because many planters were overzealous about the Christianization of slaves, but because the Obeah man represented a figure of authority who was respected and/or feared by the slave community. He competed with the slave owner for the allegiance of the slaves—an allegiance that must belong solely to the slave owner if the system of slavery was to succeed.[34] This competition for allegiance continued, and if anything increased, in the postslavery era, since it was no longer possible to resort to overt coercion as had been done during slavery. All possible challenges to the dominant hegemony had to be eradicated, and more importantly, the masses had to be made to consent to the use of force, that is, the coercive aspects of the legal system. Hence it was necessary to emphasize in the anti-Obeah campaign that Obeah was fraudulent and criminal. There is no doubt that there were fraudulent practitioners willing to exploit gullibility, as there were no doubt fraudulent Christian priests and doctors who were noted more for their moral laxity than as paragons of virtue. But in effect, describing all Obeah as fraudulent and defining Obeah so broadly that it included all religious rites of African origin criminalized African religion, made participation in the rites dangerous, undermined its authority and respect, and effectively reduced its potential as the organizing base for an attack on the hegemony of the planters.

Obeah posed a serious challenge to the rule of law and the whole judicial apparatus on which the rule of law depended for its acceptance. The authorities complained that it was difficult to get complainants to lay charges or to get witnesses before the courts—hence the dependence on entrapment. Governor Longden recognized the significance of obeah when he observed that "the very persons who need protection against the obeahmen are themselves afraid to give true evidence and every acquittal of an obeahman is attributed to the power of his obeah."[35] Many Trinidadians believed that the deliberations of the court could be affected by the Obeah man. They believed that the ability of the court to come to the "truth" of a matter did not depend on some inherent and independent ability of the law and the officers of the court, but that this process could be influenced by an effective Obeah practitioner. Many Trinidadians knew, some from cruel personal experience, that court officers were often corrupt and that very often justice was sacrificed on the altars of race and class interest. They realized that "the dispensing of justice in the magistrate's court was a mere game of cross purposes, a cynical disregard of common sense and elementary equity."[36] They therefore sought the external aid of the Obeah man—both those who were guilty and wanted to avoid detection and those who were innocent and sought to ensure success in a rather uncertain and erratic system. Every successful use of Obeah—that is, every situation where the individual believed that his good fortune before the court could be attributed to the use of Obeah—reinforced belief in the system, widened the circle of those who respected the power of the Obeah man, and reduced the aura and majesty that was supposed to surround the idea of the rule of law and the deliberations of its officers. For the latter were no longer viewed as untouchable experts in some mysterious process, external though important to litigants, but as human beings who could be manipulated by another expert, and some kind of control could be exerted on the whole process.

Trinidadians respected the rule of law, that is, they respected and sought for an arena in which the arbitration of disputes could be conducted and in which a sense of justice could be paramount. They sought and expected a significant shift from the more blatant arbitrary nature of law and justice that obtained in the slave period and that was so evidently unjust that if often bred disrespect. It should not be surprising that some former slaves brought to the postslavery period an acute sense of mistrust of the courts and therefore sought justice outside of the legal system and often by illegal means. Their descendants inherited this legacy of mistrust. By and large, however, Trinidadians respected the rule of law—even if they were often the victims of the arbitrary machinations of those who made and enforced the law and even if they often fell victim to those who camouflaged naked class interest with the empty rhetoric of law and order. They were often before the courts because they were trapped by unjust laws and dragged there by overzealous law enforcement officers, but they were also there because they voluntarily sought the jurisdiction of the courts in some of their disputes.

One newspaper editorial commented on the peculiar attraction of the courts. It observed that they were crowded with solicitors, witnesses, and friends and that the most attractive cases were "the squabbles of very low-class women."[37] The superior courts, with their bewigged and gowned personnel who used quaint terms in their deliberations, may have inspired the awe and majesty that was an essential ingredient in promoting respect for its authority. But most of the lower class found themselves before magistrates in the lower courts rather than before judges. It was much more difficult to create in the lower courts the aura of majesty that should surround the dispensation of justice. The lower courts were often conducted in overcrowded and badly ventilated rooms in either police stations or dilapidated buildings.[38] In some of these courts, the close proximity in which plaintiffs, defendants, and court officials sat reinforced suspicions of class collusion. This bred contempt rather than the awe and terror that the distance and order of the upper courts evoked in the minds of the lower class. Yet it was a contempt that demystified the law and, ironically, served to encourage participation. Although some of the lower class therefore sought their day in court because of the drama that it provided in a sometimes drab existence, many of them sincerely believed that there was value in the exercise.

There was no choice but to resort to the courts of the state, since their own legal institutions had either been destroyed or undermined and drained of validity. The law was used as a weapon to destroy, and the process of criminalization was used to deny validity and integrity to their cultural institutions, including those that served judicial functions. This was inevitable in a multicultural situation where there was a large cultural gap between ruler and ruled, essentially because the power-wielding section of the elite was from a different ethnic group than the ruled. Furthermore, the undemocratic political system denied the lower class the opportunity to ensure that their cultural interests and values were reflected in the legal framework that governed their lives.

But there could be no competing tribunals in the society. Disputes in communities could not be settled by notions or norms developed in the cultural contexts of the different ethnic communities. They were settled with reference to the ideas of law established by the dominant elite. The process of anglicizing the criminal laws of the country was completed by 1842. A few areas in criminal and civil law remained unassimilated for a while, but these were gradually changed until by and large the country was governed by English jurisprudence.[39]

If there were slave tribunals that adjudicated their own disputes, it is not likely that they survived into the postemancipation period. After slavery, there is little evidence of community tribunals or formal mechanisms for dispute settlement among the Creoles.[40] One missionary attempted to operate outside of the court system and spent "much of his time in doing what might be said more properly to be the duties of a Justice of the Peace. He even advised persons to have nothing whatever to do with the law, and in support of his advice referred them to what Jesus Christ said in his sermon on the mount."[41] There is little evidence that this was successful. It is quite likely that some religious leaders, both black and white, may have extended their religious authority to include adjudication over secular disputes.

The immigrants who came in the postemancipation period had a much better chance of establishing their own tribunals, and the evidence for independent judicial tribunals among the liberated Africans and the East Indians is slightly stronger. In Jamaica, the Yoruba selected one of their members to act as a magistrate and to settle their disputes instead of the courts. This individual also acted as a banker for the group.[42] There is no reason to doubt that the same may not have happened in Trinidad. When John Cooper's brother, Papa Nannee, the leader of the Radas, was arrested and charged for Obeah in 1886, evidence in the trial revealed that he acted as a banker for the community.[43] It is quite likely that part of his responsibilities as leader could have included judicial duties. Observers of the Yoruba community commented on their strong community ties and noted that "the cases are rare in which a Yoruba is brought before a magistrate for theft, breach of contract, or other misdemeanours."[44] This haughty spirit and discriminating attitude toward the institutions of the host society may have stemmed from the existence of their own judicial institutions to settle disputes *between* members of the group.

The East Indians stood the best chance of recreating those cultural institutions that performed judicial functions. The circumstances of their immigration and settlement—the watchdog role of the Antislavery Society, the deliberate recruitment and recognition of religious leaders, their geographical concentration and social isolation—facilitated the re-creation of a number of cultural institutions. Among those that were transferred was the panchayat—a tribunal of village elders that decided disputes. This institution functioned during the period of indentureship. It may have been particularly effective in those communities where the residents had immigrated from the same district or village, or had traveled over on the same ship, and been assigned to the same plantation, and then settled together at the end of their indentureship.

But however much Creoles, Africans, and East Indians created and used these tribunals, they were inevitably doomed to failure and demise as the corrosive effects of the colonial society took its toll. Those tribunals that depended on religious allegiance or ethnicity had their obvious limitations, since their influence or authority could extend only as far as the size of the flock or the ethnic group. The Rada and Yoruba systems may well have weakened as the ethnic core decreased—the physical community by migration and the cultural community by exogamy and the increased creolization of the second and third generations. Despite the favorable start of the panchayat, the institution was in decay long before the end of indenture in 1917. A comment on the panchayat could serve as an epitaph on the institution and a postmortem on all those cultural institutions that dared to compete with those sponsored by the state. Seepersad Naipaul, who came from eastern Ultar Pradesh sometime in the 1880s, observed at the turn of the century:

> In these amazingly modern times a *panchayat* was a rare event. The machinery of the simple village tribunal, which had in the past removed so many domestic cleavages as well as settled or imposed punishments for religious or social anomalies, had become rusty or obsolete.
>
> People preferred the law courts nowadays, because there the magistrate often imposed a heavy penalty upon the delinquent in terms of dollars and cents, and sometimes even sent him straight to jail; but here at the *panchayat* the heaviest penalty was ostracism, or alternatively a community feast that hardly cost the guilty party anything above a half bag of flour, some rice, ghee, and a few pounds of Irish potatoes. And sometimes the defaulter simply stamped his foot and walked away from the *panchayat* with impunity.
>
> After all, one did not have to serve a prison term for disobeying a *panchayat* decision. There was the penalty of social boycott of course, which proscribed the rebel from being invited to religious and social functions. But again, who cared over such ostracism in these amazingly democratic times—especially in this polygot island of many races and many creeds? Trinidad was not India.[45]

For in the final analysis, the state alone had the ability to impose and enforce sanctions, since it monopolized all the legal coercive power in the society. The use of force, or the threat of force, in getting the allegiance of the entire society to a common social and political order was a crucial aspect of the role of the state. The use of naked force was absolutely necessary during the slave period. During the postemancipation period, force and the threat of force remained an essential ingredient of social control. Governor Manners-Sutton assessed the situation in rather blunt terms and in 1866 argued that it was: "Clearly and fully recognised by the people of this colony that any attempt to substitute the force of numbers for the authority of the law would most certainly fail, and that, if successful for the moment, it would be surely and speedily visited with condign punishment by an irresistible power. . . . The principal, if not the only reliable security for the lives and properties of the minority [was] the presence of the Queen's soldiers in the colony as a symbol, clearly recognised as such by the people of the continuous support of the Mother Country."[46]

Of course, the ideal situation was not one in which force was used to discipline and evoke the allegiance of citizens, but rather one in which the citizens disciplined themselves and consented to the social and political organization of the society. The law and legal institutions represented not only the state monopoly of the coercive agencies but insofar as the law was obeyed and the jurisdiction of the courts assented to—both by those who came before it and by those who agreed with its treatment of those who came before it—the law represented the extent of consent. Every exercise of this monopoly of coercion and consent was a demonstration of the powerlessness of the masses and their institutions; and every such demonstration not only reinforced the superiority of the institutions of the elite and extended their hegemony but was a signal lesson that success in the society lay in conformity.

The law brought under its jurisdiction all cultural activities either by defining them as legal and giving consent to them, or by defining them as illegal and making participation difficult. It therefore demonstrated its power and pervasiveness and weakened the autonomy of any competing claims to hegemony. During slavery the slave owner exercised absolute control over every aspect of the life of the slave. He exercised this control in pursuit of his own interests. Sometimes this was done crudely, as in instances when he attempted to enforce patterns of personal relationships that could have the long-term effect of augmenting the size of his slave force. At other times it was done with subtlety, as in those instances when he turned a blind eye to some of their private behavior and in so doing reinforced the belief that in his hands lay absolute authority. But even before the end of slavery, the Amelioration Acts reduced the overall power of the slave owner and created a mechanism whereby slaves understood that there was something called the law that mediated between slave and owner and restricted the owner's absolute authority. As a protection against the arbitrariness of the slave owner, the slave had to recognize the jurisdiction of the law, and his descendants had to learn to respect it.

THE LAW AND PRIVATE MORALITY

This respect for law facilitated the efforts of the elites to extend the labor discipline of the plantation into personal relationships, public behavior, and leisure. The general respect for law, developed partly from fear of its coercive powers and partly out of the vacuum created by the absence of viable alternative institutions, paved the way for a gradual acceptance of the idea that the law had jurisdiction even in those sensitive areas. But it was an acceptance that did not come without struggle and without constant use of the coercive arm of the law. There was collective and individual opposition from the lower classes as some of their most intimate and cherished values were attacked. At the same time, however, there was steady defection from their ranks by those who were either awed by the retaliatory power of the state or attracted by the promise of social mobility for those who conformed. There was division even within the ranks of the elite. The English expatriate segment of the elite spearheaded the campaign, and they were often too eager to transfer all Victorian values and ideals directly from the metropole to the colony. They thus came into conflict with the local French Creole elite, who often shared some of these institutions with the lower class and had sentimental ties, if nothing else, with some of the institutions under attack. At times, therefore, some segments of the local elite came out in defense of the lower classes—some of them out of genuine concern and some of them as opportunists who seized the opportunity to advance their struggle for Creole nationalism and constitutional reform. In the struggle over cultural institutions and moral values, traditional race and class divisions often became blurred.

The most popular complaint in the nineteenth century was about the loose morality of the Trinidad lower classes. The complainers saw, or thought they saw, evidence of unbridled licentiousness at every turn and a casual attitude toward sex that paid no respect to canons of common decency and therefore permitted sexual acts to be removed from the privacy of the bedroom and to become public performances. Many of them believed that the kind of behavior that they described was inevitable among a population of non-European descent and that the Creoles were only one step removed from civilization; others, a little more optimistic, remembered that the population was but one generation removed from slavery and thought that time, religion, and education would eventually have a rehabilitative effect.

The reported casual attitude that shocked the morality of the elite of nineteenth-century Trinidad had its roots in the slave barracks rather than in the fact that the population was composed of "negroes and people who have the African element in any predominant degree in their constitutions."[47] The system of slavery was certainly not the ideal situation for some of the traditional African strictures on sexual behavior to survive. If anything, it was easier for those African attitudes that viewed sex as natural and normal (as distinct from the prudish attitude associated with Victorian morality) to survive in the climate created by slavery. Nor, for that matter, could sexual mores that emphasized prenuptial abstinence be developed during slavery. Furthermore, long-term marital arrangements and stable family life emerged and survived during slavery only under great pressure.

Sex roles and sexual attitudes were shaped by the dehumanizing conditions of slavery and were reinforced by the poverty that characterized the emancipation period. An unequal sexual ratio with its male bias influenced female attitudes, their perception of their roles, and their sexual behavior. The sexual exploitation of females that was prevalent during slavery, with a miscegenated population as the glaring evidence, helped to shape attitudes about sex and womanhood. Men developed a posture of machismo, and they proved their claims of virility by the number of women they possessed and children they fathered; women defined themselves by their ability to satisfy sexually and by their fecundity. Sex became an activity that solved the varied psychological problems created by adverse socioeconomic conditions. It became, for those who lived marginal lives, a demonstration of their alienation.

Children were given a premature introduction to sex education. The lack of privacy in the barrack rooms demystified life very early, and the young inhabitants were exposed to the full range of sexual activity. L.M. Fraser, the inspector of prisons, reported with shock the activities of three boys and three girls who entered Shure's pasture at eleven in the morning and "under a tree, in full view of the houses on Richmond Street, proceed[ed] to acts which I can merely allude to in a report." When apprehended by a watchman, the eldest girl, age fourteen, "implied that she looked upon her act as nothing more than natural."[48] On another occasion, Fraser was uncharacteristically magnanimous in his understanding and hinted that such behavior must be expected from children "who from birth breathe an atmosphere of vice and crime, hearing nothing but obscene and profane language from morning to night; and eye-witnesses, as they notoriously are, of all that takes place in the yards and rooms."[49]

It was difficult, if not impossible, for the elite to legislate about sex, and that remained one area in which the lower classes had relative freedom. But if the law could not directly attack sexual freedom, it could and did attempt to restrict it with legislation dealing with births and marriages. It was ironic that the late-nineteenth-century descendants of an elite society whose founding fathers had placed value on the fertility and fecundity of its female population complained and used that fertility as evidence of immorality. There were numerous complaints about the low marriage rate and the high rate of illegitimate births, which were seen as indications of widespread immorality.

There was a general reluctance toward formal marriage and the registration of unions. This disposition stemmed from attitudes developed during slavery and was reinforced by the economic and demographic conditions of the postemancipation period. The availability of women in the female-surplus population that developed in the cities in the nineteenth century encouraged male reluctance to marriage. On the other hand, the independence engendered by the relative freedom possible in an agricultural economy that did not discriminate in praedial jobs encouraged a female reluctance to marriage. In those ethnic groups where females were scarce, female economic independence may have encouraged attempts at challenging traditional dependence on males, and this may also have taken the form of resistance to marriage. Yoruba women were noted for being averse to marriage.[50] They may have been taking advantage of the unavailability of Yoruba women to change traditional marriage patterns. East Indian women may have been less fortunate in their struggle for independence, as reflected in the statistics on crimes of violence against women in the East Indian community.

The number of registered marriages each year was low. One cynic observed that during the cholera epidemic of 1854, there "was an increase of the morality of the lower orders, many who had previously been living in concubinage becoming married."[51] In 1861, there were only 385 registered marriages; in 1871, 416 couples registered their marriage, and ten years later there were 559 registered marriages in all of Trinidad. According to the census of 1901, 17 percent of the population was married, 4 percent widowed, and 79 percent unmarried. These figures were almost the same as those recorded forty years earlier, in 1861. But the statistics on marriage did not include marriages among the East Indian population unless they were conducted under Christian rites or before a government functionary. Hindu and Muslim marriages were not considered legal unless they were registered at the court—but few East Indians bothered to register their marriage after it had been solemnized according to their own rites.[52]

A correspondingly high level of births were registered as illegitimate. The majority of East Indian children were automatically declared illegitimate, since their parents' marriages were unregistered and therefore illegal. In 1896, of 2,698 registered East Indian births, 80 percent were recorded as illegitimate. Among the rest of the population the percentage of illegitimate births was also extremely high; in 1890, 62 percent of all births were illegitimate, and 64 percent of the births in Port-of-Spain were illegitimate.[53] This widespread illegitimacy, as defined by the elite, was seen as the result of the unbridled sexuality of the masses and evidence of their immorality.

The elite also linked the high level of infant mortality in the nineteenth century to this illegitimacy. Infant deaths cut across race and class lines, however; the white upper class and the colored middle class elite were equally affected by the infant mortality rate. Nonetheless, only for the lower classes were infant deaths attributed to immorality rather than to the paucity of medical knowledge. Some members of the elite claimed that the high death rate was caused by children being neglected by their parents. They argued that single working-class mothers struggled alone and without the support of fathers and therefore tended to neglect the proper care of their children, since most of their time was caught up in the pursuit of their daily duties to support themselves and their families. The solution, then, was to insist that fathers discharge their parental responsibility and contribute to the material well-being of their children.

The first attempt to introduce an ordinance that would force fathers to pay child support was prompted by a Colonial Office dispatch that asked Governor Freeling to consider the introduction of legislation similar to the St. Vincent Bastardy Ordinance of 1880. But the governor, backed by the Archbishop of Port-of-Spain and a number of justices of the peace, considered the enactment of such an ordinance inadvisable and unsuited to the social conditions of Trinidad. The governor agreed that concubinage was widespread but argued that this was by the deliberate choice of the women involved in the relationships. He believed that because of the economic opportunities available, the black woman found that "the protection of marriage [was] not of sufficient importance to induce her to forego her liberty." Furthermore, a bastardy ordinance would grant recognition and sanction to the practice of concubinage, either directly or indirectly. The ordinance would be of no service to those who although living in a state of concubinage, "nevertheless live together in an orderly and decent manner and are faithful to each other." Nor would the ordinance help the children for whom it was intended, since the neglect of children was not a problem. The clothing and feeding of children was a comparatively nominal expense for women who earned wages almost as high as men with little or no difficulty. Instances of neglecting to support natural children were almost unknown the governor claimed, and furthermore, there was "a generally acknowledged moral obligation by virtue of which bastard children are maintained by their natural parents." There was no positive value to be derived from the bill, but there was one hidden danger in it, since: "such a measure might probably be mischievous in its immediate results, in placing a dangerous weapon in the hands of a class of women who would not likely ever think it worth their while to apply to the courts of law under its provisions, unless for the purpose of gratifying personal resentment or causing annoyance."[54]

With such negative responses, the matter was shelved on that occasion, but the question was raised again six years later, during the term of Governor William Robinson. On this occasion a bastardy ordinance was passed, Ordinance 25 of 1888, but only after the strong objection of the unofficial nominated members, the use of Governor Robinson's casting vote, and the insertion of compromise provisions as concessions to the opposition. The unofficial members voted in a block against it, and the attack was led by Dr. L. A. De Verteuil and Dr. de Boissiere, who articulated the fears of the French Creole elite.[55]

De Verteuil claimed that he would not have opposed the bill if it had exempted married men from its penalties. In his opinion, a child born from an adulterous relationship should not be placed on the same footing as one born from the union of unmarried parents. He argued that to make married men and unmarried fathers equally liable for the payment of support for illegitimate children made a whole class susceptible to blackmail. The Honourable De Verteuil was concerned that because of the ordinance, wives would become aware of adulterous relationships, and he feared that "to publicly proclaim [his] guilt is deliberately disturbing the peace of the household, creating strife and raising in the mind of the innocent children contempt for their father."

His colleague Dr. De Boissiere, with a legislative career of twenty-two years and long experience as a planter and doctor, made a more wide-ranging attack on the ordinance. His first argument was that common-law marriages were quite popular and of long tenure, and although concubinage may imply a proportionate rate of desertion, this was not the case. The introduction of a bastardy ordinance would only remove that sense of natural obligation to support children that was common at present. Furthermore, the introduction of a legal obligation would only encourage fathers to abscond inland or back to the other West Indian islands. He claimed that many of the illegitimate children in Trinidad were the offspring of married men who had immigrated from the other islands.

He shifted his argument next to the root cause of the whole problem—the unmarried mothers. There were no deserted children, he claimed, for "desertion presupposes seduction, and seduction, in the full meaning of the word, is rare in our midst." The presence of large factories in England made the seduction of females possible, but that was not the case in Trinidad. More importantly, the moral standard of Trinidad was so low that it required "no art on the part of the man to induce the woman to give herself up to him, for she does it undeterred by any sense of shame." These women did not fear the consequences: there was no job discrimination, since no one inquired into the moral character of female applicants for jobs. And it was the moral character of these women that was at issue, according to De Boissiere: "some of them were neither prostitutes, nor reported to be such, nor known to be of immoral character but have managed so well that they have had intercourse clandestinely with several men." Like his colleague, he feared that the ordinance would encourage blackmail, since those designing women would levy blackmail on any man with wealth or social position who may have had casual intercourse with them.

The debate was also conducted outside of the legislature. Opinions expressed in the press indicated that the literate public realized what interests were being defended by the unofficial members. A petition against the bill received 306 signatures in Port-of-Spain. But the Colonial Office discounted the significance of the petition and observed that 306 names could be easily obtained in a town the size of Port-of-Spain.

The bill was passed finally, with a number of concessions made to the opposition. A clause was included that required the magistrate to satisfy himself that the claimant had reasonable grounds and reliable evidence to support her allegation before issuing a summons that would expose the alleged father. If the statements proved to be false, the woman was liable for a fine of £50 or a prison term to a maximum of six months with or without hard labor. Second, the ordinance satisfied the unofficial members by presenting a precise definition of a single woman. Since they feared that "the prostitutes of the town would use the Ordinance as an instrument wherewith they might levy blackmail on the respectable and innocent section of the community," the definition of *single woman* excluded common or reputed prostitutes or women of known immoral character.

The bill required that putative fathers be summoned either before the birth of the child or at any time within twelve months after the birth. If the alleged father had paid voluntarily for its maintenance within the first year of the child's birth, then he could be summoned at any future time. In order to guard against absconding fathers, the application could be made within one year after the return of the putative father to the colony, but no application could be made after the child was thirteen or after the death of the child. If convicted, the father was required to pay 2*s*. 6*d*. per week for the upkeep of the child until the child was sixteen years of age. The father was also responsible for funeral expenses. These clauses in the ordinance were included in order to protect the interests of those who originally opposed its promulgation.

The interest that the planters De Boissiere and De Verteuil defended had a long tradition, with roots in the slave society. It had been the right of the male slave owner to exploit his female chattels and to demand sexual favors. The support and recognition of the offspring of these relationships depended on the whim and fancy of the father and were used as evidence of the slave owner's power. They could be withheld as punishment or extended as evidence of the owner's magnanimity. There is no doubt that many planters had provided for the manumission and education of their children by slave mothers. They resented the legal compulsion to do so, however, and insisted on acting only in response to their own interpretation of their natural obligation. The right or the obligation to care for his children had been another of the planter's weapons in his fight to control his slaves.

Sexual exploitation did not end with slavery. During the slave period both coercion (the exercise of the droit du signeur) and consent (the acquiescence of women who saw sexual alliances as a way out of slavery) had been used by the slave owner to enjoy the sexual favors of his female slaves. In the postslavery period force was not used as a matter of course, although some of the elite continued to exercise this right among their domestics, and plantation owners and overseers frequently did the same with female indentured immigrants. The possible benefits to be derived from sexual alliances with the elite continued to be an attraction for those women who used sex to secure a better standard of living. The elite continued to draw their mistresses from among their social inferiors, and the support of their offspring continued to depend on the magnanimity of the fathers and their interpretation of natural obligation.

The sexual interest and right that De Boissiere and De Verteuil defended when they objected to the bastardy ordinance was connected to a larger bundle of rights that defined the ruling class in the society. These two gentlemen may not have been the fathers of illegitimate children themselves and may indeed have been honorable gentlemen.[56] In fact, De Verteuil had given valuable service during the cholera epidemic of 1872, when he and some others organized soup kitchens "to alleviate the distress existing amongst the poor inhabitants of Port-of-Spain."[57] They felt compelled to object to the bastardy ordinance, even if this objection was interpreted as a defense of a practice that was morally objectionable by their own definition of morality. Those who supported the bill may have considered that legal redress in the hands of women would mean that their private affairs would become public knowledge, but many of them were also quite aware that given the size of the society and its penchant for scandal and gossip, much of what they considered to be private was already a public secret. It was not the right to sexual favors without legal responsibility for the consequences that they defended but, more importantly, the right of the elite to distribute largesse and gifts, not as a legal obligation, but as a moral right that came with being the ruling class. This largesse included not only material gifts, as in times of distress, but also social recognition, as in the case of support for bastard children. Undermining this right to distribute material and social largesse—the transformation of moral obligation into legal compulsion—was an attack on the moral hegemony on which their right to be the ruling class depended. The local elite were in a quandary. They needed a law that would deal with those practices of the lower classes that they considered morally objectionable, and the expatriate section of the elite (the law was promoted by the Colonial Office and supported by the official members of the council) provided them with a law that would give teeth to their constant rantings about the immorality of the poor. But it was a law that attacked an entrenched practice and threatened their interest as a ruling elite. They could not promulgate one law for themselves and one law for the poor. This would have brought the whole system of justice and respect for law into disrepute and invited uncontrollable dissension. If all law was to be obeyed without the use of force, then there must be one law for the entire community—the ruling class must be disciplined by the same law that educated and guided the masses.

The compromise on the definition of *single woman* provided the way out of the quandary for the entire elite. Only those women who were not common or reputed prostitutes or of a known immoral character could apply as a single woman for child support. Not many colored females would risk the exposure and the attack on their reputation and respectability that would be involved in an attempt to compel a member of the elite to pay the cost of maintaining an illegitimate child. They would prefer to find other ways of supporting their child or would continue to depend on the magnanimity of the father. The elite could continue to father illegitimate children without much fear of exposure or threat to their sense of privilege. But it was the black lower-class females who suffered the most from this compromise.

There was always a tradition in the society that denigrated all females of non-European descent. Those of African descent were often described as lascivious and licentious, a sexual proclivity that was seen as somehow inevitable and related to their racial origin. They were viewed not merely as immoral but more often as amoral. L.M. Fraser declared that there was "no sense of shame whatever in the female criminals or quasi-criminals" and he found those who had been committed to prison "to be utterly depraved and entirely deficient of the moral sense."[58] Asian females did not escape this character slander. The female Chinese immigrants were said to have been picked up in the streets of Hong Kong and Canton and to be of the lowest class of Chinese.[59] East Indian immigrant women were considered to be of the lowest caste, morally worthless and immigrants because they had been bought by the recruiter and consigned to the highest bidder.[60] No group save the Europeans escaped this derogatory categorization of the female sex.

It is with a background of this tradition that working-class females faced the prospect of the courts in their attempts to make use of the Bastardy Ordinance. Many probably never went to the courts, quite aware of the attitude of magistrates and often secure in the ability to wring support from their paramours by traditional means. Those who had children with their social superiors knew that the use of the courts was futile, but most working-class females had children with their social equals. Those who took males to court had to be prepared to defend their moral character and to battle against accusations of immorality. If they had had paramours prior to their relationship with the putative father, that could be used as evidence to disqualify them as single women within the terms of the ordinance.

Those males who used this loophole to escape their parental responsibility unwittingly contributed to the extension of the hegemony of the ruling class. The use of the loophole created a situation in which black males joined with the nonblack ruling elite in the denigration of all black females. Some of them may have been conscious of the implications. Those who were conscious of the implications and still used the loophole denied or pretended not to understand the behavior of their class and not to be conscious of the socioeconomic conditions that contributed to the kind of behavior that was labeled immoral. Those who used the loophole because it was available, but who were unaware of the implications of their act, were no less guilty, since their defense provided added justification for the blanket label of immorality applied to the entire class.

The elite complained continually about the number of prostitutes in Trinidad as further evidence of immorality. L.M. Fraser in particular seemed to have had his eyes constantly on the prostitutes, for he remarked regularly about the increase in their numbers. In 1877 he observed "that each succeeding year shows a rapid spread of prostitution, and no one can pass through the streets of our Towns without having ample evidence of the utter degradation of our lower class females." Four years later, in 1881, he was appalled at the increase in "the number of female children who take to habits of prostitution at an age so early that the fact might almost be deemed impossible." He was also shocked at "the steady increase in the number of girls of very tender ages who unblushingly enroll themselves amongst the recognised and registered prostitutes" in 1884.[61] But how much of this was fact and how much Fraser's imagination and conjecture is difficult to determine.

The peculiar sexual structure of plantation society tended to make prostitution almost an inevitable development. During the slave period, the existence of a large number of enslaved women at the disposal of a minority of males in authority may have restricted the opportunities for women to sell themselves on the street. But there were slaves for hire as prostitutes, and mulatto women operated both as prostitutes and as brothel owners. The prostitutes serviced those males in the urban areas who had no authority over slave women. One visitor claimed that a Mrs. Perry ran the best brothel in Port-of-Spain, called "The British Coffee House," and that most of the taverns in Port-of-Spain were brothels.[62] The clientele in Port-of-Spain would have included the soldiers of the militia and the numerous sailors who regularly visited the port. In 1869, Charles Kingsley hinted at the existence of prostitution in Port-of-Spain, which he linked to the town's role as a port and which was "aggravated by the superabundant animal vigor and the perfect independence of the younger women."[63]

The plantation economy, with its peculiar demand for labor, prompted the development of a male-surplus population. This was largely rural based—first on the slave plantation and then later among the indentured immigrant population. Although this population did not have authority over an enslaved group of women, it still needed an outlet for its sexual urges. This male market therefore facilitated the emergence of a group of women who were willing to satisfy these urges for a price and outside of the confines of marriage.

The development of prostitution and increases in the number of prostitutes could be linked also to the economic distress that occurred in the 1880s. Port-of-Spain developed a female-surplus population in the postemancipation period: immediately after emancipation, women left the plantations and flocked to the urban areas, and this drift increased throughout the nineteenth century. But the marginal employment opportunities—sewing, laundering, domestic service—decreased as the supply of women increased in the urban areas. Some women may have been forced to prostitute themselves in order to survive during this period. During periods of relative prosperity, some women may also have made a conscious choice of prostitution as a career. There may have been more economic returns in that profession than in any of the low-paying, menial, nonpraedial jobs to which women were restricted in the inequitable job structure of the nineteenth century.

The statistics are not particularly useful as a guide to the extent of prostitution. The offense is not listed separately in the available statistics on total cases or convictions and we have to depend on the figures for those imprisoned (table A.39). But prostitution was a "victimless" crime. There were no complainants except if the transaction ended in a brawl between client and prostitute over payment and services. In many instances, policemen posed as prospective clients to entrap prostitutes. It was also a highly charged moral issue, and statistics on arrests, convictions, and committals reflected the moral climate, attitudes, and concern about the offense more than they did the actual extent of the offense. In many cases police raids netted women who, though charged with prostitution (or labeled as prostitutes by the press), were really only friends and neighbors of prostitutes. The statistics on committals indicated that the number imprisoned for prostitution decreased steadily after 1884. If Fraser's constantly articulated fears and the number of letters in the press that complained about prostitution were true, there should have been many more cases of this offense concealed under "miscellaneous" cases and convictions as the police responded to the clamor.

A list published in 1874 gave some indication of the age and nationality of those listed as common prostitutes. The ninety women in Port-of-Spain were all between the ages of seventeen and thirty-eight, and the thirty-eight women in San Fernando were in the same age range. In another group of fifty-three prostitutes in San Fernando, there were two girls of about eleven years. It is debatable whether these two girls were, in fact, prostitutes. They may have been arrested with their parents or older friends. At any rate, prostitution at that tender age was unusual, since their presence among the older prostitutes listed created a sensation. Creoles dominated that list. Among the ninety listed in Port-of-Spain, sixty gave their place of birth as Trinidad, eighteen as Barbados, and ten were from the other West Indian islands. There was one East Indian woman age twenty-five, born in Calcutta. In San Fernando, thirty-one of the thirty-eight women gave their place of birth as Trinidad. There was one twenty-eight year old woman listed as born in Madras, India, and a twenty-six year old woman was born in Venezuela. Unless all of these women conveniently gave their place of birth as Trinidad to avoid possible deportation, this profile contradicted the commonly held opinion that the criminals and prostitutes were drawn from the immigrant population. The list does not represent all the prostitutes in either Port-of-Spain or San Fernando; these were "only the most notorious and flagrant cases" registered under the provisions of the Contagious Diseases Ordinance.[64]

The Contagious Diseases Ordinance was one of the weapons in the campaign against prostitution. It was modeled on legislation instituted in England as a means of combating the spread of venereal diseases in towns where there were garrisons of unmarried soldiers and sailors. The ordinance required that women accused of being common prostitutes be registered, periodically examined for venereal disease, and if diseased, incarcerated in a certified hospital ward.[65] This legislation was introduced to Trinidad as Ordinance 18 of 1869, was suspended for three years but reactivated in 1875, and remained in operation until 1887.[66]

The ordinance became a tool in the hands of the police to harass not only prostitutes but all women of the lower class. The term *common prostitute* was so vaguely defined that it left the power of interpretation up to the discretion of the policemen responsible for enforcing the legislation. Women were expected to submit voluntarily to a medical examination. Those who refused were brought before a magistrate, and the onus was on them to prove that they were virtuous. Evidence of sexual activity, whether for money or not, was often all that was needed as proof of lack of virtue. Many innocent women were thus forced to register as common prostitutes and be subjected to periodic examinations. Some of the women who were harassed eventually fled the town or changed their addresses, and when the act was reactivated in 1875 after a three-year suspension, many of the registrants could not be found by the police.[67]

The ordinance was also used by unscrupulous policemen to exact sexual favors from women. Sergeant Holder, a native of Barbados, was given unlimited power to enforce the provisions of the ordinance. Those women who refused Holder's sexual advances often found themselves before the courts and registered as common prostitutes. Magistrate Mayne, in the Port-of-Spain court, accepted Holder's word on any case connected with the ordinance, and "out of twenty cases decided by Mayne against unfortunate women, victims of this man's rapacity and lust, nineteen were decided on Holder's unsupported evidence." Finally, a petition made by Elizabeth Walcott was investigated, and Holder was found guilty and dismissed from the force. He returned to Barbados, but irreparable damage had been done already to the lives of innocent women whose only crime had been that they were poor and nonwhite.[68]

Those who did not petition, as Elizabeth Walcot did, about the unfair workings of the ordinance did not necessarily accept their fate without protest. Residents of Upper Charlotte Street and St. Ann's Road, a new upper-class suburb, complained about "the scandalous scenes of obscenity and scandal occasioned on Wednesday mornings by the band of prostitutes who go up in a body to the Hospital, in compliance with the provisions of the Contagious Diseases Ordinance."[69] Without political power, unorganized and mostly illiterate, they could only deal with their powerlessness with the only tools available to them. They shouted and screamed their way to their weekly examination and flagrantly demonstrated their resentment by behaving in a way that attracted attention to them as a group. Ironically, the only way they could protest was with behavior that reinforced all the negative stereotypes "decent" society had already applied to them.

THE CONTROL OF PUBLIC BEHAVIOR

The most popular charges laid against the working class were indecent behavior, drunk and disorderly, riotous and disorderly conduct, and obscene and profane language. L.M. Fraser claimed that the bulk of the cases before the magistrate were cases of: "Gross obscenity of both words and gestures, fighting, drunkenness, street rowdyism of every description, coarse abuse of each other on the slightest provocation and an utter want of regard for the common decencies of life."[70] These charges offered policemen ample opportunity to play the role of "domestic missionaries" and to harass the working class into patterns of behavior that were acceptable to the elite. But many of these charges stemmed from the cultural gap between elite and working class, and those who were brought before the courts were the casualties of the struggle for cultural hegemony.

Every year numerous citizens were arrested, convicted, and often imprisoned on the charge of using obscene and profane language. The use of language so described was a constant source of annoyance to the elite, who complained about "the blasphemous and immodest language of the idlers and loafers, male and female, that hang about the streets of the town." An editorial in the *Port-of-Spain Gazette* supported an earlier editorial in another newspaper, the *New Era,* about the state of public morality in the lower walks of life and the widespread use of profane and obscene language in the streets and public places. It was a sore point with the ever-complaining L.M. Fraser, who observed that "the language which is to be heard at every moment from the lips of young girls scarcely more than children is not only grossly obscene, but is so clearly expressed that its meaning is forced upon the most innocent mind."[71] But this controversy over language was a reflection of the conflict immanent in the attempt to impose the domination of one language in a multiethnic society and the differences in the values attached to the use of language between the elite and the lower class.

Despite attempts to make Trinidad an English colony in law and language, by the end of the nineteenth century English was still not the dominant language in Trinidad. There were pockets of languages: Spanish, spoken by the Venezuelan peons and some of the residents of the rural areas; Indian dialects and their plantation variants, spoken by many of the East Indians in the plantation belt; French and French patois, spoken by the bulk of the Creoles; and English and its Creole variants, spoken by British expatriates in the elite and immigrants from the English-speaking Caribbean. The French-influenced Creole patois was by far the most popular language spoken by the lower classes. It was the language of everyday discourse and the one commonly used in the marketplace, so much so that Yoruba immigrants, though normally multilingual, preferred to use the popular French patois rather than English or any of the other languages with which they were also conversant.[72]

Language was an important battleground in the struggle for cultural hegemony. The English recognized that any success in their bid to control the colony depended on "the encouragement of the common use of the language in which the laws are written."[73] Both the English and French sectors of the elite understood the relationship between the possession of a language and the worldview expressed and implied by that language. The French, who had the historical and numerical advantage, jealously guarded any attempt to reduce the popularity of their language. One English Protestant minister who had dared to deliver a sermon in French received a threatening epistle from the French Catholics, who accused him of attempting to reach and seduce the minds of the Catholics.[74] Similarly, the Protestants made knowledge of English a prerequisite for baptism and entrance into the church, and on the secular level the Anglophones enforced the regulation that made English the official language of instruction in the schools.[75] But it was an uphill battle, and it as not until the end of the century, when the school system and immigration swelled the English-speaking population, that English made any serious inroads into the popularity of patois.[76]

The French-speaking elite, more often than not bilingual, could survive in a society in which the legal institutions were dominated by Anglophones. It was the lower classes who felt the brunt of this aspect of the cultural struggle. Although there were attempts to employ magistrates who understood the Creole patois, very often understanding of the language was no substitute for sympathy. Many of the court officials were often blatantly unsympathetic to those who were not conversant with the English language. Problems with language often led to miscarriages of justice, as was evident when John Cooper was on trial for Obeah: Cooper, who had a partial acquaintance with both English and French, did not understand the implications of the questions put to him during the trial.[77] More importantly, the lower classes faced daily an unsympathetic police force dominated by English speakers—at the upper and intermediate ranks by English and Irishmen and at the lower ranks by immigrants from Barbados.

It was argued that since these policemen did not understand the Creole patois, they unknowingly allowed obscene language to be used on the streets and by vendors in the market.[78] Many believed that it was difficult to stamp out the use of obscene language since: "A great deal of this foul language is spoken in the creole dialect . . . , but this in one sense only makes matters worse, for whilst thoroughly understood by the great bulk of the inhabitants it is unintelligible to most of the Police, in whose very presence words can be, and are, uttered which, were they understood, would lead to the immediate arrest of the offender."[79] But many of these policemen used their ignorance of the Creole patois to harass non–English speakers. There was no increase in patois-speaking Trinidadians on the police force between 1880 and 1894. Yet it was during this period that there were the most complaints about obscene language and the language limitations of the police, and there was a marked increase in the number imprisoned for the use of obscene and profane language. Many of those charged may have uttered phrases in another language, which the police officer conveniently translated as obscene. At the same time the lower class took advantage of the situation to taunt and harass unsuspecting policemen. Language became a defense behind which they could verbally attack the representatives of the power structure and take out some of their frustrations at their powerlessness.

The conflict over obscene language must be viewed in the context of the transfer and transformation of the African tradition of the social uses of language and the role of this reconstructed oral tradition in a situation of oppression. The ancestors of nineteenth-century Afro-Trinidadians came from African societies in which the oral tradition was an important cultural institution and in which highly developed oral skills were desirable assets.[80] In the slave society competence in oral skills was even more important. In order to communicate both among themselves and with the power structure, slaves had to be able to master not merely the European language of the slave owner but also the patois that developed out of the homogenization of African dialects. A Creole patois developed from these two imperatives of language development that utilized the vocabulary of the dominant French language and the syntax of West African languages.[81] The later introduction of English as the language of the dominant section of the elite further compounded the language problem. In the postemancipation period Creoles found it necessary to master not only the popular patois if they wished to be orally effective in the community but also English if they valued the possible social mobility that came with mastery of that language.

These two dimensions of the development of language in the plantation society served to heighten the respect and value attached to competence in oral skills. The Creole patois offered numerous possibilities for creativity and for demonstrating mastery and competence, because it was new and flexible. The education system reinforced this penchant for oral dexterity, since it often emphasized form rather than content. In those schools where the language of instruction was English, the emphasis on rote learning encouraged a concentration on and a delight in the sound of words, often at the expense of their meaning.[82] The sound of the word gave the opportunity for skilled wordsmiths to infuse new meanings into old words. Those who were orally dextrous had in their possession a weapon that could be used to defend themselves against perceived oppression.

The Creoles developed a number of word games that provided training for "the man of words." Some of these were innocent: for example, "Pierrot Grenade," which was a satire on the relationship between teacher and pupil and required the latter to utilize an intricate system of puns in order to spell words.[83] But others were overtly sexual, for example, "rhyming," an equivalent of "the dozens," a popular game among contemporary Afro-American ghetto youths.[84] In this game the individual described his sexual prowess at the expense of the female members of his opponent's family. The game channeled aggression and had its own controls, and only when these were breached did the verbal contest shift into physical conflict. It may have been this game that prompted the comments by Fraser and others about the obscenity among youths in Port-of-Spain.

There was a similar verbal contest among adults, but this

was removed from the realm of play and was more hostile and aggressive. The practice of "cussing" or "'buseing" was a demonstration of the participants' ability to use words effectively. In this case a stream of invective was used to describe the opponent's ancestry and the deficiencies of his moral behavior and to reveal to the audience the extent of poverty and deprivation experienced by the opponent. It also had its own form (without deliberate rhyme but not without rhythm) and its own rules of conduct. It was often the prelude to physical conflict for men, but for women it was more often the substitute for physical violence. Just as men used implosive violence as part of the process of self-affirmation in a situation of powerlessness, so too, women used the verbal violence implicit in obscene language as part of their struggle for self-affirmation.

The best example of the concern with oral dexterity and evidence of the extent to which the African oral tradition was reconstructed in Trinidad was the development of the calypso. This was a song that made social and political commentary either directly or by use of innuendo and that was sung both for entertainment and for information. It was used within the Creole community to disseminate information of all sorts, and since the calypso touched all aspects of life, many of them dealt with raw sexual themes. It was also used within the lower-class community as a mechanism for social control. It exposed certain patterns of behavior that the community considered undesirable and held the delinquents up to public ridicule. Many of the songs protested against the inequalities of life and the deprivations of the colonial society. The songs were also used as a forum to expose the double standards of the elite, and they employed material provided by domestics and the prostitutes and *jamettes* who had access to information about the elite. During the slave period some slave owners appreciated its potential, and one planter even hired a resident calypsonian to attack his enemies in song. The ruling class realized its potential for hegemonic subversion, for they understood that "the greatest enemy of authority [was] contempt and the surest way to undermine it [was] laughter."[85] The calypsonian was praised for his mastery of language, his skill with words, and his wit as evidenced by his use of double entendre in his songs. He became a cultural hero who represented the resistance against the cultural domination of the elite, especially since his life-style represented the antithesis of the moral values preached by the elite. Because of the use of patois (until the end of the nineteenth century), the social and political commentary, and the sexual themes, the calypso was under constant attack in the nineteenth century, and many people were arrested for singing obscene and profane ballads.[86]

This "obscene and profane language" formed part of a pattern of behavior that was prosecuted by the elite as indecent behavior and riotous and disorderly conduct. These were general charges that were vague enough to cover many kinds of lower-class activity and therefore were useful instruments in the hands of an aggressive police force. But in particular they were used to prosecute those areas of behavior among the working class that seemed to be in direct contrast to the ideals of an elite who were influenced by a European code of ethics. The elite objected to the behavior of the lower class, since it seemed to emphasize noise, turmoil, profligacy, and lack of sobriety. The definition of some areas of behavior as indecent and disorderly was an indication of the cultural confusion and the conflict of ethical systems within the colony. On the one hand, there was an ethical code that emphasized thrift, sobriety, respectability, and the individual and, on the other hand, an ethical code that was closely linked to the affirmation of community. And underlying this cultural conflict was the concern for security in the multiethnic society.

Many of the charges of indecent and disorderly conduct arose from incidents connected to the festivities of the working class. There was a distinct cultural gap between the lower-class understanding and celebration of the rites of passage—

that is, birth, marriage, and death—and the value the elite attached to the celebration of these events. The celebrations offered opportunities for the celebrant to reaffirm kinship and community links: the celebration of birth meant the selection of members of the community who would stand as substitute parents for the child; marriage was the perfect way of extending kinship links and widening contacts within the community; life itself was punctuated by numerous occasions for celebrating with friends the joy of living with dances and fetes; and at death the wake gave the community the opportunity to remember its ancestors and to communicate with the bereaved members. But for the European element of the elite (as well as some of its Creole members), these moments in the passage of life were private affairs that were restricted to the immediate family, relatives, and a few close friends. Their custom of making these celebrations public affairs brought the lower class into conflict with the elite and the police.

These events were celebrated with the consumption of considerable amounts of food and drink. The celebration of life was taken seriously, and many found in alcohol a useful mechanism for releasing inhibitions, or for drowning sorrows, or for temporarily escaping the harsh realities of everyday life. Even death became an opportunity for celebration, and at wakes and funerals alcohol was used to assist the mourners in coping with the harsh reality of death by celebrating life. But to unsympathetic observers, these events were scenes of disorder that reinforced the belief in the savage nature of the lower orders. Rituals associated with death and burial were seen as confirmation of the uncurable barbarity of the working class: the fifty people at a wake that the police interrupted, seizing three bottles of rum, were described as "a riotous and drunken mob howling over and dancing around a stiff dark corpse," and it was considered a desecration of All Souls night when a father distributed rum "to loose women over the grave of his daughter."[87] The extensive use of alcohol facilitated the degeneration of some of these events into drunken brawls. Although the unstated aim of these celebrations was to forge and/or strengthen community links, they often provided the opportunity for conflicts between individuals or groups to be resolved in combat. The elite had their accusations of barbarity confirmed by these occasions, which seemed to them evidence of the lack of sobriety and respectability among the lower orders.

The provision of large quantities of food and drink at these celebrations meant an expenditure that the provider sometimes could ill afford, and in some cases other members of the family and community made contributions to the celebration. The need to provide a lavish wedding spread sometimes meant the marriage was postponed, not only because the groom deferred until he could make the long-term commitment of supporting a family but also until the couple thought that they were capable of financing the celebration. One governor who complained about the low marriage rates noted that "the lavish expenditure they think it necessary to make on wedding festivities renders marriage a luxury in which only the provident can indulge."[88] Death observances also required refreshments for those who came to express their condolences. Many people prepared for their death by joining Friendly Societies and paid a weekly contribution that ensured a sum to cover the costs of the burial arrangements. Money was also spent on the celebration of life. The countless dances and the annual celebration of carnival seemed to the European elite a senseless waste of money. It was decidedly criminal, since this was the behavior of a people who seemed not to value honest work. The Victorian attitude toward thrift as a desirable trait was affronted by the obvious profligacy of the lower classes.

The campaign against gambling was also part of this cultural conflict in the nineteenth century. The committals for gambling offenses tripled between 1875–79 and 1885–89, and although the figure for 1890–94 decreased, it was still almost twice that for the 1875–79 period; by the end of the century it had nearly climbed back to the 1885–89 amount. In April 1879 the *Port-of-Spain Gazette* complained that "the practice of public gambling has become a serious nuisance especially at New Town and in the suburbs of Port-of-Spain," and in May of the same year it reported "a raid on a well known gambling saloon at the corner of Duke and Charlotte Streets." There were continued complaints in the 1880s, and in 1897 the *Port-of-Spain Gazette* again claimed that gambling had become a curse and reported a raid on a house in Nelson Street, where the police arrested thirty men.[89]

The elite was not against all gambling. Horse racing was legal and in fact was organized by the elites of the society. It was a popular activity, and one governor used the fact that there were eleven successful meetings in one year as evidence that the elite exaggerated the extent of distress in the 1890s.[90] Races were popular and were well attended by all sections of the community—the lower classes used the opportunity as a social outing, a time to picnic, to meet friends, and to engage in activities not always connected to the tracks.[91] But the elite were against those gambling activities organized by the lower classes. They were against the card and dice games that took place in private homes and barrack yards and on street corners. These were raided, and the participants and onlookers were charged for gambling, being incorrigible rogues or disorderly behavior. They were also against cockfights, a popular sport among the lower classes, which not only satisfied the gambling urges of the poor but were a valuable mechanism for channeling aggression. Police raids at cockfights slowly drove the sport out of the urban areas, but it survived in the rural areas, where it was much easier to take precautions against police intervention.[92]

The elite also outlawed *whe-whe,* a game similar in principle and operation to today's numbers game of the Afro-American ghetto.[93] Chinese immigrants introduced the game, and though at first restricted to that community, it became popular among all sections of the lower class. The Chinese used the profits from the game to support the distressed and to pay for the burial of the indigent within their community. The offense was prosecuted under those sections of Ordinance 6 of 1868 that covered all games of chance. But it became necessary to introduce Ordinance 5 of 1888 to deal specifically with the game of *whe-whe* after the conviction of John Crosbie was reversed by the Supreme Court on a technicality. The attorney general agreed that the new ordinance was directed at a custom peculiar to the Chinese, but the game was an intolerable nuisance that had led to much demoralization among servants and the laboring classes and therefore demanded vigorous suppression. He argued that although the stakes were small—between three and twelve pence—the game encouraged a system of petty larceny among servants, and the laboring classes were tempted to spend their savings in the hope of winning the jackpot.[94]

The elite saw no contradiction between their organization of and participation in horse races and their suppression of all forms of lower-class gambling activity. Horse races were organized with proper police control, at specific times, and in designated places. They therefore did not intrude on the rhythm of the work calendar. This was "the sport of kings," and the breeding of horses and the development of sophisticated methods of betting gave it a pseudoscientific rationality on which it depended for respectability.[95] But the gambling of the lower class was uncontrolled and without fixed timetables, and it was therefore liable to distract the working class from their purpose in life: that is, meaningful work. The elite argued that lower-class gambling, because it was unpoliced and often took place in public areas, facilitated the public display of all those patterns of behavior that they considered to be distasteful and disorderly. Lower-class gambling therefore bred further crime. Furthermore, games like *whe-whe,* in which the participants used their interpretations of dreams in order to make their wagers, defied the scientific rationality that nineteenth-century Victorians worshipped; it depended instead on chance and luck and reinforced the superstitious beliefs of the lower orders. Uncontrolled gambling among the lower class therefore encouraged a belief that material success was possible by luck and chance and not through thrift and steady work habits. It was dangerous because gambling became, not a form of entertainment, but a substitute for work.

POPULAR ENTERTAINMENT AND THE FEAR OF REVOLT

The attack on gambling was part of an overall attempt to control every form of lower-class entertainment and to impose what the elite considered to be a rational use of leisure time. Drumming and drum dances were also targets of the moral reformers. During the slave period there was no blanket prohibition against drumming, but slaves had to request permission to hold or to attend drum dances, and these were to cease at a specific time. The slave owners fantasized that these all-night affairs were wild orgiastic scenes of wantonness and debauchery that were detrimental to the health and well-being, both physical and moral, of their property.

During the postemancipation period drumming and drum dances were viewed as evidence of the persistence of African elements, despite the efforts of the pro-European segments to civilize the society. Charles Day, who lived in Trinidad towards the end of the 1840s, was attracted by "a horrible drumming on the tum-tums" and visited one of these dances. He commented that "the whole scene was truly African and showed how little the negroes are advanced in civilization." E. B. Underhill, a Baptist missionary who visited in 1861, observed that the liberated Africans retained "many African usages and are little removed from the wild life of their native country"; as evidence he pointed to "a large shed devoted to night dances and to the noisy music of the banjo or drum." Charles Kingsley, a visitor in 1869, described the dancing of the women as "violent and ungainly stampings to the music of tom-tom and chac chac, if music it can be called." But he believed that the music had immense power over the emotions, since blacks were said to be "maddened" by the drums.[96] The local critics repeated the anti-African sentiments of these visitors and argued that these dances were morally corruptive. Like their predecessors in the slave period, they saw these dances as scenes of unimaginable obscenity and immorality and the breeding ground for vice and crime.

The campaign to stamp out drumming and drum dances revealed the developing conflict between two sections of the ruling class—the embryonic Creole nationalists and the expatriates. In 1883 the governor, Sir Stanford Freeling, introduced a bill that made it illegal to play drums and other percussion instruments between six in the morning and ten at night without police permission and strictly prohibited the playing of these instruments after that hour. European instruments could be played without a license between 6 A.M. and 10 P.M., but a permit was required after ten at night. The governor had introduced the bill because of the complaints of the military officers stationed at St. James's Barracks about the drumbeating in the neighboring East Indian community, but the act affected the entire community.[97]

There was a terrible furor over the bill. In the press the division was quite clear. *Fair Play* was clearly hostile to the practice, and its editorial described drumming as crude and primitive and the dances as immoral and debased. *New Era* described the drum as barbaric and saw the need to replace it with "more civilized instruments."[98] The *New Era* was under the editorship of a colored man, and while the coloreds of the nineteenth century did not wholeheartedly reject their racial heritage, for the colored editor a defense of drums and drum dances may have meant too close an identification with what were considered the negative aspects of the African heritage. On the other hand, the *Port-of-Spain Gazette,* which was usually the conservative voice of the planters, came out *against* the bill and wrote a stirring *defense* of drums and drum dances in an editorial.[99] But at this time the newspaper was under the editorship of Phillip Rostant, a French Creole, who was one of the leading voices in the movement for constitutional reform.[100] The radical elements of the reform movement seized this opportunity and used the attack on drumming as an example of the inequities of the colonial order.

The opposition to the bill forced the governor to withdraw it and to replace it with Ordinance 11 of 1883. The new ordinance required a license for the playing of drums between 10 P.M. and 6 A.M., but the responsibility to enforce the law was now placed on the owner or occupier of the premises on which the drumming was done. The ordinance stated that the owner or occupier was guilty of an offense if he permitted "rogues and vagabonds" to assemble for the purpose of holding drumming sessions and drum dances.[101] Anyone who had been previously convicted under the Summary Convictions Ordinance, a blanket ordinance that covered all the possible offenses that came before the magistrates, was considered a rogue and a vagabond. So many people had been convicted at some time of one of the numerous possible offenses that this ordinance virtually prohibited the assembling of the lower classes.

This attitude toward assembly reflected the perennial concern of the elite for security in the plantation society. The potential for drumming and drum dances to be used as a cover for conspiracy and rebellion had not been lost on the planters during the slave period. Few had forgotten the Haitian revolution, and no one dared to forget the attempted revolt of 1805 in Trinidad. In both instances, supposedly innocent drum dances had played important roles.[102] These dances were held every Saturday night on different estates, and the slave community developed an elaborate administrative structure for the organization of the events. It was this development that was feared, since drum dances not only permitted the unsupervised congregation of slaves but facilitated the development of leadership qualities unconnected to the task of plantation production. Therefore, this form of entertainment was controlled because the planters considered it potentially dangerous or disruptive to society and to production.

Emancipation did not put an end to the fear of revolt in the plantation society. The "Angel Gabriel" riots in 1856 in British Guiana and the 1865 revolt at Morant Bay in Jamaica provided dramatic evidence of the continued potential for revolt. Nearer home, riots over prison conditions in 1849 and over attempts to regulate carnival in 1858 indicated how easily minor incidents could escalate into major disturbances. Still, the labor demands of the plantation economy continued to introduce other racial elements, which further increased the fear of revolt. The economy depended on non-Europeans as laborers, and it recruited Asians in addition to the mistrusted Africans and their descendants. British imperial adventures in Africa and Asia cast a long shadow that fell on Trinidad society. The presence of East Indians raised ugly memories of the 1857 Indian Mutiny, since some of the immigrants were ex-sepoys who could not resist reminding their hosts of their role in that affair.[103] The characteristic Victorian fear of the masses was now compounded by racism and produced a paranoia about the presence of these "alien" masses.

This paranoia often caused the security forces to overreact to minor incidents. In 1865, the inspector general of police, along with twenty-five policemen, the agent general of immigrants, and an interpreter, rushed by special steamer to put down a reported mutiny among the newly imported Chinese on the Camden and Exchange estates in Couva. It was a false alarm, however. The magistrate at Couva, Mr. Pantin, had requested an interpreter for a case of assault committed by a Chinese, and paranoia had caused this request to be translated into the need for assistance to put down a mutiny. On that occasion the *Port-of-Spain Gazette* gave a sombre warning. It pointed to the incident as a striking illustration of the secret and deep-rooted fear of insurrection by those who "live and herd by themselves." The prompt response of the police was seen as evidence that: "the authorities at least are alive to the existence of the mine which exploding under our feet, may at any moment upheave and topple down the whole of our social organisation. Our proprietors and managers live in the midst of a population of strangers—of men divided from them by a deep gulf of difference of creed, language, manners and morals."[104]

This fear of the masses prompted the passage of ordinances that prohibited convicted criminals from assembling in groups of ten or more. These ordinances, like that against the drum dances, were aimed at stamping out the bands that the law enforcement agencies considered to be the major criminal elements in the society. The bands could not be declared illegal, since any ordinance aimed directly at them would have been too obviously biased and any general ordinance would have included such organizations as the Foresters, the Good Templars, and the other associations of the elite. Therefore, the law had to be aimed at the congregation of those whose previous behavior had already earned them a conviction and who had been defined as criminals, rogues, and vagabonds. The Habitual Criminals Ordinance (no. 1 of 1870 and revised as no. 8 of 1880) provided for constant police surveillance of those convicted of felonies, and it prohibited them from congregating in groups. So many members of the bands had been convicted of felonious wounding because of their numerous intergroup clashes that the ordinance was valuable in harassing band members. The ordinance referred only to those convicted of serious offenses in the Superior Courts, so attempts were made to extend these provisions to those summarily convicted, but the Colonial Office found this to be a bit too draconian. The elite had to be satisfied with merely enforcing those clauses of Ordinance 6 of 1868 that dealt with those defined and summarily convicted as rogues and vagabonds. With this weapon in their hands, the police could raid even religious gatherings, especially those like Shango that required drums, and be sure of holding in their nets a fair number of participants. At any rate, despite these harassment measures, the bands continued to exist and to be a headache for the elite, especially at carnival.

The popular Creole festival of carnival seemed to embody all the fears of the elite and the law enforcement agency. The annual festival that developed out of African and French traditions of masked pageants had changed during the nineteenth century from a festival with popular elite participation into one dominated by the lower classes. Although the festival was never a genteel celebration completely free of scenes of disorder and obscenity, increased participation of the lower classes made such scenes far more noticeable to the elite, who had withdrawn from the festival. The *Port-of-Spain Gazette* of 25 February 1871 complained that although in former years there was amusement to be derived from carnival, it had become "thoroughly contemptible." Throughout the 1870s this was the general tone of the press, and they urged the suppression of the popular festival.

The festival was much more than contemptible—it was also dangerous, and it became increasingly so in the 1880s. The often sexually explicit presentations and the uncontrolled drinking of masqueraders and onlookers alike offended the moral sensibilities of the elite. Not only were the calypsos and the masked presentations sexually explicit, but many of them made serious social and political commentary. Some masqueraders took the opportunity to pillory and ridicule well-known members of the social establishment. This raised serious doubts about the loyalty of the masses. Much of the fighting was intraclass: that is, between bands of working-class males and females. But the possibility of transferring this implosive violence into an attack against the elite was a constant threat. The sight of an intoxicated black mass—armed with sticks, stones, bottles, and other lethal weapons, who sang obscene and profane songs—kept alive the fear of revolt.

In other societies there were similar festivals during which the elite permitted the lower orders to reverse the traditional social order. It was a brief period during which licentious behavior was temporarily sanctioned, and permission was given to transgress some of the usual moral and social taboos of the society. This served as an opportunity for the lower orders to let off steam and to deal with other aggressive tendencies in a socially approved way. The elite of those societies used such festivals as useful mechanisms for social control.[105] But those were racially homogeneous societies. The elite in Trinidad lived in a racially hetereogeneous society and were divided from the mass not only by race but, in the words of the *Port-of-Spain Gazette,* by "creed, language, manners, and morals." The therapeutic value and the social-control possibilities of carnival took second place to the very real potential of class and race revolt in the nineteenth-century plantation society. Carnival therefore had to be purged not only of its morally objectionable practices but of those potentially dangerous elements: hence, the ordinances that restricted the festival to a two-day period and to specific daylight hours; the Peace Preservation Act of 1884, which prohibited the carrying of lighted torches; and Ordinance 2 of 1891, which outlawed certain practices and carnival presentations.

The Hosein festival of the East Indians was also viewed as potentially dangerous by the elite. It was originally a Sh'ite Muslim festival that commemorated the deaths of Hussein and Hassan, the grandsons of Mohammed, at the battle of Kerbala at the hands of Sunni Muslims. Eventually, it became a pan-Indian festival in which both Muslims and Hindus participated, and it lost much of its religious significance. In 1882 six Muslim shopkeepers from San Fernando and Couva, in a petition signed by 101 other East Indians, complained about what they considered to be the degeneration of the festival.[106] The drinking and the fighting between bands drawn from different estates made the festival a secular celebration that bore a marked resemblance to carnival.

Since much of this took place in the rural areas around the estates, the festival never attracted the widespread criticism of the urban elites that carnival did. But this soon changed. In 1882 the chief of police expressed fears about that year's festival and requested a man-of-war to be on standby duty in the port.

He noted that because of the deployment of the police force at the festival, Port-of-Spain and San Fernando were left unguarded, and "the inhabitants and their property left at the mercy of a number of rogues who may at any moment take it into their heads to rise." He also declared that he had reason to believe that the East Indians at their pre-Hosein preparations had discussed the strength of the force and the feasibility of cutting off communication with Port-of-Spain.[107] The increased participation of Afro-Trinidadians raised the spectre of an Afro-Asian alliance against the elite, and therefore in the 1880s the elite sought to control the festival.

The move to control these popular forms of entertainment led to conflicts between the police and the masses, for the latter did not take this assault on their institutions without protest. It is this struggle that swelled the criminal statistics between 1880 and 1900. The period is dotted with battles—the carnival riots of 1881, 1883, and 1884;[108] the Hosein riot of 1884;[109] and the riot in Arouca over drumming in 1891.[110] These riots occurred at a time when the police force was headed by an aggressive English chief of police who was supported by a belligerent phalanx of Irish noncommissioned officers and by ranks filled with antagonistic Barbadians. They also coincided with the economic crisis occasioned by a fall in the price of sugar, which had negative effects on jobs for Afro-Trinidadians, wages and work conditions for East Indians, and the cost of living for all. The combination of these two factors made Creole Trinidadians much more conscious of the defense of their cultural institutions, especially those that provided support from both material deprivation and psychological oppression. The struggle for cultural hegemony in the nineteenth century therefore depended less on the socializing agencies of church and school to win consent and more on the coercive arms of the state to enforce compliance, and in the process, large segments of the population were forced into criminal activity.

CHAPTER NINE

Conclusion

This study does not argue that without the plantation structure there would have been no crime in Trinidad. Crimes against the person and property in particular are crimes that would occur in any society, with or without the plantation system. Trinidad was not unique, but while it shared some criminal patterns with some similarly structured plantation societies, it differed significantly from others. The level of crimes against property differed from the pattern in Barbados, for example, while the pattern of crimes against the person closely paralleled that of British Guiana. My argument is that the pursuit of plantation interests in the particular circumstances of nineteenth-century Trinidad facilitated the development of a peculiar pattern of recorded crime. In some cases the connection between the plantation structure and crime is quite clear—as in offenses against the labor regulations—while in other instances the relationship is indirect.

The nature and pattern of crime in nineteenth-century Trinidad was intimately linked to the attempts of the plantocrats and their allies to re-create the social relations of the slave society, to ensure the perpetuation of the plantation system, and, to extend the hegemony of the plantation order. The criminogenic nature of the plantation system sprang from its inherent tensions, and in the nineteenth century, the plantocrats labeled as criminal those activities that reflected the contradictions of the system.

The recorded incidence of crime—that is, the rate of committals, convictions, and total cases—fluctuated over the period 1838–1900, but in general it shows a decline. The pattern of recorded crime was affected by the nature and efficiency of those law enforcement agencies responsible for the annual compilation of criminal statistics. The statistics, therefore, mirror the changes within these agencies, that is, their perception of their role in a plantation society, their organization, and the composition of their personnel. In the nineteenth century, these agencies considered themselves to be in the forefront of a battle to bring civilization to a non-European population and as the first defense against a reversion to barbarism. Because of this attitude, they conducted a war against the lower-class members of the society, especially during the latter part of the nineteenth century, and this resulted in the swollen statistics on crime. In the process of defending the plantocrats, they unwittingly made criminals of large segments of the population.

The vulnerability of the economic structure of the plantation system contributed to the criminal behavior that is recorded as crimes against property, social-economy offenses, and the Immigration and Master and Servants Ordinances. The plantation economy depended on an external market for the sale of its major staple product. Fluctuations in world prices for sugar had its repercussions on the cost of living, which in turn produced pauperizing conditions that some people sought to alleviate by theft. Before the 1880s, however, the uneven development of Trinidad prevented widespread pauperization and therefore reduced the incidence of theft. The availability of land that was not alienated by export-crop production meant that opportunities existed for the growth of a peasantry oriented towards production of food crops for internal consumption. It also meant that the working class were in a position to take advantage of the labor market and to demand high wages for their services. Furthermore, the growth of the cocoa sector of the export economy reduced the dependence of the economy on the sugar monopoly. Overall, crimes against property was the smallest category in total cases, convictions, and committals to prison throughout the nineteenth century, although there was a slight increase in theft, chiefly in urban areas, that coincided with the sugar crisis of the 1880s and the urban migration generated by this crisis.

The planters moved to redress the imbalance in the land-labor ratio—and therefore to maintain their control over labor—principally by importing an indentured labor force. The attempts of the planters to exercise the same extent of control over the indentureds as they had formerly exercised over the slave force produced the third largest category of "crime" that could be identified among the total cases before the courts. These attempts to control indentured labor were accompanied by increased efforts to control the nonindentured work force. The elite designed legal measures to monitor the growth of the labor force that was not indentured to the plantation, and many of these measures resulted in criminal cases. Altogether, the control of labor in the nineteenth century resulted in a group of offenses that constituted the second largest category (labor and social economy offenses) among both total convictions and committals to prison. In the nineteenth century, the attempt to control labor tended to criminalize all industrial relations.

A conscious effort to maintain the social and economic relations of the slave period contributed indirectly to the pattern of violence in the nineteenth century. Crimes against the person was the second largest category in total cases and the third largest in convictions and committals. In their effort to introduce a controlled labor force, the planters influenced the demographic patterns that developed, especially among the rural based population. This sector was male dominated, and the incidence of crimes against women and uxoricide was directly linked to a male-biased pattern of immigration and the creation of a female-deficient indentured population. Furthermore, rapid immigration influenced an internal migration to the urban areas, especially during the economic crisis of the 1880s. This migration put a strain on the availability and quality of urban housing. But the planters and their allies turned a blind eye to the atrocious living conditions that developed in the urban barracks. The pattern of impulsive and implosive violence that characterized the closing decades of the nineteenth century was directly linked to the quality of life created in part by poor housing conditions and in part by a deteriorated economic situation.

The domination of the planters over the society was enhanced by their ability to exploit the contradictions of the political structure of nineteenth-century Trinidad. The undemocratic Crown Colony system gave the planter elite access to and influence over the decision-making process, and from this priviledged position, they were able to defend their interests and extend their hegemony. The bias within the society toward European civilization produced another area of conflict. This conflict over the cultural orientation of the society was responsible for the largest category of offenses (social order) among those convicted and among those committed to prison. A crucial element in the ideology of the plantation system was the cultural supremacy of Europe and the congenital inferiority of non-Europeans. During the slave period, there was a tendency to overlook the African elements among the work force, so long as these did not interfere with plantation production. But during the nineteenth century, the emerging Creole culture was viewed increasingly as being counterproductive and a challenge to the hegemony of the plantocrats. They therefore criminalized all those cultural activities that they viewed as inimical to their interests. Much of the collective violence of the period stemmed from the actions of a politically powerless class in conscious or unconscious defense of their cultural interests.

A brief look at the period beyond the time limits of this

study reveals a changing pattern of recorded criminal activity. These changes are linked to the changes in the political organization of the plantation system. The political structure came under attack by some segments of the elite as well as by those who aspired to elite status. The latter, in particular, felt restricted by the inequities of the colonial system and advocated constitutional reform. Some of this reform related strictly to internal organization, but later, some of the radical members even questioned the wider imperial connections. The activities of this movement had its effect on crime.

Those offenses associated with indentured labor disappeared as a major category of recorded crime when the system of indentured immigration ended in 1917. Indentured immigration fell victim to internal agitation by those who linked the need for constitutional reform to the economic distress that was fueled by indentureship and immigration and to external agitation organized by nationalist groups in colonial India. This does not mean that all crimes against labor disappeared: the category of social-economy offenses continued to contain the victims of the planters' attempts to control the labor market. Furthermore, the discovery and commercial exploitation of oil began another phase of industrial conflict that would erupt in the riots of 1937 as labor sought its second emancipation. The political conflict that began in the late nineteenth century continued into the twentieth and culminated in the grant of political independence in 1962. The emerging political elite, essentially a black middle class, found it politically convenient to advocate the decriminalization of some of those cultural activities that were under attack by the plantocrats. Thus, some of these cultural activities were decriminalized and elevated to respectable status in the process of political emancipation.

But it would be naive to suggest that political changes have completely eradicated the wellsprings of violence and conflict—or, for that matter, of pauperization and theft—in the neocolonial society. Moreover, in the era of political independence a Creole nationalist government found it convenient to use laws from the colonial era to prosecute its political enemies who protested neocolonial conditions during the civil disorders of 1970.

But these changes are all in the twentieth century. In the nineteenth century, Trinidad experienced a period of fluctuating crimes against property, persistent crimes against the person, deliberate crimes against labor, and the consistent criminalization of Creole culture—all of this derived from the direct or indirect actions of the plantocrats in their pursuit of short-term economic interests and long-term hegemony.

Appendix: Criminal Statistics

Table A.1 Prison Statistics, 1838–54

Year	Estimated Population	No. in Confinement on September 29
1838	36,655	55
1839	39,436	59
1840	42,217	77
1841	44,998	63
1842	47,880	76
1843	53,847	77
1844	59,815	95
1845	61,214	100
1846	62,613	97
1847	64,012	130
1848	69,411	102
1849	66,810	127
1850	68,209	140
1851	68,600	—
1852	71,091	180
1853	72,573	215
1854	74,055	168

Source: PRO, C.O. 300/51–65: Prison Statistics.

Table A.2 Committals for Principal Offenses, 1848–54

	1848	1849	1850	1851	1852	1853	1854
Person							
Assault	146	122	140	137	104	146	72
Cutting and wounding	2	12	12	9	13	19	10
Murder and manslaughter	2	2	2	0	2	2	7
Rape	1	1	1	2	2	8	5
Social Order							
Cursing and swearing	58	78	44	42	34	54	26
Drunkenness	128	203	132	112	75	75	20
Keeping a disorderly house	0	1	4	4	2	0	0
Self-exposure	26	35	33	25	20	18	4
Resistance to police	10	20	36	32	50	37	34
Property							
Arson	2	1	0	3	3	2	1
Burglary	3	1	2	11	4	12	6
Theft	226	229	293	248	224	265	266
Social Economy and Labor							
Debts	312	221	237	247	245	233	226
Breach of contract	0	127	110	142	121	237	230
Immigration ordinance	0	0	0	0	38	50	194

Sources: Blue Books for 1848–49, in PRO, 60.300/59–60; L. A. A. De Verteuil, *Trinidad,* 205.

Table A.3 Principal Committals, 1848–54

Type of Offense	1848	1849	1850	1851	1852	1853	1854	Total	% of All Principal Committals
Person	151	137	155	148	121	175	94	981	13.40
Social Order	241	351	284	228	185	189	89	1,567	21.40
Property	231	231	295	262	231	279	273	1,802	24.61
Social Economy and Labor	312	348	347	389	404	520	650	2,970	40.57
Total	935	1,067	1,081	1,027	941	1,163	1,106	7,320	
Total Committals	1,431	1,411	1,174	1,176	1,055	1,270	1,168	8,585	

Sources: Blue Books for 1848–49, in PRO, C.O. 300/59–60; L. A. A. Verteuil, *Trinidad,* 205.

Note: Total gives the figures for those offenses which the authorities considered principal offenses.
Total committals gives the figures for committals for *all* offenses as well those who had been imprisoned while awaiting trial, imprisoned for safe custody although not officially charged, and convicted of any offense.

Table A.4 Crime Rates per 1,000 of the Population, 1870–99

Years	Prison Committals		Court Convictions		Total Cases	
	Annual	Rate	Annual	Rate	Annual	Rate
1870–74	2,500	21.55	5,224	45.03	—	—
1875–79	3,154	23.19	7,332	53.91	15,147	111.37
1880–84	4,166	26.36	9,252	58.55	17,351	109.81
1885–89	3,946	21.80	9,389	51.87	16,763	92.61
1890–94	4,082	19.81	10,805	52.45	18,225	88.47
1895–99	4,474	19.20	12,746	54.70	20,453	87.78

Sources: Blue Books for 1870–99, in PRO, C.O. 300/81–10: Criminal Statistics.

Table A.5 Pattern of Recommittals, 1870–95 (%)

Year	Once Before	Twice Before	Thrice Plus
1870	59.10	19.26	21.62
1875	52.42	18.74	28.83
1880	37.43	21.86	40.69
1885	35.54	19.94	44.50
1890	33.19	21.82	44.98
1895	36.93	21.41	41.65

Sources: Blue Books for 1870–95, in PRO, C.O. 300/81–106: Prison Statistics.

Table A.6 Disposition of Imprisonment Terms, 1874–99 (%)

Years	5 Years Plus	1–4 Years	3–11 Months	3 Months or Less
1874–79	0.55	3.03	8.32	88.09
1880–84	0.66	2.78	9.13	87.42
1885–89	0.81	2.02	7.03	90.12
1890–94	0.67	1.92	6.90	90.48
1895–99	0.25	1.37	5.61	92.75

Sources: Blue Books for 1874–99, in PRO, C.O. 300/85–110: Prison Statistics.

Table A.7 Disposition of Convictions, 1871–1900 (%)

Years	Fines	Imprisonment in Lieu	Peremptory Imprisonment	Bound Over, etc.
1871–76	44.07	14.08	32.23	9.62
1877–82	47.37	11.92	21.30	19.47
1882–88	43.30	13.88	19.98	22.83
1889–94	48.56	13.77	13.89	23.75
1895–1900	50.58	14.40	12.13	23.05

Sources: Blue Books for 1871–1900, in PRO, C.O. 300/85–111: Criminal Statistics.

Table A.8 Disposition of Cases: Magistrates' Courts, 1870–99

Years	Total	Discharged (%)	Dismissed (%)	Convicted (%)	Sent to Superior Courts (%)
1870–74	37,134	34.43	21.76	42.71	1.08
1875–79	75,739	29.00	21.54	48.40	1.03
1880–84	86,755	29.32	16.26	53.32	1.10
1885–89	83,817	24.46	18.40	56.00	1.12
1890–94	91,125	22.63	16.89	59.28	1.18
1895–99	102,265	22.52	14.43	62.31	0.71

Sources: Blue Books for 1870–99, in PRO, C.O. 300/81–110: Criminal Statistics.

Table A.9 Disposition of Cases: Superior Courts, 1871–1900

Years	Total	Convicted (%)	Acquitted (%)	Insane (%)	Nolle Prosequi (%)
1871–75	707	62.08	35.92	0.28	1.69
1876–80	678	64.60	26.99	0.56	7.81
1881–85	1074	56.61	25.13	0.55	17.69
1886–90	963	54.30	20.04	0.31	25.33
1891–95	1065	56.24	23.94	0.18	19.62
1896–1900	672	59.37	24.85	0.29	15.47

Sources: Blue Books for 1871–1900, in PRO, C.O. 300/82–111: Criminal Statistics.

Table A.10 Police Strength and Population Increase, 1848–1900

Year	Police Strength	Per 1,000 of Population	Population	Total Cases
1848	91	1.4	65,411	N.A.
1851	114	1.62	69,609	N.A.
1861	142	1.69	84,438	N.A.
1866	176	1.81	97,038	N.A.
1871	204	1.85	109,638	11,267
1883	405	2.42	162,508	17,468
1897	537	2.30	233,100	20,735
1900	574	2.25	255,148	19,399

Sources: Blue Books for 1848–1900, in PRO, C.O. 300/59–111: Police Statistics.

Table A.11 Location of Police, 1871

District	Police Strength	Population
Port-of-Spain	130	23,561
North Naparima	8	12,879
Tacarigua	14	12,472
South Naparima	2	10,433
Couva	9	10,233
St. Ann's	10	7,549
Diego Martin	5	7,283
San Fernando	42	5,006
Caroni	5	4,714
Arima	8	4,390
Cedros	5	4,241
Montserrat	1	3,388
Mayaro	3	1,915
Toco	2	1,278
Moruga	1	969
Total	245	110,311

Source: For population figures see Census of 1871 in PRO, C.O. 295/256 no. 113.

Table A.12 Distribution of Police Strength: Northern and Southern Divisions, 1883

Station	Dist. From Div. HQ (miles)	Strength
Northern Division		
Port-of-Spain	HQ	215
Mayaro	61	3
Toro	58	3
Blanchisseuse	35	1
Tunapuna	21.5	3
Chaguanas	18	5
Arima	16	9
Southern Division		
San Fernando	HQ	50
Cedros	34	4
Erin	28	3
Moruga	26	2
La Brea	16	2
Montserrat	13	4
Couva	12	9
Princess Town	9	11
Claxton Bay	7	4
Oropouche	7	3

Source: Freeling to Derby, 25 March 1884, PRO, C.O. 295/301 no. 65.

Table A.13 Nationality of Trinidad Police Force, 1895 (total strength = 537)

Country of Origin	No.	Country of Origin	No.
Africa	1	Jamaica	8
Antigua	1	Montserrat	1
Barbados	301	Nevis	4
British Guiana	4	St. Kitts	15
Dominica	1	St. Vincent	65
England	13	Sweden	1
Grenada	8	Tobago	45
Ireland	14	Trinidad	47

Source: Annual Report on the Police, 1895, in *T.C.P.* 30 of 1896.

Table A.14 Cases by Category, 1875–99 (%)

	1875–79	1880–84	1885–89	1890–94	1895–99
Total cases	75,739	86,755	83,817	91,125	102,269
Property	9.71	13.90	16.39	15.33	13.30
Labor and Social Economy	19.82	19.37	17.36	19.44	16.01
Person	26.39	27.81	26.43	23.45	18.61
Social Order	44.68	39.51	40.23	42.42	52.37

Sources: Blue Books for 1875–99, in PRO, C.O. 300/86–110: Criminal Statistics.

Table A.15 Convictions by Category, 1875–99 (%)

	1875–79	1880–84	1885–89	1890–94	1895–99
Total convictions	36,636	46,272	46,932	54,005	63,722
Property	7.45	10.05	11.86	10.47	9.03
Person	17.58	19.62	19.28	17.08	13.37
Labor and Social Economy	26.96	28.90	27.12	29.33	37.06
Social Order	47.95	41.40	41.71	43.08	40.51

Sources: See table A.14.

Table A.16 Committals by Category, 1875–99 (%)

	1875–79	1880–84	1885–89	1890–94	1895–99
Total committals	13,312	15,878	15,486	14,789	17,243
Property	12.35	20.28	23.61	24.63	19.48
Person	13.69	15.20	13.90	12.02	9.65
Labor and Social Economy	25.09	29.24	26.58	30.71	38.80
Social Order	48.85	35.26	35.89	32.61	32.05

Sources: See table A.14.

Table A.17 Property Offenses as Percent of Total Offenses, 1875–99

Years	Property-offense	Convictions	Committals
1875–79	9.30	8.11	10.43
1880–84	13.71	10.86	15.48
1885–89	17.38	12.89	18.53
1890–94	14.83	11.44	17.85
1895–99	13.07	9.57	15.01

Sources: See table A.14.

Table A.18 Property Offenses, 1875–99

	Total Property-offense Cases			Convictions			Committals		
Years	Total	Average Annual Rate	Per 1,000 of Population	Total	Average Annual Rate	Per 1,000 of Population	Total	Average Annual Rate	Per 1,000 of Population
1875–79	6,799	1,359	9.99	2,730	546	4.0	1,645	329	2.41
1880–84	11,555	2,311	14.62	4,652	930	5.92	3,221	644	4.07
1885–89	13,373	2,674	14.77	5,569	1,113	6.14	3,657	731	4.03
1890–94	13,244	2,648	12.83	5,655	1,131	5.51	3,644	728	3.53
1895–99	13,208	2,461	11.33	5,757	1,151	4.73	3,359	671	2.87

Sources: See table A.14.

Table A.19 Committals for Debt, 1838–99

Years	No.	Years	No.	Years	No.
1838–43	73	1870–74	541	1885–89	151
1848–52	1,193	1875–79	50	1890–94	186
1860–67	1,244	1880–84	100	1895–99	132

Note: During the Period 1838–69 the committals for debt were not always recorded every year.

Sources: Blue Books for 1838–99, in PRO, C.O. 300/50–110: Prison Statistics.

Table A.20 Praedial Larceny Offenses, 1875–99 (%)

Years	Disposition of Cases			Disposition of Convictions		
	Discharged	Dismissed	Convicted	Fine	Imprisonment	Whipped/Bound Over
1875–79	28.08	22.44	49.47	50.00	47.68	2.31
1880–84	27.40	14.43	58.15	44.40	54.85	3.77
1885–89	26.78	18.35	54.85	27.95	59.05	12.92
1890–94	23.37	24.78	51.93	12.34	67.37	20.27
1895–99	24.12	22.84	53.03	12.65	66.26	21.08

Sources: Blue Books for 1875–99, in PRO, C.O. 300/86–110: Criminal Statistics.

Table A.21 Prison Committals for Offenses against Property, 1875–99

Offense	1875–79	1880–84	1885–89	1890–94	1895–99
Burglary, breaking and entering	214	69	46	57	47
Larceny and theft	1,916	2,222	2,229	2,037	1,372
Praedial larceny	247	305	300	442	220
Robbery	4	15	23	30	17
Receiving stolen property	244	312	372	351	441
Unlawful entry	116	87	138	81	151
Trespass	164	266	252	269	289
Malicious injury to property	86	100	95	120	85
Arson	11	17	2	21	7
Fraud, embezzlement	34	59	67	58	84
Forgery	6	17	21	16	14
Counterfeiting and uttering	1	3	8	10	17
Obtaining money and goods under false pretenses	64	68	92	89	89

Sources: Annual Report on the Prisons: *T.C.P.* 45 of 1878, tables E; *T.C.P.* 53 of 1882, table E,F,G; *T.C.P.* 47 of 1886, table I,J,K; *T.C.P.* 55 of 1891, table H; T.C.P. 55 of 1896, table D; *T.C.P.* 33 of 1900, table D. For praedial larceny see Blue Books for 1875–99, in PRO, C.O. 300/86–110: Prison Statistics.

Table A.22 Offenses against the Person as Percent of All Offenses, 1870–99

Years	Total Offenses Against the Person	Percentage of All Offenses	Average Annual Rate
1870–74	18,109	—	3,622
1875–79	19,910	26.28	3,982
1880–84	24,119	27.80	4,824
1885–89	22,115	26.38	4,423
1890–94	21,271	23.34	4,254
1895–99	18,978	18.55	3,796

Sources: Blue Books for 1870–99, in PRO, C.O. 300/81–110: Criminal Statistics.

Table A.23 Offenses against the Person: Total Cases, Superior Courts, 1870–99

Offense	1870–74	1875–79	1880–84	1885–89[a]	1890–94	1895–99
Murder	51	27	44	42	27	44
Manslaughter	16	37	21	43	39	39
Attempted murder	3	4	2	9		2
Rape	17	17	26	56	50	40
Other offenses	202	246	349	263	410	234
Total offenses	289	331	442	413	533	359

[a]The figures for 1888 (Superior Courts) were not published and are not included.

Sources: Blue Books for 1870–99, in PRO, C.O. 300/81–110: Criminal Statistics.

Table A.24 Disposition of Offenses against the Person: Magistrates' Courts, 1875–99 (%)

	Discharged	Dismissed	Convicted	Sent to Superior Courts
1875–79	42.67	23.09	32.35	1.87
1880–84	38.58	21.92	37.66	1.82
1885–89	31.99	24.72	40.92	2.35
1890–94	30.76	22.92	43.40	2.90
1895–99	32.47	20.64	44.84	2.04

Sources: Blue Books for 1875–99, in PRO, C.O. 300/86–110: Criminal Statistics.

Table A.25 Disposition of Offenses against the Person: Superior Courts, 1875–99

	Total	Convictions (%)	Acquittals (%)	Fell Thru (%)	Judged Insane (%)
1875–79	327	70.64	24.15	4.58	0.61
1880–84	454	65.41	24.88	9.25	0.44
1885–89[a]	376	62.23	18.88	17.81	1.06
1890–94	551	62.25	22.68	14.51	0.54
1895–99	384	60.41	25.26	13.80	0.52

[a]The figures for 1888 were not published and are not included.

Sources: Blue Books for 1875–99, in PRO, C.O. 300/86–110: Criminal Statistics.

Table A.26 Disposition of Convictions for Offenses against the Person: Magistrates' Courts, 1875–99

	Total Convictions	Fined (%)	Imprisoned in Lieu of Fine (%)	Peremptorily Imprisoned (%)	Bound Over (%)
1875–79	6,441	55.82	8.92	19.37	15.86
1880–84	9,085	49.19	9.76	16.81	24.22
1885–89	9,050	49.76	11.84	11.94	26.44
1890–94	9,233	52.52	12.83	6.43	28.20
1895–99	8,524	45.81	13.57	5.95	34.65

Sources: Blue Books for 1875–99, in PRO, C.O. 300/86–110: Criminal Statistics.

Table A.27 Committals for Offenses with Weapons: Magistrates' Courts, 1875–99

Offense	1875–79	1880–84	1885–89	1890–94	1895–99
Armed to commit a felony	9	0	33	75	79
Discharging a fire-arm in the street	0	0	3	5	2
Possession of un-licensed firearm	0	0	3	9	11
Shooting with in-tent	0	2	6	13	3
Throwing missiles	38	104	159	92	88

Sources: See table A.21.

Table A.28 Population of Trinidad, 1844–1901

Census Year	Population	Density	Colony-born (%)	Immigrant Population (%)
1844	59,815	32	55.38	44.61
1851	68,600	37	58.18	41.81
1861	84,438	45	55.58	44.41
1871	109,638	59	55.85	44.14
1881	153,128	82	53.61	46.38
1891	200,028	107	55.78	44.21
1901	255,148	136	58.96	41.03

Sources: for 1844, *P.P. 1845,* 31:354; for 1851, *P.P. 1845–53,* 62:170; for 1861, Blue Book for 1861 in PRO, C.O. 300/72; for 1871, 27 June 1871, PRO, C.O. 295/257, no. 113; for 1881, Blue Book for 1881 in PRO, C.O. 300/92; for 1891, *T.C.P.* 59 of 1891; for 1901, Blue Book for 1901 in PRO, C.O. 300/113.

Table A.29 Population of Port-of-Spain by Sex and Age, 1861–81

	1861	Percent	1871	Percent	1881	Percent
			Sex			
Male	8,544	45.01	11,065	46.96	15,342	48.10
Female	10,436	54.98	12,496	53.03	16,534	51.89
			Age			
Under 20	8,011	42.20	9,304	39.48	12,588	39.51
20–40	7,032	37.04	9,442	40.07	12,871	40.40
40–60	2,798	14.74	3,696	15.68	4,885	15.53
Over 60	1,139	6.00	1,119	4.71	1,514	4.75
Total population	18,980		23,561		31,858	

Sources: Census of 1861: PRO, C.O. 300/72; Census of 1871: 27 June 1871, PRO, C.O. 295/256, no. 113; Census of 1881: *T.C.P.* 52 of 1881.

Table A.30 Committals for Crimes of Violence: Magistrates' Courts, 1875–99

	1875–79	1880–84	1885–89	1890–94	1895–99
Affray and riot	40	151	128	71	22
Assault and battery	1,382	1,793	1,786	1,463	1,372
Cutting and wounding	132	158	157	173	100
Disturbing the peace	224	338	427	0[a]	0[a]
Fighting	977	843	1,068	1,443	1,705
Riotous and disorderly conduct	528	429	218	308	301

[a]From 1890 the committals for disturbing the peace were included under fighting.
Sources: See table A.21.

Table A.31 Murders among East Indian Immigrants, 1872–1910

	Reported	Male Victims	Female Victims	No. of Wives Among Female Victims
1872–80	22	0	22	22
1881–89	45	18	27	24
1890–99	49	13	36	20
1901–10	62	42	20	10

Sources: Annual Report of the Protector of Immigrants: *T.C.P.* 68 of 1891, p. 5; *T.C.P.* 92 of 1893, p. 6; *T.C.P.* 175 of 1896, p. 5; *T.C.P.* 93 of 1900, p. 6; *T.C.P.* 143 of 1911, p. 5.

Table A.32 East Indian Population, 1891

	Male		Female		Total
Under 15	10,740		9,457		20,197
15–50	27,251		15,540		42,791
Over 50	4,914		2,316		7,230
Total	42,905	(61%)	27,313	(39%)	70,218

Source: Census of Trinidad, 1891, table 37 in PRO, C.O. 300 v. 102.

Table A.33 Offenses under the Immigration and Masters and Servants Ordinances, 1875–1917

	Total Cases			Convictions			Committals		
	Total Offenses	% of All Offenses	Annual Average	Total	% of All Convictions	Annual Average	Total	% of All Committals	Annual Average
1875–79	15,350	20.26	3,070	8,290	22.61	1,658	3,175	20.14	635
1880–84	16,789	19.35	3,357	11,483	24.82	2,296	4,425	21.24	885
1885–89	14,556	17.36	2,911	10,677	22.74	2,135	3,715	18.12	743
1890–94	17,773	19.50	3,554	12,772	23.64	2,554	4,196	20.55	839
1895–99	16,578	16.21	3,315	12,089	18.96	2,417	5,237	23.40	1047
1900–05/6	18,848	17.64	3,769	14,448	21.41	2,889	7,561	31.97	1512
1906/7–10/11	19,568	16.16	3,913	14,152	17.79	2,830	6,811	28.22	1362
1911/12–1917	15,062	10.66	3,012	10,958	12.04	2,191	4,852	20.65	970

Sources: Blue Books for 1875–1917, in PRO, C.O. 300/86–128.

Table A.34 Disposition of Offenses under the Immigration and Masters and Servants Ordinances, 1875–1906

	Total Cases			Convictions		
	Discharged	Dismissed	Convicted	Imprisoned	Fine	Bound Over
1875–79	27.39	18.59	54.00	38.29	38.96	22.73
1880–84	27.00	4.59	68.39	38.53	30.13	31.13
1885–89	21.96	4.68	73.35	34.79	25.93	39.27
1890–94	23.14	4.99	71.86	32.85	33.78	33.36
1895–99	22.69	4.37	72.92	42.32	33.86	22.81
1900–1905/06	19.71	3.62	76.65	52.33	24.30	23.42

Sources: Blue Books for 1875–1905/06 in PRO, C.O. 300/86–116: Criminal Statistics.

Table A.35 Committals under the Immigration Ordinances, 1870–99

Offense	1870–74	1875–79	1880–84	1885–89	1890–94	1895–99
Breach of contract and indenture	1,700	1,509	2,413	1,771	2,490	3,319
Immigrants without pass	1,550	912	1,713	1,442	1,477	1,627
Escaping estate hospital	0	34	91	69	0	0
Inciting immigrants to strike	0	4	31	31	0	0
Harboring immigrants	5	7	6	2	12	3
Miscellaneous/not specifically listed	727	709	171	400	217	289

Sources: For 1870, see *P.P. 1872,* 42:78–79; For 1871, see enclosure in no. 242, Rennie to Kimberley, 25 Nov. 1872, PRO, C.O. 295/264; For 1872, see enclosure in no. 77, Garcia to the Colonial Secretary, 20 April 1873, PRO, C.O. 295/267; For 1873–74, see *T.C.P.* 43 of 1875 p. 7; For 1875–99, see table A.21.

Table A.36 Committals for Some Labor-Related Offenses, 1870–99

Offense	1870–74	1875–79	1880–84	1885–89	1890–94	1895–99
Begging alms	23	22	107	88	58	51
Gambling	41	84	129	256	149	217
Squatting	24	10	1	3	11	24
Vagrancy	241	281	253	260	270	644
Social economy	—	166	218	402	347	1,455

Sources: For 1870–74, see sources in table A.35. For 1875–99, see sources in table A.21.

Table A.37 Disposition of Convictions for Social-Economy Offenses, 1875–99

Years	Total	Prison Committals (%)	Fines (%)	Bound Over (%)	As % of All Convictions
1875–79	1,592	10.42	63.50	26.06	4.34
1880–84	1,897	11.49	80.70	7.80	4.10
1885–89	2,059	19.52	62.84	17.62	4.38
1890–94	3,074	11.28	71.08	17.63	5.38
1895–99	11,528	12.62	71.51	15.85	18.08

Sources: Blue Books for 1875–99, in PRO, C.O. 300/86–110: Criminal Statistics.

Table A.38 Social-Order Offenses, 1875–99

	Convictions		Disposition of Convictions			Committals	
	Total	As % of All Convictions	Fine	Prison	Bound Over	Total	As % of All Committals
1875–79	17,582	47.95	47.25	36.98	15.75	6,503	48.85
1880–84	19,157	41.40	53.42	29.22	17.34	5,599	35.26
1885–89	19,577	41.70	53.85	28.28	17.74	5,559	35.89
1890–94	23,270	43.07	59.91	20.72	19.35	4,824	36.61
1895–99	25,824	40.51	56.80	21.40	21.79	5,527	32.05

Sources: Blue Books for 1875–99 in PRO, C.O. 300/86–110: Criminal Statistics.

Table A.39 Committals for Social-Order Offenses, 1875–99

	1875–79	1880–84	1885–89	1890–94	1895–99
Exposing person	52	39	49	16	—
Indecent behavior	122	91	77	159	245
Obscene and profane language	470	843	985	869	668
Drunk and disorderly	790	690	554	474	574
Riotous and disorderly conduct	528	429	218	308	301
Dancing to and beating drum	1	93	18	0	0
Disturbing divine worship	0	2	9	3	4
Obeah	6	7	14	4	8
Illegal assembly of convicted felons	0	0	86	0	0
Carnival regulations	0	0	0	38	65
Hosein regulations	0	0	3	5	0
Habitual and alien criminals	0	17	15	21	19
Procession ordinance	0	24	25	0	0
Incorrigible rogues	25	33	0	0	0
Gambling	84	129	256	149	217
Prostitution	0	49	32	23	11
Disturbing the peace	224	338	427	375	340
Obstructing street or wharf	488	301	163	103	42

Sources: See table A.21.

Notes

CHAPTER 1

1. For studies of the plantation see Vera Rubin, ed., *Plantation Systems of the New World;* George L. Beckford, *Persistent Poverty;* Jay R. Mandle, *The Plantation Economy;* Sidney W. Mintz, *Caribbean Transformations;* Egar T. Thompson, *Plantation Societies, Race Relations, and the South;* Franklin W. Knight, *The Caribbean.*

2. Scholarly concern with crime is not new, but it is only within recent times that historians have concerned themselves with the study of crime and its relationship to the structure of society. For an excellent review of criminological theory, see Ian Taylor, Paul Walton, and Jack Young, *The New Criminology,* and L. Radzinowicz, *Ideology and Crime.* For a bibliographical review of the historical study of crime, see Patricia O'Brien, "*Crime and Punishment as Historical Problems.*"

3. Elsa V. Goveia, *Slave Society in the British Leeward Islands at the End of the Eighteenth Century;* Orlando Patterson, *The Sociology of Slavery;* Edward Braithwaite, *The Development of Creole Society in Jamaica, 1770–1820;* Richard S. Dunn, *Sugar and Slaves;* Carl Bridenbaugh and Roberta Bridenbaugh, *No Peace Beyond the Line;* B. W. Higman, *Slave Population and Economy in Jamaica, 1807–1834;* Michael Craton, *Testing the Chains.*

4. The chief argument for the plural society is found in M.G. Smith, *The Plural Society in the British West Indies.*

5. Phillip D. Curtin, *Two Jamaicas;* Douglas Hall, *Free Jamaica, 1838–1865.*

6. Alan H. Adamson, *Sugar without Slaves.* For another interest-

ing view, see William A. Green, *British Slave Emancipation*. See also Walter Rodney, *A History of the Guyanese Working People, 1881–1905*.

7. Eric Williams, *History of the People of Trinidad and Tobago*, viii.

8. James Millette, *The Genesis of Crown Colony Government*. See also Linda A. Newson, *Aboriginal and Spanish Colonial Trinidad*.

9. Donald Wood, *Trinidad in Transition*, 39.

10. Bridget Brereton, *A History of Modern Trinidad, 1783–1962*.

11. Vidia S. Naipaul, *The Loss of El Dorado*.

12. Wood, *Trinidad in Transition*, 238.

13. Bridget Brereton, *Race Relations in Colonial Trinidad, 1870–1900*.

14. Wood, *Trinidad in Transition*, 301; Brereton, *Race Relations*, 1. The term *colored* refers to light-complexioned individuals of mixed European and African descent.

15. Brereton, *Race Relations*, 125, 211.

16. Wood, *Trinidad in Transition*, 299.

17. Chandra Jayawardena, *Conflict and Solidarity in a Guianese Plantation*.

18. R. Brana-Shute and G. Brana-Shute, *Crime and Punishment in the Caribbean*.

19. David J. Dodd, "The Well-Springs of Violence: Some Historical Notes on East Indian Criminality in Guyana"; David J. Dodd and Michael Parris, "An Urban Plantation: Socio-cultural Aspects of Crime and Delinquency in Georgetown, Guyana"; David J. Dodd, "The Role of Law in Plantation Society: Reflections on the Development of a Caribbean Legal System."

20. For example, J.J. Tobias, *Crime and Industrial Society in the Nineteenth Century;* Howard Zehr, *Crime and the Development of Modern Society;* Eric H. Monkkonen, *The Dangerous Class*. For interesting studies of the preindustrial period in England, see Douglas Hay et al., *Albion's Fatal Tree;* Joel Samaha, *Law and Order in Historical Perspective;* and J.B. Given, *Society and Homicide in Thirteenth-Century England*.

21. For example, V.A.C. Gatrell and T.B. Hadden, "Criminal Statistics and Their Interpretation."

22. For example, U.R.Q. Henriques, "The Rise and Decline of the Separate System of Prison Discipline"; Robert D. Storch, "The Policeman as Domestic Missionary"; David Phillips, *Crime and Authority in Victorian England*. Of interest also was Michel Foucault, *Discipline and Punish*, and Michael Ignatieff, *A Just Measure of Pain*.

23. Marshall B. Clinard and Daniel J. Abbott, *Crime in Developing Countries;* W. Clifford, *An Introduction to African Criminology;* A.A.

Yang, "The Agrarian Origins of Crime." See also Colin Summer, ed., *Crime, Justice, and Underdevelopment,* for interesting studies of crime in colonial areas.

24. For an intelligent defense of the unique nature of colonialism in the Caribbean, see Mintz, *Caribbean Transformations.*

25. For example, Y.B. Mathur, "Jail Administration in the Punjab, 1849–1875"; Robert B. Seidman, "The Ghana Prison System"; T. N. Tamuno, *The Police in Modern Nigeria, 1861–1965;* Galen Broeker, *Rural Disorder and Police Reform in Ireland, 1812–1836.*

26. For a critique of contemporary criminological theory and its development, see Taylor, Walton, and Young, *The New Criminology.* See also Richard Quinney, *Class, State, and Crime.*

27. Public Record Office, London, Colonial Office records (hereafter cited as PRO, C.O.) 295/267, no. 77 and enclosures, Gov. Rennie to Sec. of State Kimberley, 26 April 1873.

28. Blue Book for 1872, in PRO, C.O. 300/83.

29. Trinidad Council Paper (hereafter cited as *T.C.P.*) 22 of 1872, Royal Commonwealth Society Library, London.

CHAPTER 2

1. The islands of Trinidad and Tobago comprise the contemporary political state called Trinidad-Tobago. The island of Tobago was linked administratively to Trinidad in 1898. But this study refers only to the island of Trinidad. For a comprehensive description of Trinidad in the nineteenth century, see L.A.A. De Verteuil, *Trinidad.*

2. See 4 June 1866, PRO, C.O. 295/235, no. 67; and José M. Bodu, *Trinidadiana,* 73.

3. For the problems of communication and road transport in the nineteenth century, see Charles Kingsley, *At Last, a Christmas in the West Indies;* PRO, 7 December 1878, PRO, C.O. 295/282, no. 255; and J.N. Brierley, *Trinidad;* esp. 179–82.

4. On this early period of transformation in Trinidad, see Jean F. Dauxion-Lavaysee, *A Description of Venezuela, Trinidad, Margarita, and Tobago;* Eric E. Williams, *History of the People of Trinidad and Tobago;* James Millette, *The Genesis of Crown Colony Government;* and Linda A. Newson, *Aboriginal and Spanish Colonial Trinidad.* For the sugar revolution in the Caribbean see J.H. Parry and P. Sherlock, *A Short History of the West Indies;* Richard Sheridan, *The Development of*

the Plantations to 1750; Richard S. Dunn, *Sugar and Slaves;* and Franklin W. Knight, *The Caribbean,* 67–92.

5. On the condition of the sugar industry in the nineteenth century, see W.G. Sewell, *The Ordeal of Free Labour in the British West Indies,* and report of the West India Royal Commission, in *Parliamentary Papers* (hereafter cited as *P.P.*), *1898,* vol. 50, esp. pp. 40–45. For secondary treatments see R. W. Beachey, *The British West Indian Sugar Industry in the Late Nineteenth Century;* William A. Green, *British Slave Emancipation;* Walter Rodney, *A History of the Guyanese Working People, 1881–1905.*

6. See statistical abstracts in *P.P. 1890,* 78:90–91; on the development of cocoa in Trinidad, see C.Y. Shepherd, "Economic Survey of the Cocoa Industry of Trinidad, British West Indies."

7. On the introduction of Crown Colony rule, see Millette, *Genesis of Crown Colony Government.*

8. See Donald Wood, *Trinidad in Transition,* especially chapters 4–8, and K. O. Laurence, *Immigration Into the West Indies in the Nineteenth Century.*

9. Anthony Trollope, *The West Indies and the Spanish Main,* 229, and Wood, *Trinidad in Transition,* especially chapters 9–12.

10. F.W. Knight, *The Caribbean,* 115–17.

11. E.J. Hobsbawm, *Industry and Empire.*

12. See V.G. Kiernan, *The Lords of Human Kind.*

13. See census figures cited in Millette, *Genesis,* tables 2, 7, and 9.

14. For the census of 1821, see Eric Williams, ed., *Documents on British West Indian History,* 1807–1833, 382.

15. Ibid.

16. There is little published work on the free coloreds in Trinidad. See Millette, *Genesis,* for the slave period; for the postemancipation period, see Bridget Brereton, *Race Relations in Colonial Trinidad, 1870–1900.* For their counterparts in other territories, see David Cohen and J. Greene, *Neither Slave nor Free.*

17. On the slave trade to Trinidad, see Phillip D. Curtin, *The Atlantic Slave Trade.* See also Eric Williams, "The British West Indian Slave Trade after 1807," and D. Eltis, "The Traffic in Slaves between the British West Indian Colonies, 1807–1833."

18. See K.O. Laurence, "The Settlement of Free Negroes in Trinidad before Emancipation," and Carl Campbell, "Jonas Mohammed Bath and the Free Mandingoes in Trinidad."

19. For the census of 1813 and the supporting figures, see B. Higman, "African and Creole Slave Family Patterns in Trinidad." For the ethnic profiles of the earlier period see Curtin, *The Atlantic Slave Trade.*

20. See J.U.J. Asiegbu, *Slavery and the Politics of Liberation, 1787–1861.*

21. See M. Warner, "Africans in Nineteenth Century Trinidad," and D.V. Trotman, "The Yoruba and Orisha Worship in Trinidad and British Guiana." For Jamaica, see Monica Schuller, *"Alas, Alas, Kongo."*

22. For an intriguing discussion of this, see Sidney W. Mintz and Richard Price, *An Anthropological Approach to the Afro-American Past.*

23. See Melvin J. Herskovitts and Francis S. Herskovitts, *Trinidad Village.*

24. *Port-of-Spain Gazette,* Saturday, 13 December 1856.

25. 27 October 1884, PRO, C.O. 295/303, no. 263.

26. J.R. Mandle, *The Plantation Economy,* 12.

27. See H.A. Will, *Constitutional Change in the British West Indies, 1880–1903,* 154, and Williams, *History,* 120.

28. Will, *Constitutional Change,* 153.

29. 17 September 1887, PRO, C.O. 295/315, no. 254 with enclosures.

30. See Williams, *History,* 120, and Howard Johnson, "Immigration and the Sugar Industry in Trinidad during the Last Quarter of the Nineteenth Century."

31. Mandle, *The Plantation Economy,* 10.

32. The cost of indentured immigration was financed partly from the general revenue and partly from taxes paid by the planters. Before the abolition of income taxes in 1873, general revenue funds contributed one-third of the cost of immigration. Between 1873 and 1888, three-tenths of the cost came from general revenues. Beginning in 1888, in the midst of the sugar crisis, public funds again paid for one-third. The planter's share was derived from a combination of indenture fees and the revenue from special export taxes voted annually on sugar and other agricultural products. The whole society was forced to pay a significant amount for a system of labor that benefited the sugar planters and a few big cocoa planters.

33. On the limitations of a conflict-of-interests model for dealing with all aspects of criminal law see W.G. Carson, "The Sociology of Crime and the Emergence of Criminal Laws," in P. Rock and M. McIntosh, *Deviance and Social Control,* 67–90.

CHAPTER 3

1. See James Millette, *The Genesis of Crown Colony Government;* Eric Williams, *History of the People of Trinidad and Tobago;* and Donald Wood, *Trinidad in Transition.*

2. A.C. Carmichael, *Domestic Manners and Social Conditions of the White, Coloured, and Negro Population of the West Indies,* 2:334–35.

3. Governor Smith to Goderich, PRO, C.O. 295/87, 13 July 1831, extracted in Eric Williams, ed., *Documents on British West Indian History,* 1807–1833, 190.

4. Elgin to Stanley, 5 August 1845, PRO, C.O. 137/284. See extracts in K. N. Bell and W. P. Morell, eds., *Select Documents on British Colonial Policy, 1830–1860,* 426.

5. 27 October 1884, PRO, C.O. 295/303, no. 263.

6. Wood, *Trinidad in Transition,* 46.

7. W.H. Burnley, *Observations on the Present Condition of the Island of Trinidad,* 83.

8. Blue Books for 1839–53 in PRO, C.O. 300.

9. For population figures for 1838 see PRO, C.O. 295/125 no. 19; for 1844 see House of Commons Paper no. 426 of 1845, p. 26; for 1851 see census figures in *P.P. 1852–53,* 62:166.

10. Stipendiary magistrates reports in *P.P. 1842,* 29:396–411.

11. Frantz Fanon, *The Wretched of the Earth.*

12. *Port-of-Spain Gazette,* April-October 1839.

13. Ibid.

14. See, for example *P.P. 1842,* 29:407–9.

15. *P.P. 1846,* 30:669; and Wood, *Trinidad in Transition,* 91–93.

16. Carmichael, *Domestic Manners,* 184–85.

17. *P.P. 1842,* 29:379, and W. G. Sewell, *The Ordeal of Free Labour in the British West Indies,* 113–14.

18. L.A.A. De Verteuil, *Trinidad,* 44–45.

19. Ibid., 29.

20. Wood, *Trinidad in Transition,* 48.

21. Burnley, *Observations,* 65.

22. The entire report, entitled "Minutes of Evidence Taken by the Sub-Committee of the Agricultural and Immigration Society," was reprinted in *P.P. 1842,* vol. 29: "Papers Relative to the Affairs of Trinidad."

23. Maxwell quoted in Burnley, *Observations,* 53, 51.

24. *P.P. 1842,* 29:397. (*Magass* or *bagasse* is the remainder of the cane after the juice had been extracted from it.)

25. Burnley, *Observations,* 65.

26. Wood, *Trinidad in Transition,* 54.

27. Burnley, *Observations,* 99.

28. On James Stephen see Paul Knaplund, *James Stephen and the British Colonial System, 1813–1847.*

29. During the period of slavery the free coloreds performed the police office of Alguacil, which the British had inherited from the Spaniards. See Wood, *Trinidad in Transition,* 41. At the end of apprenticeship in 1838, the stipendiary magistrates and their police no longer had any authority. There was, therefore, an especially urgent need to set up a police force, especially for the rural areas. See *P.P. 1839,* 36:552–54.

30. Knaplund, *James Stephen,* 123.

31. See "Acts Passed by Colonial Legislatures of Councils—Disallowed by the Colonial Secretary of State," *P.P. 1847–48,* 45:488–96.

32. On immigration in general, see K.O. Laurence, *Immigration into the West Indies in the Nineteenth Century.* See also Burnley, *Observations,* 176, and "Return of Immigrants and Liberated Africans 1843–1861," *P.P. 1862,* 36:418.

33. On African immigration, see J.U.J. Asiegbu, *Slavery and the Politics of Liberation, 1787–1861;* Laurence, *Immigration,* 13–16; G.W. Roberts, "Immigration of Africans into the British Caribbean"; Wood, *Trinidad in Transition,* 63–80; Monica Schuler, "*Alas, Alas, Kongo.*"

34. See Wood, *Trinidad in Transition,* 81–106.

35. Ibid., 107–67.

36. Report with the Blue Book for 1846, in *P.P. 1847,* 37:352.

37. Enclosure in no. 2, *P.P. 1847,* 39:222.

38. For the crises see *P.P. 1847,* vol. 46: "Correspondence Relative to Distress in the Sugar Growing Colonies."

39. This is merely a suggestion, which is supported with concrete evidence for the period 1870–1900 in later chapters.

40. Governor's message to the Legislative Council, 2 September 1850, PRO, C.O. 295/171, no. 206; see also Harris to Grey, 19 July 1848, in *P.P. 1849,* 37:576.

41. *P.P. 1847,* 39:127–29. Ordinance 13 of 1841, which regulated the granting of licenses for rum and other spiritous liquors, also restricted the issuing of rum by unlicensed persons. See also *P.P. 1842,* 29:408.

42. See *P.P. 1852–53,* 67:401–9.

43. See De Verteuil, *Trinidad,* 21, 199.

44. Ibid., 24.

45. Ibid., 198.

46. This aspect is developed in chapter seven.

47. Governor Harris's report on the Blue Book, *P.P. 1849,* 34:298.

CHAPTER 4

1. Elliot to Labouchere, 4 October 1856, PRO, C.O. 295/192, no. 85.

2. Report with Blue Book of 1879, in PRO, C.O. 295/288, no. 263.

3. See, for example, W. A. Bonger, *Criminality and Economic Conditions*.

4. *Port-of-Spain Gazette,* 8 December 1895, cited in PRO, C.O. 295/361, no. 15.

5. Report of the inspector of prisons, 1873, p. 2, in *T.C.P.* 42 of 1874.

6. Ibid., p. 3.

7. The increased use of fines as a substitute for imprisonment developed in a number of European countries during the nineteenth century. See G. Rusche and Otto Kircheimer, *Punishment and Social Structure,* 166–76.

8. The figures for the period 1870–74 do not include the years 1870 and 1873, since these are not available. The total cases for the period should be nearer 59,483 if we use approximate averages for the missing years. Convictions were approximately 46.53 percent, and the combined number of acquittals, that is, both discharged and dismissed, was approximately 31,268 or 53.46 percent.

9. Attorney general's report to the colonial secretary on the criminal statistics for 1877, 30 November 1878, PRO, C.O. 295/284, no. 148.

10. Attorney general's report on criminal statistics for 1883, in Bushe to Derby, 5 April 1884, PRO, C.O. 295/302, no. 77.

11. L.A.A. De Verteuil, *Trinidad,* 222.

12. 30 November 1879, PRO, C.O. 295/284, no. 148.

13. Colonial Office minute, PRO, C.O. 295/266, no. 37, pp. 269–75.

14. Enclosed in no. 37, Judge Fitzgerald to Gov. Longden, ibid.

15. Garcia to the colonial secretary, 26 February 1873, ibid.

16. Report with Blue Book for 1871, in *P.P. 1873,* 48:91.

17. Broome to Ripon, 30 May 1894, PRO, C.O. 295/353, no. 205.

18. The duties of the solicitor general were to attend and prosecute indictments in the Second Court and at the assizes in Port-of-Spain while the attorney general was engaged in the more important cases before the chief justice. The solicitor general also attended and prosecuted for the Crown in the assizes at the Supreme Court held at

San Fernando. See Longden to Kimberley, 7 January 1871, PRO, C.O. 295/225, no. 5.

19. Private and confidential, Longden to Kimberley, 7 January 1871, PRO, C.O. 295/255. For an overly sympathetic view of M.M. Philip, see C.L.R. James, "Michael Maxwell Philip: 1829–1888," in the *Beacon* 1, no. 6 (September 1931), reprinted in Reinhard W. Sander, ed., *From Trinidad,* 253–69.

20. Irving to Carnarvon, 21 February 1876, PRO, C.O. 295/276, no. 34 with enclosures. For Charles Warner's career, see Wood, *Trinidad in Transition.*

21. See Bridget Brereton, "The Development of an Identity."

22. See *T.C.P.* 21 and 22 of 1896.

23. See *Hansard Legislative Debates,* 4th series, 5 October 1903, pp. 171–76.

24. The stipendiary magistrates adjudicated in the minor courts, and their jurisdiction was limited to fines not exceeding ten pounds sterling and to imprisonment with or without hard labor not exceeding three months. See De Verteuil, *Trinidad,* 222.

25. *Trinidad Chronicle,* 21 February 1865.

26. Broome to Ripon, 4 September 1893, PRO, C.O. 295/347, no. 312.

27. Irving to Hicks-Beach, confidential, 9 July 1879, PRO, C.O. 295/284.

28. 15 May 1894, PRO, C.O. 295/353, no. 175. Many of the petitioners may have been cocoa farmers who depended on the West Indian immigrant labor force.

29. Quoted in J.J. Thomas, *Froudacity,* 99.

30. Lt. Gov. Rennie to Kimberely, 3 February 1873, PRO, C.O. 295/266, no. 24; Thomas, *Froudacity,* 108.

31. Acting Gov. Fowler to Knutsford, 16 July 1889, PRO, C.O. 295/323, no. 251.

32. Havelock to Derby, 8 July 1885, PRO, C.O. 295/306, no. 190; Robinson to Knutsford, 26 March 1889, PRO, C.O. 295/321, no. 93.

33. Freeling to Kimberley, 5 February 1881, PRO, C.O. 295/289, no. 41.

34. Confidential, MacLeod to Stanley, 2 February 1845, PRO, C.O. 295/146.

35. Harris to Grey, 19 June 1848, in P.P. 1847–48, 46:645.

36. W. H. Gamble, *Trinidad,* 20.

37. Colonial Office memo, 25 October 1884, PRO, C.O. 295/303, no. 258.

38. See, for example, reports on the Chapman case in the *San Fernando Gazette,* 29 March 1879.

39. *Port-of-Spain Gazette,* Saturday, 3 September 1881.

40. Longden to Kimberley. 19 May 1871, PRO, C.O. 295/256, no. 90. *Obeah* is a religiomagical complex of African origin.

41. Letter in *New Era,* 1 March 1880, enclosed in Irving to Hicks-Beach, 23 April 1880, PRO, C.O. 295/286, no. 90.

42. See letter from Captain Baker enclosed in Robinson to Holland, 7 December 1887, in PRO, C.O. 295/315, no. 257.

43. Broome to Knutsford, 9 July 1892, PRO, C.O. 295/339, no. 200 and enclosures. For an unsympathetic view of Chief Justice Gorrie, see James, "Michael Maxwell Philip," in Sander, *From Trinidad;* for another assessment of Gorrie, see Bridget Brereton, "Sir John Gorrie."

44. See, for example, complaints reported in the *Trinidadian,* 8 April 1852. The question of language and the law for East Indians was so problematic that Chief Justice Gorrie made it a rule never to take a plea of guilty in "a case of murder from an Indian who did not know our language, or our system of law, and in whose own language there was no word which expresses the difference as we understand it between murder and manslaughter." See PRO, C.O. 295/315, no. 301.

45. Garcia to the colonial secretary, 26 February 1973, PRO, 295/266, enclosure in no. 37.

46. See *The Trial of N. W. Brunton,* enclosed in confidential report, Longden to Kimberely, 8 May 1871, PRO, C.O. 295/256.

47. See V.A.C. Gatrell and T.B. Hadden, "Criminal Statistics and Their Interpretation," 336 ff.

48. Donald Wood, *Trinidad in Transition,* 182–89. See also H. A. Alcazar, "The Evolution of English Law in Trinidad."

49. Bushe to Kimberley, 1 October 1974, PRO, C.O. 295/273, no. 201.

50. Des Voeux to Carnarvon, 24 July 1877, PRO, C.O. 295/278, no. 125 and enclosure.

51. Of the 130 men assigned to Port-of-Spain in 1871, at least 56 were not available for active police duties. Insp. comm. of police to the colonial secretary, 8 August 1877, in PRO, C.O. 295/279, enclosure in no. 167.

52. Kortright to Buckingham, 24 October 1868, PRO, C.O. 295/245, no. 173.

53. Gordon to Granville, 24 June 1868, PRO, C.O. 295/244, no. 95.

54. Gamble, *Trinidad,* 20.

55. 8 November 1881, PRO, C.O. 295/291, no. 308: Ordinance 16 of 1880, calling for the appointment of additional constables.

56. See C.W. Lovesy quoted in Longden to Kimberley, 23 October 1873, PRO, C.O. 295/270, no. 216.

57. Robinson to Knutsford, 8 February 1889, PRO, C.O. 295/321, no. 42. In fact, Baker's earlier career is shrouded in mystery. When he was appointed to act for Fraser in 1876, he was listed as having previously been inspector general of the Gold Coast constabulary, but there was doubt as to whether he had actually had any connection with Hausa police. See Irving to Carnarvon, confidential, 9 July 1876, PRO, C.O. 295/277.

58. Confidential, 19 February 1889, PRO, C.O. 295/321.

59. Longden to Kimberley, 7 February 1874, PRO, C.O. 295/272, no. 41.

60. Sir Charles Jefferies, *The Colonial Police* (London, 1952), 30–31, quoted in Galen Broeker, *Rural Disorder,* 242.

61. Quoted in J.N. Brierley, *Trinidad: Then and Now,* 117.

62. Irving to Carnarvon, confidential, 9 July 1876, PRO, C.O. 295/277.

63. Harris to Grey, 19 July 1848, in *P.P. 1849,* 37:176.

64. *T.C.P.* 16 of 1893, in PRO, C.O. 295/344.

65. *P.P. 1849,* 37:576.

66. Letter signed "Shikaree" in *Trinidad Chronicle,* 24 November 1865.

67. Robinson to Knutsford, 24 May 1890, PRO, C.O. 295/328, no. 137.

68. Robinson to Knutsford, 13 April 1889, PRO, C.O. 295/322, no. 146.

69. *Committals for Assaulting or Resisting Police*

1872–76	224	1887–91	98
1877–81	173	1892–96	156
1882–86	122	1897–1901	162

Source: Extracted from annual reports of the inspector of prisons published in *T.C.P.*, 1872–1901.

70. 29 November 1881, PRO, C.O. 295/291, no. 333.

71. *T.C.P.* 16 of 1893; police report for 1892 in PRO, C.O. 295/344.

72. Gordon to Granville, 24 June 1868, PRO, C.O. 295/244, no. 95 and enclosure.

73. *Trinidad Palladium,* Saturday, 19 November 1881.

74. 8 December, 1888, Robinson to Knutsford, confidential, PRO, C.O. 295/319, and Robinson to Knutsford, 8 February 1889, PRO, C.O. 295/321, no. 42; *Trinidad Palladium,* Saturday, 10 December 1881; Harris to Grey, 19 July 1848, in *P.P. 1849,* 37:576.

75. Broome to Ripon, 2 December 1892, PRO, C.O. 295/341, no. 325.

76. Robinson to Holland, 28 October 1887, PRO, C.O. 295/315, no. 297. Chief Justice Gorrie, who had considerable experience with the police force in Mauritius and their treatment of East Indians, made this sweeping but justified condemnation about perjury in the Trinidad police force.

77. Freeling to Kimberley, 8 November 1881, PRO, C.O. 295/291, no. 308.

78. Freeling to Kimberley, 25 June 1881, PRO, C.O. 295/290, no. 175; Robinson to Granville, PRO, C.O. 295/311, no. 284; PRO, C.O. 295/312, 806; Bushe to Derby, 22 August 1884, PRO, C.O. 295/303, no. 201 with enclosure.

79. Supplement to the *Port-of-Spain Gazette,* 18 June 1881.

CHAPTER 5

1. R.W. Beachey, *The British West Indian Sugar Industry in the Late Nineteenth Century,* 40–60.

2. Hugh Tinker, *A New Kind of Slavery,* 32, 185–86; Gov. Havelock to Earl of Derby, 6 May 1885, PRO, C.O. 295/306, no. 121.

3. December 1895, PRO, C.O. 295/361, no. 15; *T.C.P.* 248 of 1894.

4. Gov. Knolly to Chamberlain, 11 May 1898, private, PRO, C.O. 295/386.

5. *P.P. 1898,* 5:41; the motion was made by Mr. Agostini and seconded by Mr. Finlayson and passed at a meeting of the Legislative Council on 1 December 1881, but was disapproved by the Colonial Office—see 9 December 1891, PRO, C.O. 295/292, no. 345.

6. During the governorship of Sir Henry Irving (1874–80), the sugar planters did not object to the program of public works. But during the crisis they objected to the development of the railway at a cost of £60,000. Yet they benefited directly from railway expansion, which linked the sugar estates on the western seaboard and provided a land route to the wharves at Port-of-Spain as an alternative to the plunder-prone sea route. With typical shortsightedness, they com-

plained that the higher wages paid on railway construction attracted labor from the estates. See Governor Robinson's reply to the West India Committee on the State of Affairs in Trinidad: 21 July 1890, PRO, C.O. 295/329, no. 217.

7. For the earlier restrictive land policy see *P.P. 1846,* 30:669, and Brian W. Blouet, "Land Policies in Trinidad, 1838–1850." See also Donald Wood, *Trinidad in Transition,* 91–97, 271–72.

8. See immigration report for 1874–75 in *T.C.P.* 16 of 1876, p. 4; and Gov. Havelock to Earl of Derby, 6 May 1885, PRO, C.O. 295/306, no. 121.

9. Gov. Havelock to Earl of Derby, 16 April 1885, PRO, C.O. 295/306, no. 93.

10. PRO, C.O. 295/313, no. 64; *T.C.P.* 27 of 1887 in 20 April 1887, PRO, C.O. 295/313, no. 64.

11. Gov. Havelock to Earl of Derby, 16 April 1885, PRO, C.O. 295/306, no. 93.

12. PRO, C.O. 295/313, no. 64; see *T.C.P.* 27 of 1887 in 20 April 1887, PRO, C.O. 295/313, no. 64.

13. Gov. Robinson to Knutsford, 17 March 1890, PRO, C.O. 295/327, no. 72.

14. Ibid.

15. *P.P. 1898,* 50:741; J.H. Collens, *A Guide to Trinidad,* 49.

16. Gov. Young to Kimberley, 26, October 1880, PRO, C.O. 295/288, no. 273; *T.C.P.* 47 of 1891, p. 3; on the savings bank during slavery see Henry Nelson Coleridge, *Six Months in the West Indies in 1825,* 94–98.

17. On the communal savings system, see W. R. Bascom, "The Esusu," on West Africa; and see Melvin J. Herskovitts and Frances S. Herskovitts, Trinidad Village on Trinidad. The Indians apparently used a similar system; see Tinker, *A New Kind of Slavery,* 214.

18. Wood, *Trinidad in Transition,* 242. The inspector general of immigrants also reported that the Yoruba in Trinidad were known to be "guided, in a marked degree, by the sense of association; and the principle of combination for the common weal has been fully sustained wherever they have settled in many numbers" (L.A.A. De Verteuil, *Trinidad,* 175).

19. Basil Matthews, *Crisis of the West Indian Family,* 98, claims that Bishop Richard Smith introduced the Friendly Society movement to Trinidad "on the morrow of emancipation," that is, on his appointment as apostolic missionary in 1828. But A.F. Wells and D. Wells report in *Friendly Societies in the West Indies* the existence of Friendly Societies during the slave period in other West Indian islands. It is

reasonable to believe that—given the existence of similar institutions in West Africa—a parallel institution developed among the slaves in Trinidad before Bishop Smith's time, both among the Creole transfers from other islands and among the Africans imported directly from Africa. The existence of groups, albeit labeled dancing societies, that were responsible for the organization and planning of the attempted insurrection of 1805 reveals a level of organization that could have permitted the earlier development of mutual-aid societies. At any rate, in 1841 Bishop Smith reported the existence of "twenty [societies] now established amongst the different trades and laborers, comprising 2800 members, most of whom are heads of families, who pay from 5*d.* to 1*s.* 8*d.* sterling per month, amounting in the aggregate to 1,750 pounds sterling per annum, from which fund they receive when sick, subsistence, medicine, and occasional medical attendance; and funeral expenses in case of death" (W.H. Burnley, *Observations on the Present Condition of the Island of Trinidad,* 98). On the role of these societies in other parts of the African diaspora see A.J.R. Russell-Wood, "Black and Mulattoo Brotherhoods in Colonial Brazil."

20. *Trinidad Reviewer, 1900,* 274–75; see also the Blue Book for 1900 in PRO, C.O. 300/111.

21. Blue Books for 1895 and 1900, in PRO, C.O. 300/106 and 111.

22. Ordinance 18 of 1888—To Regulate and Provide for the Registration of Friendly Societies.

23. *T.C.P.* 47 of 1891, p. 8; *T.C.P.* 108 of 1896, p. 9; *T.C.P.* 96 of 1910, p. 9.

24. Blue Books for 1895 and 1900, in PRO, C.O. 300/106 and 111.

25. *T.C.P.* 6 of 1890, p. 9.

26. Enclosure by receiver-general, Robinson to Stanley, 14 January 1886, PRO, C.O. 295/310, no. 13.

27. Freeling to Derby, 26 July 1883, PRO, C.O. 295/297, no. 157 pp. 458–82, ten years later a magistrate in charge of a savings bank embezzled £4,000 and absconded. *See P.P. 1895,* 60:599–600.

28. Tinker, *A New Kind of Slavery,* 174–76.

29. Wood, *Trinidad in Transition,* 157–58.

30. *Port-of-Spain Gazette,* Saturday, January 18, 1879.

31. Report of the inspector of prisons, 1873, p.2., in *T.C.P.* 42 of 1874.

32. Charles Kingsley, *At Last, A Christmas in the West Indies,* 71.

33. Fowler to Ripon, 20 July 1893, PRO, C.O. 295/347, no. 248.

34. Manners-Sutton to Cardwell, 8 July 1865, PRO, C.O. 295/231, no. 94 and enclosures.

35. Havelock to Derby, 15 April 1885, PRO, C.O. 295/306, no. 92 and enclosures.

36. Jermingham to Chamberlain, 10 March 1898, PRO, C.O. 295/385, no. 90.

37. On the development of the peasantry in Barbados, see W.K. Marshall, "The Establishment of a Peasantry in Barbados, 1840–1920."

38. Report to governor, 18 March 1870, PRO, C.O. 295/251, enclosure in no. 116.

39. Inspector-commandant of police to governor's private secretary, 4 May 1871, enclosed in Longden to Kimberley, confidential, 9 May 1871, PRO, C.O. 295/256.

40. Gordon to Granville, 24 June 1868, PRO, C.O. 295/244, enclosure in no. 95.

41. See J. Davy, *The West Indies before and after Slave Emancipation,* 525, and José M. Bodu, *Trinidadiana,* 44.

42. *Port-of-Spain Gazette,* 27 September 1879.

43. *Trinidad Palladium,* 29 October 1881.

44. Inspector-commandant of police to governor's private secretary, confidential, 4 May 1871, PRO, C.O. 295/256.

45. *Port-of-Spain Gazette,* 27 January 1877; Rushe to Carnarvon, 24 January 1877, PRO, C.O. 295/278, no. 11.

46. Rushe to Carnarvon, 24 January 1877, PRO, C.O. 295/278, no. 11. C.O. minute, p. 43, ibid.

47. On social banditry see E.J. Hobsbawm, *Primitive Rebels* and *Bandits.*

48. Havelock to Earl of Derby, 12 May 1885, PRO, C.O. 295/306, no. 126.

49. Gordon to Granville, 25 January 1870, PRO, 295/250, no. 8 and enclosures.

50. *T.C.P.* 12 of 1892.

51. Walker to Newcastle, 22 February 1860, PRO, C.O. 295/208, no. 31.

52. Bushe to Derby, 17 June 1884, PRO, C.O. 295/302, no. 145.

53. Robinson to Holland, 17 March 1887, PRO, C.O. 295/313, no. 66.

54. Acting governor to Carnarvon, 25 January 1878, PRO, C.O. 295/280, no. 18 with enclosures.

55. Ibid.

56. See Wood, *Trinidad in Transition,* 291–94.

57. Irving to secretary of state, confidential, 25 September 1878, PRO, C.O. 295/281.

58. Ibid.

CHAPTER 6

1. Report on criminal statistics for 1877, PRO, C.O. 295/284, no. 148 and enclosures.

2. P.P. 1893–94, 70:389; Blue Book for 1892 in PRO, C.O. 300/103.

3. For secondary literature on the relationship between violence and social and political structures see Frantz Fanon, *The Wretched of the Earth;* Hannah Arendt, *On Violence;* Rollo May, *Power and Innocence;* Fredric Wertham, *A Sign for Cain.*

4. *Trinidad Chronicle,* 17 March 1865.

5. Longden to Kimberley, 22 February 1872, PRO, C.O. 295/260, no. 34 and enclosures. See Robinson to Holland, July 1887, PRO, C.O. 295/314, no. 122 and enclosures, for Chief Justice Gorries' comments on medical men and their evidence before the courts.

6. 18 May 1899, PRO, C.O. 295/392, no. 183 and enclosures.

7. Report on immigration, February 1870, PRO, C.O. 295/250, p. 441.

8. Longden to Kimberley, 3 January 1871, PRO, C.O. 295/255, no. 1 with enclosures.

9. *T.C.P.* 143 of 1911, p. 5.

10. For example, Irving to Hicks-Beach, 23 June 1880, PRO, C.O. 295/286, no. 25, reports the case of Benjamin Joseph, a black executed for the murder of a male Indian during a robbery. Donald Wood makes a similar argument for the period 1838–69, *Trinidad in Transition,* 137–38. For an alternative view, see Carl Campbell, "Immigration into Trinidad in the Middle of the Nineteenth Century."

11. This does not mean that there were no instances of riots between laborers of different races. See, for example, the report of a riot on the St. Clair Estate in April 1879 in the *Port-of-Spain Gazette,* 21 April 1879.

12. See Longden to Kimberley, confidential minute no. 5354, 29 June 1871, in PRO, C.O. 295/256, p. 389, for response to complaints made by Dr. Bakewell.

13. Longden to Kimberley, enclosure in confidential despatch, 8 May 1871, in PRO, C.O. 295/256.

14. Robinson to Holland, June 1887, PRO, C.O. 295/314, no. 122, with enclosures.

15. Rush to Carnarvon, 24 January 1877, PRO, C.O. 295/278,

no. 11 and enclosures; and Des Voeux to Carnarvon, 22 August 1877, ibid., no. 138.

16. Des Voeux to Carnarvon, 22 August 1877, PRO, C.O. 295/278, no. 138.

17. See Blue Books for 1880, 1882, and 1900 in PRO, C.O. 300 / 91, 93, 111.

18. MacLeod to Russell, 31 May 1845, confidential, PRO, C.O. 295/146.

19. *Port-of-Spain Gazette,* 3 June 1871.

20. Ibid., 2 September 1871; and see also Longden to Kimberley, 29 January 1872, PRO, C.O. 295/260, no. 23.

21. Longden to Kimberley, 6 April 1872, PRO, C.O. 295/261, no. 74.

22. Report of the agent general for immigration, 1872, PRO, 295/267.

23. Registrar general's report for 1890, *T.C.P.* 45 of 1891, pp. 20–21.

24. Enclosure from H. Mitchell, Protector of Immigrants, PRO, C.O. 295/290, no. 241.

25. Enclosure from surgeon general, 6 August 1881, PRO, C.O. 295/290, no. 241.

26. See Blue Book for 1875, in PRO, C.O. 300/86.

27. Immigration Report for 1873, p. 4. See *T.C.P.* 11 of 1874 in PRO, C.O. 300/84.

28. See Blue Book for 1881, in PRO, C.O. 300/91.

29. Of course, there were those who lived to ripe old ages. In 1895 among the registered deaths were four persons of the reputed ages of 110, 111, 125, and 131 (report with Blue Book for 1895 in *P.P. 1897,* 59:477.

30. Blue Book for 1894, in *P.P. 1895,* 69:607; Blue Book for 1897 in *P.P. 1899,* 62:605.

31. See comments of surgeon general in Gov. Broome to Ripon, 10 January 1893, PRO, C.O. 295/343, no. 7.

32. *T.C.P.* 6 of 1880.

33. See K.O. Laurence, *Immigration into the West Indies in the Nineteenth Century,* and R.R. Kuckzynski, *Demographic Survey of the British Colonial Empire,* 9–15.

34. These are the figures for Port-of-Spain proper and do not include the population of the suburban districts. If those are included, the population for 1891 would be as high as 50,000. See Bridget Brereton, *Race Relations in Colonial Trinidad, 1870–1900,* 12.

35. The cholera epidemic of 1855 may also have been responsible

for the decline in females between 1851 and 1861. Dr. Clarke, the principal medical officer, reported that female mortality predominated particularly among the colored population, but that both sexes were affected equally among the black Creoles. See Elliott to Labouchere, 1 January 1856, PRO, C.O. 295/191, no. 1.

36. Kuckzynski, *Demographic Survey,* 15.

37. On housing for indentured immigrants, see Judith Ann Weller, *East Indian Indenture in Trinidad,* chap. 6.

38. See C.L.R. James, "Triumph," in Reinhard W. Sanders, ed., *From Trinidad,* 86, and James Cummings, "Barrack-Rooms," in ibid., 42. For other descriptions see H.J. Clark, *The Material and Moral Progress of Trinidad during the Last Fifty Years,* 8 and Brereton, *Race Relations,* 116–17.

39. José M. Bodu, *Trinidadiana,* 28.

40. See Fowler to Ripon, 27 May 1893, PRO, C.O. 295/345, no. 171; Fowler to Broome, 12 August 1893, PRO, C.O. 295/347, no. 283; Broome to Ripon, 30 June 1894, PRO, C.O. 295/351, no. 33; Broome to Ripon, June 1894, PRO, C.O. 295/356, no. 361.

41. *T.C.P.* 45 of 1891, p. 18. On the extent of overcrowded rooms and its connection with contaminative lung diseases, see A. Balfour and Henry H. Scott, *Health Problems of the Empire,* 291.

42. See, for example, prison report for 1882, in *T.C.P.* 30 of 1883, p. 2; Charles Kingsley, *At Last a Christmas in the West Indies,* 70; C. W. Eves, *The West Indies,* 175.

43. Blue Book for 1894, in *P.P. 1895,* 69:607.

44. *T.C.P.* 69 of 1891, p. 10.

45. Keate to Newcastle, 20 September 1862, PRO, C.O. 295/219, no. 170.

46. *Port-of-Spain,* Saturday, 25 February 1871.

47. On the lunatic asylum, see R. Seheult, *A Survey of the Trinidad Medical Services, 1814–1944,* and M.H. Beaubrun et al., "The West Indies."

48. Longden to Kimberley, 3 September 1870, PRO, C.O. 295/252, no. 144.

49. Robinson to Stanley, 8 January 1886, PRO, C.O. 295/310, no. 11.

50. Surgeon general's report, *T.C.P.* 130 of 1911.

51. Surgeon general's report, *T.C.P.* 46 of 1891.

52. See Blue Book for 1875, in PRO, C.O. 300/86.

53. L.A.A. De Verteuil, *Trinidad,* 163.

54. Longden to Kimberley, 6 March 1871, PRO, C.O. 295/255, no. 38 with enclosure.

55. Report on the lunatic asylum for 1869, PRO, C.O. 295/251, pp. 39–40.
56. Longden to Kimberley, 16 March 1871, PRO, C.O. 295/255, no. 38 and enclosures.
57. *T.C.P.* 32 of 1884.
58. Report on the lunatic asylum for 1877, *T.C.P.* 14 of 1878.
59. See stipendiary magistrates reports in *P.P. 1842,* 29:396–411.
60. Broome to Chamberlain, 26 October 1896, PRO, C.O. 295/375, no. 337 with enclosures.
61. Keate to Newcastle, 23 July 1861, PRO, C.O. 295/213, no. 112 with enclosures.
62. *Port-of-Spain Gazette,* Saturday 18 March, 1882.
63. Ibid., Saturday, 26, July 1879.
64. Quoted in Havelock to Stanley, 2 October 1885, PRO, C.O. 295/308, no. 277.
65. Bushe to Derby, 17 August 1884, PRO, C.O. 295/303, no. 195.
66. Broome to Ripon, 23 August 1894, PRO, C.O. 295/356, no. 402.
67. Jerningham to Chamberlain, 17 July 1899, PRO, C.O. 295/392, no. 252 and enclosure.
68. Ibid.; see also Brian Inglis *The Forbidden Game,* 99–109.
69. Irving to Hicks-Beach, 21 June 1879, PRO, C.O. 295/283, no. 119.
70. Report of the agent general for immigration, 1872, PRO, C.O. 295/267.
71. Keate to Cardwell, 21 May 1864, PRO, C.O. 295/277, no. 79 and enclosures.
72. Longden to Kimberley, 21 August 1873, PRO, C.O. 295/269, no. 161.
73. Ibid.
74. Longden to Kimberley, 6 April 1872, PRO, C.O. 295/261, no. 74.
75. See Louis Wharton to colonial secretary, enclosed in Robinson to Knutsford, May 1887, PRO, C.O. 295/313, no. 88.
76. A.C. Carmichael, *Domestic Manners and Social Conditions of the White, Colored, and Negro Population of the West-Indies,* 140–47.
77. De Verteuil, *Trinidad,* 75; Brereton, Race Relations, 131–22.
78. See education reports for 1876 and 1877 in PRO, C.O. 295/279, no. 186, and PRO, C.O. 295/281, no. 201.
79. See Merle Hodge, "The Shadow of the Whip," in Orde

Coombs, ed., *Is Massa Day Dead?* 111–18, for some insightful comments on this.

80. The offense "assaulting female or child" was not distinguished from "assault and battery" in the statistics prior to 1901. In the decade 1901–10, 275, persons (256 males and 19 females) were imprisoned for "assaulting female or child."

81. For example, see rape cases reported in the *Port-of-Spain Gazette,* 19 October 1892.

82. Quoted from L. Fraser, inspector of prisons, enclosure in Des Voeux to Carnavon, 18 May 1877, PRO, C.O. 295/278, no. 87.

83. Gordon to Granville, 8 May 1869, PRO, C.O. 295/247, no. 59 and enclosure.

84. Report of the law officers on Ordinance 1 of 1889, enclosed in Robinson to Knutsford, 11 April 1889, PRO, C.O. 295/322, no. 127.

85. Robinson to Knutsford, 11 April 1889, PRO, C.O. 295/322, no. 127; Robinson to Knutsford, 8 October 1890, PRO, C.O. 295/330, no. 312; Robinson to Knutsford, 27 November 1891, PRO, 295/334, no. 311.

86. Harris to Grey, 5 January 1850, PRO, C.O. 295/170, no. 1.

87. See J.D. Elder, "Kalinda, Song of the Battling Troubadours of Trinidad," *Journal of the Folklore Institute* 3 no. 2 (1966): 192–203, and Elder, "Evolution of the Traditional Calypso of Trinidad and Tobago," 90–92.

88. See Seepersad Naipaul, *The Adventure of Gurudeva and Other Stories,* 46.

89. *Trinidad Chronicle,* 23 December 1864.

90. Andrew Pearsen, ed. and arranger, "Mitto Sampson in Calypso Legends of the Nineteenth Century."

CHAPTER 7

1. On the problems of reconstruction in the postemancipation period see W.G. Sewell, *The Ordeal of Free Labor in the British Indies;* Phillip D. Curtin, *Two Jamaicas;* Douglas Hall, *Free Jamaica, 1838–1865;* Douglas Hall, *Five of the Leewards, 1838–1870;* Alan H. Adamson, *Sugar without Slaves;* Walter Rodney, *A History of the Guyanese Working People, 1881–1905.* See also William A. Green, *British Slave Emancipation;* O.N. Bolland, "Systems of Domination after Slavery"; and the exchange between Green and Bolland in *Comparative Studies in Society and History* 26, no. 1 (1984): 112–25.

2. *P.P. 1847–48,* 66:632–33.

3. Harris to Gladstone, 30 July 1846, *P.P. 1847–48,* vol. 23, pt. 3, p. 263, for all references to the regulations. See also Wood, *Trinidad in Transition,* pp. 119–20.

4. In fact, the regulations were also used "to counteract the seducing away of coolies by rival planters": *P.P. 1847–48,* vol. 23, pt. 2, p. 436.

5. Grey to Harris, 15 September 1846, *P.P. 1847–48,* vol. 23, pt. 3, p. 263.

6. Immigration report, 1874–75, in *T.C.P.* 16 of 1876.

7. Longden to Kimberley, 21 August 1873, PRO, C.O. 295/269, no. 160.

8. Havelock to Derby, 25 March 1885, PRO, C.O. 295/305, no. 75.

9. Freeling to Kimberley, 23 February 1883, PRO, C.O. 295/296, no. 44.

10. *T.C.P.* 68 of 1901, p. 5.

11. *P.P. 1898,* 50:600.

12. *P.P. 1898,* 50:747; and *Hansard Legislative Debates,* 4th series, 5 October 1903, pp. 171–76.

13. At one time it was suggested that indentured East Indians be made to wear some distinctive mark on their dress. The agent general for immigrants also reported that "Slaves, where is your free paper?" was an occasional salutation from the West Indian to the East-Indian laborer. Rennie to Kimberley, 17 April 1873, see PRO, C.O. 295/267, no. 74, enclosures and minute pages.

14. For a more extensive discussion of resistance among East Indian workers, see Kusha Haracksingh, "Control and Resistance among Overseas Indian Workers." See also Ron Ramdin, *From Chattel Slave to Wage Earner.*

15. L.A.A. De Verteuil, *Trinidad,* 383–86.

16. Hon. De Verteuil to Gov. Manners-Sutton, 25 May 1866, in *T.C.P.* 9 of 1875.

17. *P.P. 1864,* 40:33.

18. *P.P. 1846,* 30:669.

19. Gordon to Granville, 10 March 1869, PRO, C.O. 295/247, no. 29.

20. Gordon to Granville, 20 January 1870, PRO, C.O. 295/250, no. 7.

21. Longden to Kimberley, 15 April 1871, PRO, C.O. 295/256, no. 61.

22. Blue Book for 1897, in PRO, C.O. 300/108.

23. *T.C.P.* 15 of 1876, p. 5.
24. See Howard Johnson, "The Origins and Early Development of Canefarming in Trinidad, 1882–1906.
25. Warden's report for 1885, *T.C.P.* 6 of 1886; see also, L.P. Pierre, the warden for Toco in 1886, in *T.C.P.* 27 of 1887.
26. C.Y. Shepherd, "The Cacao Industry of Trinidad: Some Economic Aspects." *Tropical Agriculture* 9, nos. 5 and 6 (1932).
27. Havelock to Derby, confidential, 7 May 1885, PRO, C.O. 295/306; PRO, C.O. 295/315, no. 254, with enclosures; report with Blue Book for 1888, in *P.P. 1889,* 54:809–10.
28. Robinson to Knutsford, 14 January 1889, PRO, C.O. 295/321.
29. Robinson to Holland, 6 December 1887, PRO, C.O. 295/315, no. 254 with enclosures.
30. J.H. Collens, *A Guide to Trinidad,* 168.
31. *T.C.P.* 43 of 1875, P.5.
32. *P.P. 1870,* 50:679.
33. Charles Kingsley, *At Last, a Christmas in the West Indies,* 70.
34. *Port-of-Spain Gazette,* 22 July 1871.
35. Kingsley, *At Last, a Christmas in the West Indies,* 70.
36. Annie Brassey, *In The Trades, the Tropics, and the Roaring Forties,* 128.
37. Warden's report, *T.C.P.* 60 of 1887.
38. *P.P. 1898,* 50:737.
39. *T.C.P.* 42 of 1876, p. 4.
40. *P.P. 1847–48,* 45:488–96.
41. Ibid.
42. Longden to Kimberley, 14 February 1871, PRO, C.O. 295/255, no. 3.
43. See *T.C.P.* 40 of 1919, p. 3.

CHAPTER 8

1. *Hegemony* is defined as "an order in which a certain way of life and thought is dominant, in which one concept of reality is diffused throughout society in all its institutional and private manifestations, informing with its spirit all taste, morality, customs, religious and political principles, and all social relations, particularly in their intellectual and moral connotation." See Gwyn A. Williams, "The Concept of 'Egemonia' in the Thought of Antonio Gramsci, p. 586, and

see also Q. Hoare and J. Nowell-Smith, eds., *Selections from the Prison Notebooks of Antonio Gramsci;* for an interesting treatment of the concept and its relationship with crime, see Stuart Hall et al., *Policing the Crisis.*

2. R.T. Smith, "Social Stratification, Cultural Pluralism, and Integration in West Indian Societies," 235.

3. On the problems of education in Trinidad in the postemancipation period, see Donald Wood, *Trinidad in Transition,* 212–37; on education and its role in the creation of a black and colored middle class, see Bridget Brereton, *Race Relations in Colonial Trinidad, 1870–1900,* 64–109.

4. For the Latrobe Report see *P.P. 1839,* vol. 34. For excerpts from both reports see Shirley Gordon, *A Century of West Indian Education;* for the Keenan Report, see *P.P. 1870,* 50:450ff.

5. Report of the inspector of schools for 1877, PRO, C.O. 295/281, no. 201.

6. See Gordon, *A Century of West Indian Education,* 119.

7. See report of the inspector of schools for 1877, PRO, C.O. 295/281, no. 201.

8. Report of the inspector of schools in for 1875, PRO, C.O. 295/277, no. 160; report for 1876, in PRO, C.O. 295/279, no. 186; and report for 1877, PRO, C.O. 295/281, no. 201.

9. *P.P. 1852–53,* vol. 68, nos. 33 and 37, pp. 475–86.

10. Robinson to Knutsford, 17 December 1888, PRO, C.O. 295/319, no. 339.

11. See Gordon, *A Century of West Indian Education,* 199.

12. Ibid., 207.

13. Ibid., 170.

14. Registrar general's report for 1885, *T.C.P.* 10 of 1886, in PRO, C.O. 295/310, no. 58.

15. *T.C.P.* 45 of 1891.

16. *T.C.P.* 55 of 1891, report on prisons for 1890, appendix Q, 20.

17. W.G. Gamble, Jr., to Baynes, 21, July 1888, Baptist Missionary Society Records, W1/9.

18. On the Spiritual Baptists in Trinidad, see *Melvin J. Herskovitts and Frances S. Herskovitts, Trinidad Village.*

19. On Shango, see ibid., 321–39; George Simpson, *The Shango Cult in Trinidad;* and Frances Mischel, "African 'Powers' in Trinidad"; D.V. Trotman, "The Yoruba and Orisha Worship in Trinidad and British Guiana." On Rada, see Andrew Carr, "A Rada Community in Trinidad."

20. On Obeah, see Herskovitts and Herskovitts, Trinidad Village, 224–55.

21. Inspector of police to colonial secretary, PRO, C.O. 295/261, enclosure in no. 101.

22. See *Laws of Trinidad and Tobago* (Port-of-Spain: Government Printing Office, 1905), vol. 1, no. 5, p. 123.

23. Ibid.

24. Gov. Longden to Kimberley, 9, May 1872, PRO, C.O. 295/261, enclosure in no. 101.

25. Ibid.

26. *Trinidad Chronicle,* 9 April 1872; see also Brereton, *Race Relations,* 154.

27. See Donald Wood, *Trinidad in Transition,* 242.

28. Andrew Pearse, "Mitto Sampson on Calypso Legends of the Nineteenth Century."

29. Herskovitts and Herskovitts, *Trinidad Village,* 346.

30. On medical service in Trinidad, see R. Seheult, *A Survey of the Trinidad Medical Services. 1814–1944,* and K.O. Laurence, "The Development of Medical Services in British Guiana and Trinidad, 1841–1873."

31. Fowler to Ripon, 21 July 1891, PRO, C.O. 295/333, no. 154 and enclosures.

32. Ibid.

33. Charles Kingsley, *At Last, a Christmas in the West Indies,* 239.

34. For a brief but interesting exploration of this theme, see Michael Mullin, "Slave Obeahmen and Slaveowning Patriarchs in an Era of War and Revolution."

35. Longden to Kimberley, 9 May 1872, PRO, C.O. 295/261.

36. J.J. Thomas, *Froudacity,* 99.

37. *Trinidad Chronicle,* 3 October 1865.

38. 28 June 1881, PRO, C.O. 295/290, no. 185.

39. H. A. Alcazar, "The Evolution of English Law in Trinidad," and Wood, *Trinidad in Transition,* 182–89.

40. The possibility of the existence of a parallel system of justice among the peasantry is raised for Jamaica, but I have uncovered no similar evidence for Trinidad. See Noelle Chutkan, "The Administration of Justice in Jamaica as a Contributing Factor in the Morant Bay Rebellion of 1865."

41. W.H. Gamble, Jr., to Baynes, 21 July 1888, Baptist Missionary Society Report, W1/9.

42. See Monica Schuler, "The Experience of African Immigrants in Nineteenth Century Jamaica," 15.

43. See Brereton, *Race Relations,* 155.
44. L.A.A. De Verteuil, *Trinidad,* 175.
45. Seepersad Naipaul, *The Adventures of Gurudeva and Other Stories,* 157–58.
46. Governor Manners Sutton to Cardwell, confidential, 22 January 1866, PRO, C.O. 295/294.
47. Reports on prison discipline, 7 July 1882, PRO, C.O. 295/294, no. 192.
48. L. M. Fraser, Report on prisons, 1884, enclosure in PRO, C.O. 295/306, no. 107.
49. L.M. Fraser, Report on prisons, 1882, in *T.C.P.* 30 of 1883, p. 3.
50. *P.P. 1952–53,* 67:486.
51. José Bodu, M. *Trinidadiana,* 17.
52. See J.C. Jha, "The Background of the Legislation of Non-Christian Marriages in Trinidad and Tobago." See also "Petition from Certain Indian Immigrants Praying for an Enactment of an Ordinance for the Registration of Coolie Marriages," *Port-of-Spain Gazette,* Saturday, 5 February 1881.
53. *T.C.P.* 56 of 1896 and *T.C.P.* 35 of 1891, table S.
54. Gov. Freeling to Kimberley, 8 May 1882, PRO, C.O. 295/293, no. 121.
55. Gov. Robinson to Knutsford, 24 December 1888, PRO, C.O. 295/319, no. 363 and enclosures. The debate on the ordinance and all the comments by De Verteuil and De Boissiere quoted in the paragraphs that follow are from this source.
56. On the De Verteuils and the bastard wing of the family see Brereton, *Race Relations,* 40.
57. *Port-of-Spain Gazette,* 3 February 1872.
58. L.M. Fraser, Report on prisons in W. Des Voeux to Carnavon, 18 May 1877, enclosure from PRO, C.O. 295/278, no. 87; see also *T.C.P.* 27 of 1877, p. 3.
59. 18 July 1862, PRO, C.O. 295/218, no. 137.
60. 21 May 1864, PRO, C.O. 295/227, no. 79.
61. Report of the inspector of prisons, 1877, in *T.C.P.* 45 of 1878, p. 2; Report of the inspector of prisons, 1881, in *T.C.P.* 53 of 1882, p. 3; enclosure from the inspector of prisons in 1884, PRO, C.O. 295/306, no. 107.
62. Vidia S. Naipaul, *The Loss of El Dorado,* 162.
63. Kingsley, *At Last,* 72.
64. See *T.C.P.* 17 of 1875.
65. See J.R. Walkowitz and D.G. Walkowitz, "We are not beasts of the field."

66. On the ordinance in Trinidad see *T.C.P.* 17 of 1875; *P.P. 1887,* 62:675–87; and Robinson to Knutsford, 21 January 1891, PRO, C.O. 295/332, no. 26.

67. *T.C.P.* 17 of 1875.

68. *Port-of-Spain Gazette,* Saturday, 10 December 1881, and *Trinidad* Palladium, Saturday, 19 November 1881.

69. *Port-of-Spain Gazette,* Saturday, 5 November 1881.

70. L.M. Fraser, Inspector of Prisons in *T.C.P.* 30 of 1883, p. 3.

71. *Trinidad Chronicle,* 6 October 1865; *Port-of-Spain Gazette,* 7 October 1871; L.M. Fraser, Inspector of Prisons in *T.C.P.* 30 of 1883, p. 2.

72. See W. H. Gamble, *Trinidad: Historical and Descriptive,* 40.

73. Elliot to Labouchere, 4 October 1856, PRO, C.O. 295/192, no. 85.

74. E.B. Underhill, *The West Indies,* 41.

75. *P.P. 1852–53,* vol 67, enclosure 1 in no. 13, 418–19.

76. Brereton, *Race Relations,* p. 165; see also comments by the chief justice, 17 March 1894, PRO, C.O. 295/351, no. 78, and *Port-of-Spain Gazette,* 8 March 1894.

77. Longden to Kimberley, 9 May 1872, PRO, C.O. 295/261 enclosure in no. 101.

78. *Port-of-Spain Gazette,* Saturday, 16 August 1881.

79. *T.C.P.* 30 of 1883, p. 2.

80. See Janheinz Jahn, *Muntu.*

81. For an example of the homegenization of Yoruba dialects, see M. Warner, "Trinidad Yoruba—Notes on Survivals," 46. On the development of Creole see Sidney W. Mintz, *Caribbean Transformations,* 16–17.

82. J.H. Collens, *A Guide to Trinidad,* 200.

83. D.J. Crowley, "The Traditional Masques of Carnival," for the tradition in oral skills and the development of the "Man of Words," see R.D. Abrahams, *The Man of Words in the West Indies: Performance and the Emergence of Creole Culture* (Baltimore: John Hopkins University Press, 1983).

84. R.D. Abrahams, *Deep Down in the Jungle,* 39–60, and Ulf Hannerz, *Soulside,* 129 ff.

85. Hannah Arendt, *On Violence,* 45.

86. On the calypso, see Pearse, "Mitto Sampson on Calypso Legends of the Nineteenth Century"; J.D. Elder, "Evolution of the Traditional Calypso"; Errol Hill, *The Trinidad Carnival;* F. Gordon Rohlehr, "Forty Years of Calypso"; and "Patrick Jones—Calypso Lore and Legend," Cook Phonograph Recording, #5016, 1956.

87. *Trinidad Chronicle,* 3 March 1865, and *Port-of-Spain Gazette,* 5 November 1881.
88. Rennie to Kimberley, 14 April 1873, PRO, C.O. 295/267, no. 72.
89. *Port-of-Spain Gazette,* 27 April 1879, 24 May 1879, and 7 February 1897.
90. Private, Knolly to Chamberlain, 11 May 1898, PRO, C.O. 295/386.
91. See Kingsley, *At Last,* 303–8.
92. For an example of a cockfight raid, see *Port-of-Spain Gazette,* 17 May 1879.
93. See Hannerz, *Soulside,* 140–44.
94. Robinson to Knutsford, 30 July 1888, PRO, C.O. 295/318, no. 197; see also *Port-of-Spain Gazette,* 12 November 1881, for a description of the game.
95. See D.M. Downes, *Gambling, Work, and Leisure.*
96. Charles Day, *Five Years Residence in the West Indies,* 294–96; Underhill, The West Indies, 24; Kingsley, *At Last,* 307. See also newspaper articles cited extensively in Brereton, *Race Relations.* 160.
97. Bodu, Trinidadian, 49.
98. See Brereton, Race Relations, p. 160; see also her chapter on "The Colored and Black Middle Class."
99. The editorial is reprinted in Hill, *The Trinidad Carnival,* 44.
100. See H.A. Will *Constitutional Change in the British West Indies, 1888–1903,* 163–65.
101. Freeling to Derby, 24 July 1883, PRO, C.O. 295/297, no. 155.
102. On the Haitian revolution see C.L.R. James, *The Black Jacobins;* for Trinidad, see V.S. Naipaul, *The Loss of El Dorado,* and Michael Craton, *Testing the Chains,* 233–38.
103. J.C. Jha, "The Indian Mutiny cum Revolt of 1857 and Trinidad."
104. *Trinidad Chronicle,* 21 April 1865.
105. Peter Burke, *Popular Culture in Early Modern Europe,* and Robert Malcolmson, *Popular Recreation in English Society, 1700–1850.*
106. *T.C.P.* 26 of 1882.
107. Freeling to Kimberley, 25 October 1882, PRO, C.O. 295/295, no. 260 with enclosures.
108. PRO, C.O. 884, vol. 4, confidential print (West Indies), no 40: "Report on the causes and circumstances of the disturbances in connection with Carnival in Trinidad"; Freeling to Kimberley, 17

February 1883, PRO, C.O. 295/296, no. 35; and Freeling to Derby, 8 March 1884, PRO, C.O. 295/301, nos. 56 and 60 with enclosures.

109. "Report on the Coolie Disturbances in Trinidad," *T.C.P.* 26 of 1885.

110. 25 July 1871, PRO, C.O. 295/374, no. 241, and *T.C.P.* 25 of 1891.

Bibliography

ARCHIVAL SOURCES

Public Record Office, London (PRO)

Original Correspondence, Trinidad, 1838–1900. Colonial Office (C.O.) 295, vols. 120–400.

Blue Books of Statistics, Trinidad, 1838–1900. C.O. 300, vols. 50–128.

Confidential Print [West Indies]: "Report on the Causes and Circumstances of the Disturbances in Connection with Carnival in Trinidad." C.O. 884, vol. 4, no. 40.

Reports, Minutes of Evidence of Select Committees, Correspondence and Returns, 1838–1900: *Parliamentary Papers* (*P.P.*).

Royal Commonwealth Society Library, London

Trinidad Council Papers, 1870–1900 (*T.C.P.*).

British Museum, Newspaper Library, Colindale, London

Trinidad Newspapers: (consulted selectively)

Fair Play.

New Era.

Port-of-Spain Gazette.

Trinidad Chronicle.

Trinidad Palladium.

The Trinidadian.

Crime in Trinidad

British Missionary Society Library, London
Papers relating to the West Indies, Boxes W19 and W10.

Contemporary Books

Billouin, H.S. *Guide Book to the Masonic and Friendly Societies of Trinidad.* Port-of-Spain, 1900.

Bodu, José M. *Trinidadiana, Being a Chronological Review of Events.* Port-of-Spain, 1890.

Brassey, Annie. *In the Trades, the Tropics, and the Roaring Forties.* London, 1885.

Brierley, J.N. *Trinidad Then and Now.* Port-of-Spain, 1912.

Burkett, A.A. *Trinidad, a Jewel of the West.* London, 1914.

Burnley, W.H. *Observations on the Present Condition of the Island of Trinidad.* London, 1842.

Carmichael, A.C. *Domestic Manners and Social Conditions of the White, Colored, and Negro Population of the West Indies.* 2 vols. London, 1834.

Clark, H.J. *The Material and Moral Progress of Trinidad during the Last Fifty Years.* Port-of-Spain, 1888.

———. *Iere the Land of the Humming Bird.* Port-of-Spain, 1893.

Coleridge, Henry Nelson. *Six Months in the West Indies in 1825.* London, 1826.

Collens, J.H. *A Guide to Trinidad.* London, 1888.

Dauxion-Lavaysee, Jean F. *A Description of Venezuela, Trinidad, Margarita, and Tobago.* London, 1820.

Davy, J. *The West Indies before and after Slave Emancipation.* London, 1859.

Day, Charles. *Five Years Residence in the West Indies.* London, 1852.

De Verteuil, L.A.A. *Trinidad: Its Geography, Natural Resources, Administration, Present Condition, and Prospects.* London, 1858; 2d ed., 1884.

Eves, C.W. *The West Indies.* London, 1893.

Fraser, L.M. *History of Trinidad from 1781 to 1839.* 2 vols. Port-of-Spain, 1891, 1892.

Froude, J.A. *The English in the West Indies.* London, 1888.

Gamble, W.H. *Trinidad: Historical and Descriptive: Being a Narrative of Nine Years' Residence in the Island.* London, 1866.

Innis, L.O. *Trinidad and Trinidadians: A Collection of Papers, Historical, Social, and Descriptive, about Trinidad and Its Peoples*. Port-of-Spain, 1910.

Joseph, E.L. *History of Trinidad*. London, 1838.

Kingsley, Charles. *At Last, a Christmas in the West Indies*. London, 1869.

Paget, J. *Illustrated Guide to Trinidad*. Port-of-Spain, 1801.

Paton, W.A. *Down the Islands: A Voyage to the Caribbees*. London, 1888.

Sewell, W. *The Ordeal of Free Labour in the British West Indies*. New York, 1860.

Stark, J.H. *Guide Book and History of Trinidad*. London, 1897.

Thomas, J.J. *Froudacity*. London, 1889; rpt. London: New Beacon Books, 1969.

The Trial of N.W. Brunton. Port-of-Spain, 1870.

Trollope, A. *The West Indies and the Spanish Main*. London, 1860.

Underhill, E.B. *The West Indies: Their Economic and Social Condition*. London, 1862.

SECONDARY SOURCES

Books

Abrahams, R.D. *Deep Down in the Jungle: Negro Narrative Folklore from the Streets of Philadelphia*. Chicago: Aldine, 1973.

———. *The Man of Words in the West Indies: Performance and the Emergence of Creole Culture*. Baltimore: Johns Hopkins Univ. Press, 1983.

Adamson, Alan H. *Sugar without Slaves: The Political Economy of British Guiana, 1838–1904*. New Haven: Yale Univ. Press, 1972.

Arendt, Hannah. *On Violence*. New York: Harcourt Brace Jovanovich, 1969.

Asiegbu, J.J. *Slavery and the Politics of Liberation, 1787–1861: A Study of Liberated African Emigration and British Anti-Slavery Policy*. New York: Africana, 1969.

Balfour, A., and H.H. Scott. *Health Problems of the Empire*. Vol. 5. London: W. Collins, 1924.

Beachey, R.W. *The British West Indian Sugar Industry in the Late Nineteenth Century*. London: Oxford Univ. Press, 1957.

Beckford, George L. *Persistent Poverty: Underdevelopment in Plantation Economies of the Third World.* New York: Oxford Univ. Press, 1972.

Bell, K.N., and W.P. Morrell, eds. *Select Documents on British Colonial Policy, 1830–1860.* London: Oxford Univ. Press, 1928.

Bonger, W.A. *Criminality and Economic Conditions.* Boston: Little, Brown, 1916.

Brana-Shute, R., and G. Brana-Shute. *Crime and Punishment in the Caribbean.* Gainesville: Univ. of Florida, Centre for Latin American Studies, 1980.

Brathwaite, Edward. *The Development of Creole Society in Jamaica, 1770–1820.* Oxford: Clarendon Press, 1971.

Brereton, Bridget. *Race Relations in Colonial Trinidad, 1870–1990.* London: Cambridge Univ. Press, 1979.

———. *A History of Modern Trinidad, 1783–1962.* Port-of-Spain: Heinemann, 1981.

Bridenbaugh, Carl, and Roberta, Bridenbaugh. *No Peace beyond the Line: The English in the Caribbean, 1624–1690.* New York: Oxford Univ. Press, 1972.

Broeker, Galen. *Rural Disorder and Policy Reform in Ireland, 1812–1836.* Toronto: Univ. of Toronto Press, 1970.

Burke, Peter. *Popular Culture in Early Modern Europe.* New York: Harper, 1978.

Chapman, J.K. *The Career of Arthur Hamilton Gordon, First Lord Stanmore, 1829–1912.* Toronto: Univ. of Toronto Press, 1964.

Chesney, Kellow. *The Victorian Underworld.* London: Penguin, 1972.

Clifford, W. *An Introduction to African Criminology.* London: Oxford Univ. Press, 1974.

Clinard, Marshall B., and Daniel J. Abbott. *Crime in Developing Countries: A Comparative Perspective.* New York: Wiley, 1973.

Cohen, David, and J. Greene. *Neither Slave nor Free: The Freedmen of African Descent in the Slave Societies of the New World.* Baltimore: Johns Hopkins Univ. Press, 1972.

Coombs, Orde, ed. *Is Massa Day Dead? Black Moods in the Caribbean.* New York: Doubleday, Anchor, 1974.

Crahan, M., and F. Knight. *Africa and the Caribbean: The Legacies of a Link.* Baltimore: Johns Hopkins Univ. Press, 1979.

Craton, Michael. *Testing the Chains: Resistance to Slavery in the British West Indies.* Ithaca, N.Y.: Cornell Univ. Press, 1982.

Curtin, Phillip D. *Two Jamaicas: The Role of Ideas in a Tropical Colony, 1830–1865*. Cambridge, Mass.: Harvard Univ. Press, 1955.

———. *The Atlantic Slave Trade: A Census*. Madison: Univ. of Wisconsin Press, 1969.

Downes, D.M. *Gambling, Work, and Leisure*. London: Routledge and Kegan Paul, 1976.

Dunn, Richard S. *Sugar and Slaves: The Rise of the Planter Class in the English West Indies, 1624–1713*. Chapel Hill: Univ. of North Carolina, 1972.

Fanon, Frantz. *The Wretched of the Earth*. New York: Grove, 1968.

Foucault, Michel. *Discipline and Punish: The Birth of the Prison*. New York: Pantheon, 1977.

Given, J.B. *Society and Homicide in Thirteenth-Century England*. Stanford, Calif.: Stanford Univ. Press, 1977.

Gordon, Shirley. *A Century of West Indian Education: A Source Book*. London: Longmans, 1963.

Goveia, Elsa V. *Slave Society in the British Leeward Islands at the End of the Eighteenth Century*. New Haven: Yale Univ. Press, 1965.

Green, W.A. *British Slave Emancipation: The Sugar Colonies and the Great Experiment, 1830–1865*. London: Oxford Univ. Press, 1976.

Hall, Douglas. *Free Jamaica, 1838–1865: An Economic History*. London: Caribbean Universities Press, 1969.

———. *Five of the Leewards, 1834–1870: The Major Problems of the Post-Emancipation Period in Antigua, Barduda, Montserrat, Nevis, and St. Kitts*. Barbados: Caribbean Universities Press, 1971.

Hall, Stuart, et al. *Policing the Crisis: Mugging, the State, and Law and Order*. London: Macmillan, 1978.

Hannerz, Ulf. *Soulside: Inquiries into Ghetto Culture and Community*. New York: Columbia Univ. Press, 1969.

Hay, Douglas, et al. *Albion's Fatal Tree: Crime and Society in Eighteenth Century England*. New York: Pantheon, 1975.

Herskovitts, M.J., and F. Herskovitts. *Trinidad Village*. New York: Knopf, 1947.

Higman, B.W. *Slave Population and Economy in Jamaica, 1807–1834*. London: Cambridge Univ. Press, 1976.

Hill, Errol. *The Trinidad Carnival: Mandate for a National Theatre*. Austin: Univ. of Texas Press, 1972.

Hoare, Q., and J. Nowell-Smith, eds. *Selections from the Prison Note-*

books of Antonio Gramsci. New York: International Publishers, 1971.

Hobsbawm, E.J. *Primitive Rebels: Studies in Archaic Forms of Social Movement in the Nineteenth and Twentieth Centuries.* New York: Norton, 1965.

———. *Industry and Empire.* London: Penguin, 1968.

———. *Bandits.* London: Penguin, 1972.

Howell, J.G., ed. *World History of Psychiatry.* London: Baillere Tindall, 1975.

Ignatieff, Michael. *A Just Measure of Pain: The Penitentiary in the Industrial Revolution, 1750–1850.* New York: Pantheon, 1978.

Inglis, Brian. *The Forbidden Game: A Social History of Drugs.* London: Coronet, 1977.

Innis, L.O. *Reminiscences of Old Trinidad.* Port-of-Spain, 1932.

Jahn, Janeinz. *Muntu: The New African Culture.* New York: Grove, 1961.

James, C.L.R. *The Black Jacobins: Toussaint L'Ouverture and the Santo Domingo Revolution.* New York: Vintage, 1963.

Jayawardena, Chandra. *Conflict and Solidarity in a Guianese Plantation.* London: Athlone, 1963.

Jones, Howard. *Crime, Race, and Culture: A Study in a Developing Country.* London: Wiley, 1981.

Kiernan, V.G. *The Lords of Human Kind.* Boston: Little, Brown, 1969.

Knaplund, Paul. *James Stephen and the British Colonial System, 1813–1847.* Madison: Univ. of Wisconsin Press, 1953.

Knight, F.W. *The Caribbean: The Genesis of a Fragmented Nationalism.* New York: Oxford Univ. Press, 1978.

Kuckznski, R. *Demographic Survey of the British Colonial Empire.* Vol. 3. London: Harvester, 1977.

LaGuerre, John, ed. *Calcutta to Coroni: The East Indians of Trinidad.* London: Longmans Caribbean, 1974.

Laurence, K.O. *Immigration into the West Indies in the Nineteenth Century.* Barbados: Caribbean Universities Press, 1971.

Malcolmson, Robert. *Popular Recreations in English Society, 1700–1850.* London: Cambridge Univ. Press, 1973.

Mandle, Jay R. *The Plantation Economy: Population and Economic Change in Guyana, 1838–1960.* Philadelphia: Temple Univ. Press, 1973.

Matthews, Basil. *Crisis in the West Indian Family.* Trinidad: Government Printing Works, 1953.

May, Rollo. *Power and Innocence: A Search for the Sources of Violence.* New York: Delta, 1972.

Millette, James. *The Genesis of Crown Colony Government: Trinidad, 1783–1810.* Trinidad: Moko, 1970.

Mintz, Sidney W. *Caribbean Transformations.* Chicago: Aldine, 1974.

Mintz, Sidney W., and Richard Price. *An Anthropological Approach to the Afro-American Past: A Caribbean Perspective.* ISHI Occasional Papers in Social Change, no. 2. Philadelphia: Institute for the Study of Human Issues, 1976.

Monkkonen, Eric H. *The Dangerous Class: Crime and Poverty in Columbus, Ohio, 1860–1885.* Cambridge, Mass.: Harvard Univ. Press, 1975.

Naipaul, Seepersad. *The Adventures of Gurudeva and Other Stories.* London: Andre Deutsch, 1976.

Naipaul, Vidia S. *The Loss of El Dorado: A History.* New York: Knopf, 1970.

Newson, Linda A. *Aboriginal and Spanish Colonial Trinidad: A Study in Culture Contact.* London: Academic Press, 1976.

Parry, H., and P. Sherlock. *A Short History of the West Indies.* London: St. Martin's, 1971.

Patterson, Orlando. *The Sociology of Slavery: An Analysis of the Origins, Development, and Structure of Negro Slave Society in Jamaica.* Rutherford, N.J.: Fairleigh Dickinson Univ. Press, 1967.

Phillips, David. *Crime and Authority in Victorian England: The Black Country, 1835–1860.* London: Croom Helm, 1977.

Quinney, Richard. *Class, State, and Crime: On the Theory and Practice of Criminal Justice.* New York: David McKay, 1977.

Radzinowicz, L. *Ideology and Crime: A Study of Crime in Its Social and Historical Context.* London: Heinemann, 1966.

Ramdin, Ron. *From Chattel Slave to Wage Earner: A History of Trade Unionism in Trinidad and Tobago.* London: Martin Brian and O'Keefe, 1982.

Rock, P., and M. McIntosh. *Deviance and Social Control.* London: Tavistock, 1974.

Rodney, Walter. *A History of the Guyanese Working People, 1881–1905.* Baltimore: Johns Hopkins Univ. Press, 1981.

Rubin, Vera, ed. *Plantation Systems of the New World.* PAU-RISM

Social Science Monograph no. 7. Washington, D.C.: Pan American Union and Research Institute for the Study of Man, 1959.

Rubin, Vera, and A. Tuden, eds. *Comparative Perspectives on Slavery in New World Plantation Societies*. Annals of the New York Academy of Sciences, vol. 292. New York: New York Academy of Sciences, 1977.

Rusche, G., and O. Kircheimer. *Punishment and Social Structure*. New York: Russell and Russell, 1934.

Samaha, Joel. *Law and Order in Historical Perspective: The Case of Elizabethan Essex*. New York: Academic Press, 1976.

Sander, R.W., ed. *From Trinidad: An Anthology of Early West Indian Writing*. London: Hodder and Stoughton, 1978.

Schuler, Monica. *"Alas, Alas Kongo": A Social History of Indentured African Immigration into Jamaica*. Baltimore: Johns Hopkins Univ. Press, 1980.

Seheult, R. *A Survey of the Trinidad Medical Services, 1814–1944*. London, 1948.

Sheridan, Richard. *The Development of the Plantations to 1750*. Barbados: Caribbean Universities Press, 1970.

Simpson, George. *The Shango Cult in Trinidad*. I.C.S. Caribbean Monograph Series, no. 2. Puerto Rico: Institute for Caribbean Studies, 1965.

Smith, M.G. *The Plural Society in the British West Indies*. Berkeley: Univ. of California Press, 1965.

Sumner, Colin, ed. *Crime, Justice, and Underdevelopment*. London: Heinemann, 1982.

Tamuno, T.N. *The Police in Modern Nigeria, 1861–1965*. Ibadan: Ibadan Univ. Press, 1970.

Taylor, Ian, Paul Walton, and Jock Young. *The New Criminology: For a Social Theory of Deviance*. London: Routledge and Kegan Paul, 1973.

Thompson, Edgar. *Plantation Societies, Race Relations, and the South: The Regimentation of Populations*. Durham, N.C.: Duke Univ. Press, 1975.

Tinker, Hugh. *A New Kind of Slavery*. London: Oxford Univ. Press, 1974.

Tobias, J.J. *Crime and Industrial Society in the Nineteenth Century*. London: Penguin, 1972.

Weller, Judith Ann. *East Indian Indenture in Trinidad*. I.C.S. Caribbean Monograph Series, no. 4. Puerto Rico: Institute for Caribbean Studies, 1968.

Wells, A.F., and D. Wellso. *Friendly Societies in the West Indies*. London: Colonial Research Publications, 1953.

Wertham, Fredric. *A Sign for Cain: An Exploration of Human Violence*. New York: Warner, 1966.

Will, H.A. *Constitutional Change in the British West Indies, 1880–1903*. London: Oxford Univ. Press, 1970.

Williams, Eric, ed. *Documents on British West Indian History 1807–1833*. Port-of-Spain: Trinidad Publishing Co., 1952.

———. *History of the People of Trinidad and Tobago*. Port-of-Spain: PNM Publishing Co., 1962.

Wood, Donald. *Trinidad in Transition: The Years after Slavery*. London: Oxford Univ. Press, 1968.

Zehr, Howard. *Crime and the Development of Modern Society*. London: Croom Helm, 1976.

Articles, Unpublished Papers, and Theses

Alcazar, H.A. "The Evolution of English Law in Trinidad." In *Minutes of the Canadian Bar Association,* vol. 12, 1927. Toronto: Carswell, 1928 pp. 159–167.

Bascom, W.R. "The Esusu: A Credit Institution of the Yoruba." *Journal of The Royal Anthropological Society* 72 (1952): 63–69.

Beaubrun, M.H., et al. "The West Indies." In *World History of Psychiatry,* ed. J.G. Howell. London: Baillere Tindall, 1975.

Blouet, Brian W. "Land Policies in Trinidad, 1838–1850." *Journal of Caribbean History* 9 (1976): 43–59.

Bolland, O.N. "Systems of Domination after Slavery: The Control of Land and Labour in the British West Indies after 1838." *Comparative Studies in Society and History* 24, no. 4 (1981): 591–619.

———. "Reply to William A. Green's "The Perils of Comparative History." *Comparative Studies in Society and History* 26, no. 1 (January 1984): 120–25.

Brereton, Bridget. "The Development of an Identity: The Negro Middle Class of Trinidad in the Late Nineteenth Century." Pp. 50–65 in *Social Groups and Institutions in the History of the Caribbean*. Puerto Rico: Association of Caribbean Historians, 1975.

———. "Sir John Gorrie: A Radical Chief Justice of Trinidad (1885–1892)." *Journal of Caribbean History* 13 (1980): 44–72.

Campbell, Carl. "Jonas Mohammed Bath and the Free Mandingoes in Trinidad." *Pan African Journal* 7, no. 2 (Summer 1974): 129–51.

———. "Immigration into Trinidad in the Middle of the Nineteenth Century: A Note on Race Relations in a West Indian Colony." *Journal of Indian History* 54, no. 2 (1976): 407–39.

Carr, Andrew. "A Rada Community in Trinidad." *Caribbean Quarterly* 3, no. 1 (1953): 36–54.

Chutkan, Noelle. "The Administration of Justice in Jamaica as a Contributing Factor in the Morant Bay Rebellion of 1865." *Savacou* 11/12 (September 1975): 78–85.

Crowley, D.J. "The Traditional Masques of Carnival." *Caribbean Quarterly* 4, nos. 3, 4 (1956): 194–223.

Dodd, David J. "The Well-springs of Violence: Some Historical Notes on East Indian Criminality in Guyana." *Caribbean Issues* 2, no. 3 (1976): 3–16.

———. "The Role of Law in Plantation Society: Reflections on the Development of a Caribbean Legal System." *International Journal of the Sociology of Law* 7 (1979): 275–96.

Dodd, David J., and M. Parris. "An Urban Plantation: Socio-cultural Aspects of Crime and Delinquency in Georgetown, Guyana." *International Journal of Criminology and Penology* 5 (1977): 31–61.

Elder, J.D. "Color, Music, and Conflict: A Study of Aggression in Trinidad with Reference to the Role of Traditional Music." *Ethnomusicology* 8, no. 2 (1964): 128–36.

———. "Evolution of the Traditional Calypso of Trinidad and Tobago: A Socio-Historical Analysis of Social Change." Ph.D. diss., Univ. of Pennsylvania, 1966.

———. "Kalinda, Song of the Battling Troubadours of Trinidad." *Journal of the Folklore Institute,* no. 2 (1966): 192–203.

Eltis, D. "The Traffic in Slaves between the British West Indian Colonies, 1807–1833." *Economic History Review,* no. 25 (February 1972): 55–64.

Gattrell, V.A.C., and T.B. Hadden. "Criminal Statistics and Their Interpretation." Pp. 336–96 in *Nineteenth Century Society,* ed. E.A. Wrigley, Cambridge, London: 1972.

Green, William A. "The Perils of Comparative History: Belize and the British Sugar Colonies after Slavery." *Comparative Studies in Society and History* 26, no. 1 (January 1984): 112–19.

Hall, Neville. "Law and Society in Barbados at the Turn of the Nineteenth Century." *Journal of Caribbean History* 5 (1972): 20–45.

Haracksingh, Kusha. "Control and Resistance among Overseas Indian Workers: A Study of Labour on the Sugar Plantations of Trinidad, 1875–1917." *Journal of Caribbean History* 14 (1981): 1–17.

Henriques, U.R.O. "The Rise and Decline of the Separate System of Prison Discipline." *Past and Present* 54 (Feb. 1972): 61–93.

Higman, B. "African and Creole Slave Family Patterns in Trinidad." Pp. 41–64 in *Africa and the Caribbean,* ed. M. Crahan and F. Knight. Baltimore: Johns Hopkins Univ. Press, 1979.

James, C.L.R. "Michael Maxwell Phillip, 1829–1888." *The Beacon* 1, no. 6 (Sept. 1931). Reprinted in R.W. Sander, *From Trinidad: An Anthology of Early West Indian Writing,* 253–69. London: Hodder and Stoughton, 1978.

Jha, J.C. "The Indian Mutiny cum Revolt of 1857 and Trinidad." *Journal of Indian History* 50, no. 149 (1972): 441–58.

———. "The Background of the Legislation of Non-Christian Marriages in Trinidad and Tobago." Paper presented at Conference on East Indians in the Carribbean, Univ. of the West Indies, St. Augustine, Trinidad, June 1975.

Johnson, Howard. "Immigration and the Sugar Industry in Trinidad during the Last Quarter of the Nineteenth Century." *Journal of Caribbean History* 3 (Nov. 1971): 28–72.

———. "The Origins and Early Development of Cane-Farming in Trinidad, 1882–1906." *Journal of Caribbean History* 5 (Nov. 1972): 46–74.

———. "Barbadian Immigrants in Trinidad, 1870–1897." *Carribbean Studies* 13, no. 3 (1973): 5–30.

Laurence, K.O. "The Settlement of Free Negroes in Trinidad before Emancipation." *Caribbean Quarterly* 9, nos. 1, 2 (1963): 26–52.

———. "The Development of Medical Services in British Guiana and Trinidad, 1841–1873." *Jamaica Historical Review* 4 (1964): 59–67.

———. "The Evolution of Long-Term Labour Contracts in Trinidad and British Guiana, 1834–1863." *Jamaica Historical Review* 5 (1965): 9–27.

Marshall, W.K. "The Establishment of a Peasantry in Barbados, 1840–1920." Pp. 85–104 in *Social Groups and Institutions in the History of the Caribbean.* Puerto Rico: Association of Caribbean Historians, 1975.

Mathur, Y.B. "Jail Administration in the Punjab, 1849–1875." *Journal of Indian History* 43, no. 2 (1965): 159–82.

Mischel, Frances. "African 'Powers' in Trinidad: The Shango Cult." *Anthropological Quarterly* 30, no. 2 (April 1957): 45–59.

Mullin, Michael. "Slave Obeahmen and Slaveowning Patriarchs in an Era of War and Revolution." Pp. 481–90 in *New World Plantation Societies Comparative Perspectives on Slavery,* ed. Vera Rubin and A. Tuden. New York: New York Academy of Sciences, 1977.

O'Brien, Patricia. "Crime and Punishment as Historical Problems." *Journal of Social History* 11 (Summer 1978): 508–20.

Pearse, Andrew. "Carnival in Nineteenth Century Trinidad." *Caribbean Quarterly,* 4, nos. 3, 4 (March, June 1956): 175–93.

———. "Mitto Sampson on Calypso Legends of the Nineteenth Century." *Caribbean Quarterly* 4, nos. 3, 4 (March, June 1956): 250–62.

Pyrce, Ken. "Towards a Caribbean Criminology." *Caribbean Issues* 2, no. 2 (Aug. 1976): 3–21.

Riviere, W.E. "Labour Shortage in the British West Indies after Emancipation." *Journal of Caribbean History* 4 (May 1972): 1–30.

Roberts, G.W. "Immigration of Africans into the British Caribbean." *Population Studies* 20 (1966): 123–34.

Rohlehr, Gordon. "Forty Years of Calypso." *TAPIA* 2, (Sept.-Oct. 1972): no. 1, pp. 1–4; no. 2, pp. 4–5; no. 3, pp. 6–7.

Russell-Wood, A.J.R. "Black and Mulatto Brotherhoods in Colonial Brazil: A Study in Collective Behaviour." *Hispanic American Historical Review* 54, no. 4 (1974): 567–602.

Schuler, Monica. "The Experience of African Immigrants in Nineteenth Century Jamaica." Paper presented at the Fourth Annual Conference of Caribbean Historians, University of the West Indies, Mona, Jamaica, 1972.

Seidman, Robert B. "The Ghana Prison System: An Historical Perspective." Pp. 429–72 in *African Penal Systems,* ed. Alan Milner. London: Routledge and Kegan Paul, 1969.

Shepherd, C.Y. "Economic Survey of the Cocoa Industry of Trinidad, British West Indies." *Economic Geography* 3, no. 2 (1927): 239–58.

———. "The Cacao Industry of Trinidad: Some Economic Aspects." *Tropical Agriculture* 9, nos. 5, 6 (1932).

———. "Some Economic Aspects of Cacao Production in Trinidad with Special Reference to the Montserrat District." *Tropical Agriculture* 13, no. 4 (April 1936): 85–90.

Smith, R.T. "Social Stratification, Cultural Pluralism, and Integration in West Indian Societies." Pp. 226–58 in *Caribbean Integration: Papers on Social, Political and Economic Integration,* ed. S. Lewis and T. Matthews. Puerto Rico: Institute of Caribbean Studies, 1967.

Storch, R.D. "The Policeman as Domestic Missionary: Urban Discipline and Popular Culture in Northern England, 1850–1880." *Journal of Social History* 9, no. 4 (Summer 1976): 481–509.

Trotman, D.V. "The Yoruba and Orisha Worship in Trinidad and British Guiana, 1838–1870." *African Studies Review* 19, no. 2 (1976): 1–17.

Walkowitz, J.R., and D.J. Walkowitz. "'We are not beasts of the field': Prostitution and the Poor in Plymouth and Southampton under the Contagious Diseases Act." Pp. 192–225 in *Clio's Consciousness Raised: New Perspectives on the History of Women,* ed. M. Hartman and L. Banner. New York: Harper and Row, 1974.

Warner, M. "Trinidad Yoruba: Notes on Survivals." *Caribbean Quarterly* 17, no. 2 (June 1971): 40–49.

———. "Africans in Nineteenth Century Trinidad." *African Studies Association of the West Indies Bulletin,* no. 5 (1972) pp. 27–59 and no. 6 (1973) pp. 13–37.

Williams, Eric. "The British West Indian Slave Trade after 1807." *Journal of Negro History* 27, no. 2 (April 1942): 175–91.

Williams, Gwyn A. "The Concept of Egemonia in the Thought of Antonio Gramsci: Some Notes on Interpretation." *Journal of the History of Ideas* 21, no. 4 (Oct.-Dec. 1960): 586–99.

Yang, A.A. "The Agrarian Origins of Crime: A Study of Riots in Saran District, India, 1866–1920." *Journal of Social History* 13, no. 2 (Winter 1979): 289–306.

Index